MIRACULOUS

A FASCINATING HISTORY OF SIGNS, WONDERS, AND MIRACLES

KEVIN BELMONTE

THOMAS NELSON
Since 1798

NASHVILLE   DALLAS   MEXICO CITY   RIO DE JANEIRO

Published in Nashville, Tennessee, by Thomas Nelson. Thomas Nelson is a registered trademark of Thomas Nelson, Inc.

Published in association with Rosenbaum & Associates Literary Agency, Brentwood, Tennessee.

Thomas Nelson, Inc., titles may be purchased in bulk for educational, business, fund-raising, or sales promotional use. For information, please e-mail SpecialMarkets@ThomasNelson.com.

Unless otherwise noted, Scripture quotations are taken from THE NEW KING JAMES VERSION. © 1982 by Thomas Nelson, Inc. Used by permission. All rights reserved.

Scripture quotations marked AMP are from THE AMPLIFIED BIBLE: OLD TESTAMENT. ©1962, 1964 by Zondervan (used by permission); and from THE AMPLIFIED BIBLE: NEW TESTAMENT. © 1958 by the Lockman Foundation (used by permission).

Scripture quotations marked NASB are from the NEW AMERICAN STANDARD BIBLE®. © The Lockman Foundation 1960, 1962, 1963, 1968, 1971, 1972, 1973, 1975, 1977. Used by permission.

Scripture quotations marked NIV are from the HOLY BIBLE: NEW INTERNATIONAL VERSION®. © 1973, 1978, 1984 by International Bible Society. Used by permission of Zondervan Publishing House. All rights reserved.

Scripture quotations marked KJV are from the KING JAMES VERSION.

Library of Congress Cataloging-in-Publication Data

Belmonte, Kevin Charles.
    Miraculous : a fascinating history of God's signs and wonders / Kevin Belmonte.
        p. cm.
    Includes bibliographical references and index.
    ISBN 978-1-59555-495-6 (alk. paper)
    1. Miracles--Anecdotes. 2. Miracles--Biblical teaching. 3. Bible--Biography. 4. Christian biography. I. Title.
    BT97.3.B46 2012
    231.7'3--dc23
                                    2012013215

Printed in the United States of America

12 13 14 15 QG 6 5 4 3 2 1

To Joel Miller, for the privilege of writing this book;
to my parents, and all my friends from Oxbridge

Beyond saying sweet, past telling of tongue,
Thou art lightning and love . . .

—Gerard Manley Hopkins[1]

For Thou, O Lord, in every age didst send testimonies from
heaven . . . miracles of power and mercy.

—Jeremy Taylor[2]

Great floods have flown
From simple sources; and great seas have dried
When miracles have by the greatest been denied.

—William Shakespeare[3]

CONTENTS

PREFACE

The most incredible thing about miracles is that they happen.

—G. K. Chesterton[1]

Seek the Lord and His strength; seek His face evermore! Remember His marvelous works which He has done, [and] His wonders.

—Psalm 105:4-5

D efinitions matter. They are where we begin to better understand things we've been interested in but may not know much about.

The subject of miracles, to cite a case in point, is one that holds great fascination. Yet many may not know a lot about what miracles actually are.

Here we may turn to a distinguished scholar whose writings have long been a source of blessing to the church. Dr. Walter Elwell wrote that "a miracle is an extraordinary event . . . accomplished by God as a sign of some purposes of his own."[2]

Billy Graham, America's pastor, has told us still more. "A miracle," he wrote, "is an event beyond the power of any known physical law to produce, it is a spiritual occurrence produced by the power of God, a marvel, a wonder."[3]

"Miracles," it has been said, "are a conspicuous feature of the Bible."[4] And so they are. In the Old Testament, for example, God performed many miracles during the time when Moses led the children of Israel. In the New Testament, the miracles performed by Jesus were signs for a watching world. Their purpose then and now was and is to show that Jesus "is the Christ, the Son of God, and that believing [we] may have life in His name" (John 20:31).

Our word for miracle comes from the Latin word *mirari*, "to wonder." And well might we wonder when we consider the nature of miracles and their purpose. For always, Scripture teaches, the emphasis is on what God has revealed through the miracles He has bestowed on humanity.[5] Miracles are all about Him, and what He has revealed is extraordinary.

"In the whole Scripture there is nothing but Christ. He is the sun and truth in Scripture."[6] These are the words of Martin Luther, and they confirm one of the great miracles to be found in Scripture—some might say the greatest of all. There are sixty-six books in the Bible, written by some forty different authors over a period of fifteen centuries. There were kings among them, as well as fishermen, tax collectors, shepherds, prophets, and a physician—an incredible diversity of writers—and yet each book points to Christ.[7]

In the chapters to follow, we will look at great and representative miracles from the Old and New Testaments. But at the outset, it is deeply important to keep in view the central truth stated above. To once again cite Luther, "The whole Scripture is about Christ alone."[8] He is the heart of the greatest story ever told.

It may also be said that miracles have a profoundly important history. From ancient times to the present, wondrous things have taken place. In our age of constant innovation, technological achievement, and the sad tendency to see ourselves as the captains of our fates, we may be tempted to make little time for miracles or give little credence to them. But to live our lives without a sense of the miraculous is to live impoverished lives.

Of course, no one can pretend to have the last word on the subject of miracles, and no definition of them will satisfy everyone. Some see miracles as things that unfold over a lifetime; others as events that take place in a tightly focused window of time. Some see miracles as phenomena that shape the destiny of nations; others perceive them as moments that are profoundly personal in nature. There are divergent opinions, and all of this is readily admitted. The best one can do is to consult widely respected sources and seek to be fair and judicious in speaking of them.

Such methods have served as guiding principles for this book.

Between its covers are some of the best and most eloquently considered thoughts about miracles that have ever been given to us. During my research, I've been privileged to keep company with, and learn from, some of the finest men and women whose words adorn the pages of Christian history. May something of the grace and wisdom that attended their ways be ours also. And may we, like them, come to see something more of the blessing and richness that flow from a deeper understanding of what miracles are.

The question of what miracles are prompts the onset of a fascinating journey—a pilgrimage unlike any other. In the pages of this book, a grand and memorable conversation beckons—one that leaves no doubt that God has been our help in ages past and that He is our hope for years to come. This book aspires to join that enduring conversation, and contribute to it in meaningful ways. In short, may the conversation continue.

I would only add one further note. It follows that since this text seeks to be comprehensive—though not exhaustive—discussions of teachings about miracles from the major Christian communions—Protestant, Catholic, and Orthodox alike—will be taken into account. In doing so, I have tried to be guided by the best elements of "mere Christianity"—to write respectfully, charitably, and helpfully about traditions beyond my own, which is the Protestant tradition. I have family members and friends who worship within the Catholic and Orthodox communions, and their love and devotion for God has been a source of blessing to me. I hope I may in some small way return the favor with what follows in this book.

PART I

Miracles of the Ancient Word

The heavens," Scripture tells us, "declare the glory of God" (Psalm 19:1). Look at a night sky, shrouded in a mantle of deepest blue, studded with numberless constellations of stars. Each is a point of light, each a celestial shard of glory bestowing glimpses of the eternal.

Miracles in Scripture are like the stars. They help us glimpse the eternal. And they, like the heavens, declare the glory of God.

To gaze upon miracles in the Old and New Testaments is to look upon the great tapestry of redemption, to look upon scenes and lives touched by eternity, settings of almighty declaration, moments marked by deliverance, by mercy, or by visionary unfoldings of God's holy purpose.

Creation. The birth of humanity. The fall, and the matchless promise of redemption to come. God's dealings with Noah, Abraham, Moses, and Elisha. The incarnation. The miracles of Jesus. His death and resurrection. The triumph and purchase of our redemption. An apostle's conversion. The advent of the church. To learn of these holy events and people—supremely, to look upon the Savior—is to see the power of God, and to see how God has always sought to draw us to Himself. He is our eternal home. Miracles point the way there.

1 ✦ In the Beginning:
The Miracle of Our World

Thou hast brought us into being out of nothing.
—The Liturgy of Saint John Chrysostom[1]

God calls for things that are not, and they come.
—William Cowper[2]

And where are all His miracles which our fathers told us about?"(Judg. 6:13). For Jews and Christians alike, the answer to this ancient question from the book of Judges must be traced to the origin of the world itself.

What is the first miracle? God created the heavens and the earth. All that we know—this world and the universe in which it resides—were spoken into existence through a mighty, matchless word.

"Then God said, 'Let there be . . . ' "; it was the soaring refrain an omnipotent God gave to the song of creation (Gen. 1:3). Each time it was voiced, something more of the world we know became a reality: light, the heavens and earth, flora, fauna, and humanity itself. All have their origin in God.

As we have seen, every miracle is "accomplished by God as a sign of some purposes of his own."[3] The first miracle reveals that God is the king of creation—the heavens and earth His royal decree. They show forth His glory.

The psalmist told us this: "The heavens declare the glory of God; and the firmament shows His handiwork. . . . Their line has gone out through all the earth, and their words to the end of the world" (Ps. 19:1, 4).

The writer of Psalm 93 heard this celestial hymn of praise. It called forth stirring reflections in which he saw God, the king of creation, "clothed with majesty . . . [and] strength" (v. 1).

And that is how we should see God in this first of all miracles. It shows Him to be the majestic Creator, the gifting God who decreed the world's existence because it was His good will and pleasure. He is our beneficent, almighty sovereign.

This truth is captured beautifully in lines from the poet William Cowper, which tell us that "a ray of heav'nly light gilds all forms . . . in the vast and the minute." In them we see "the unambiguous footsteps of God."[4]

~

The foregoing paragraphs speak of the majesty of God as reflected in the colossal act of creation. It ought to inspire within us an enduring, overwhelming sense of awe. And so it does whenever we see a sunset that far surpasses any skyscape rendered by J. M. W. Turner, mountains whose beauty far transcends any sculpture Michelangelo crafted, or a sea alongside which any painting of Winslow Homer pales in comparison. "I am the LORD, who makes all things," we read in Isaiah 44:24, "who stretches out the heavens all alone, who spreads abroad the earth by Myself."

But lost in wonder at such sights, we may tragically miss asking ourselves a question that gets to the heart of the miracle of creation: why did God do it?

No one has written more beautifully in framing an answer to this question than Bishop Kallistos Ware, whose reflections grace a subsequent chapter in this book—one exploring the faith heritage of the Orthodox Church. "If nothing compelled God to create," Bishop Ware asked rhetorically, "why then did He choose to do so?" It is a staggering question, he admitted, but

> in so far as such a question admits of an answer, our reply must be: God's motive in creation is His love. Rather than say that He created the universe out of nothing, we should say that he created it out of His own self, which is love. We should think, not of God the Manufacturer or God the Craftsman, but of God the Lover. . . . God's love is, in the literal sense of the word, "ecstatic"—a love that causes God to go out from Himself. By voluntary choice God created the world in "ecstatic" love, so that there might be besides Himself other beings to participate in the life and love that are His.[5]

This moving description of God's purpose in creation is one rooted and complemented in Scripture. Do we remember the description given in Job 38, when the Lord spoke out of the whirlwind? "I laid the foundations of the earth" (v. 4), the Lord told Job, but do you know where its foundations are fastened, or who laid its cornerstone? Were you there "when the morning stars sang together, and all the sons of God shouted for joy?" (v. 7). As this passage shows, there was an ecstasy that marked the creation of the world. The very heavens and earth rejoiced in what God had done.

Does this sound strange? It shouldn't. For 1 Chronicles 16:31 is just one of many passages that declares, "Let the heavens rejoice, and let the

earth be glad; and let them say among the nations, 'The LORD reigns.'"
So, too, we read in Psalm 96:11: "Let the heavens rejoice, and let the
earth be glad; let the sea roar, and all its fullness."

And if love and joy were woven into the fabric of creation, other aspects
of God's divine intent are present within that matchless tapestry. Consider
Isaiah 45:8: "Rain down, you heavens, from above, and let the skies pour
down righteousness; let the earth open, let them bring forth salvation, and
let righteousness spring up together. I, the LORD, have created it."

All of these passages, in concert, only deepen our sense of what God
imparted to us in the miracle that is the creation of the world. Creation
was God's opening movement in the symphony of our reality, and there
is none other like it.

~

Moving from the creation of the world to the flow of human history in
the Old Testament, we begin to learn more about the nature of miracles
as they transpired among men and women whose lives were closely associated with the purposes of God.

Here, *The Oxford Companion to the Bible* has done a good service in
describing the several kinds of miracles that occur in the Old Testament.
Among them are *confirmatory* miracles, "through which God shows
his choice and support of certain individuals or groups." Confirmatory
miracles were displayed prominently in God's dealings with the patri-
archs Abraham and Jacob, as well as Moses, who led the Israelites out of
bondage in Egypt.[6]

A second kind of Old Testament miracle is that which is *judgmental*
in nature. We see them in the plagues God visited on the Egyptians
because they refused to obey the commands of God spoken to them by
Moses or in the fall of the walls of Jericho because its citizens resisted
Israel's entry into the promised land.[7]

Miracles of *mercy* are a third type of miracle displayed in the Old Testament. In the book of 2 Kings, for example, the prophet Elisha is the mediator through whom God performs miraculous healings.[8]

Miracles of *deliverance* represent a fourth kind of miracle found in the Old Testament. The preservation of Daniel in the lions' den is one famous example, as is the saving of his friends from death in the fiery furnace.[9]

Lastly, a fifth type of miracle described in the Old Testament is a miracle of *divine vision*. Isaiah, Ezekiel, and Daniel were three prophets of God who were favored with such visions from God. These visions were given to "reveal God's purpose for his people, or to achieve some form of deliverance or punishment in behalf of individuals, of the Israelite nation, of her enemies, or of the minority who remain faithful to God."[10]

～

Now that each of these kinds of miracles has been described in brief, we may take time to explore them more fully. We cannot take every instance of these types of miracles into discussion, but we can select representative examples of each and consider what they tell us about God. For miracles are all about God and what He wishes us to know of Himself.

2 + Creation:
The Miracle of Humanity

Try to conceive a man without the ideas of God, eternity, freedom, will, absolute truth; of the good, the true, the beautiful, the infinite. An animal endowed with a memory of appearances and facts might remain. But the man will have vanished, and you have instead a creature more subtle than any beast of the field, but likewise cursed above every beast of the field. Upon the belly must it go, and dust must it eat all the days of its life.

—SAMUEL TAYLOR COLERIDGE[1]

In *Paradise Lost*, the poet John Milton said to look upon Adam and Eve in the splendor of the garden of Eden was to see that "the image of their glorious Maker shone."[2] Once the heavens and earth had been created, a meeting unlike any other took place: a council to consider the creation of humanity. How matchless a scene must it have been when the Triune God—Father, Son, and Holy Spirit—met in holy conference for this task. We do not know what that scene looked like, but we do know what was said. And so we read in Genesis 1:26–27: "Then God said, 'Let Us make man in Our image, according to Our likeness; let them have dominion over the fish of the sea, over the birds of the air, and over the cattle, over all the earth and over every creeping thing that creeps on the earth.' So God created man in His own image; in the image of God He created him; male and female He created them."

In the act of creation, God extended the mighty power of His royal scepter to bestow the gift of life upon Adam and Eve—with all its attendant blessings. What were these? For a classic description of the creation of humanity, we could do no better than to turn to the great seventeenth-century biblical commentator Matthew Henry. With great eloquence and insight, he described the gifts God bequeathed to Adam and Eve.

At the outset, Henry noted that the creation of Adam "was a more signal and immediate act of divine wisdom and power" than that of the other creatures to which God had given life earlier in the Genesis account. "Man," Henry continued, "was to be a creature different from all that had been hitherto made. Flesh and spirit, heaven and earth, [were] put together in him, [that he might] be allied to both worlds."[3]

This was wondrous in itself, but Henry placed special emphasis on the divine council God convened as Adam was to be given life. In no other place within the Genesis account did God do this. That unique and most sacred fact impressed Henry deeply. Where Adam was concerned,

[God] called a council to consider of the making of him; *Let us make man.* The three persons of the Trinity, Father, Son, and Holy Ghost, consult about it, and concur in it, because man, when he was made, was to be dedicated and devoted to Father, Son, and Holy Ghost. Into that Great Name we are, with good reason, baptized, for to that Great Name we owe our being.[4]

Henry moved next to a play on words born of wonder over what God had wrought in creating Man. "God made the worlds," Henry marveled, "not only the great world, but man, *the little world*, [and]

formed the human body." But there was more besides, and Henry knew it. The soul of Adam, *therein* lay the essence of our humanity. "It is the soul," he wrote, "the great soul of man, that does especially bear God's image. The soul is a spirit, an intelligent immortal spirit . . . resembling God, the Father of Spirits, and the Soul of the world." Then followed one of the most beautiful phrases in all commentary literature: "The spirit of man," Henry wrote, "*is the candle of the Lord.*"[5]

Next, the great commentator turned to Eve—Adam's gift from the Lord. All that has been said of Adam was most certainly true of her. Fashioned as she was from one of Adam's ribs, she was endowed—no less than he—with all the gifts that Adam had before God. But then, Henry also noted that since Eve was given to Adam because "it was not good for him to be alone," there were things about her creation and its intent that were unique to her. And what Henry said here is one of the finest, most eloquent descriptions ever given of Eve and her place at the fountainhead of our humanity. "The woman," Henry noted, "was made of a rib out of the side of Adam; not made out of his head to top him, not out of his feet to be trampled upon by him, but out of his side to be equal with him, under his arm to be protected, and *near his heart to be beloved.*"[6]

When we consider the creation of Adam and Eve further, we might say a great deal about the capacity for creativity that led to all the arts as we know them or the physical prowess we so often see displayed in athletics. A great catalog might list all the things history has revealed of the richness of our humanity. God was indeed generous beyond measure to our first parents.

But the chief gift, the capstone of all the gifts God gave humanity, was woven into the gift of life itself. For far beyond the physical aspect of our being, the matchless gift is one that lies within: our souls.

No one has written more helpfully about the nature of our souls, or in words more readily understood, than Billy Graham. He said,

> The Bible teaches that the person is more than just a body. . . . Our
> souls are created in the image of the living God. Just as our bodies have
> certain characteristics and appetites, so do our souls. The characteris-
> tics of the soul are personality, intelligence, conscience and memory.
> [Moreover,] the human soul (or spirit) longs for peace, contentment
> and happiness. Most of all, the soul has an appetite for God—a yearn-
> ing to . . . have fellowship with Him forever.[7]

Many beautiful thoughts are expressed here. Let us consider the
first great statement that Dr. Graham introduced: the personality, intelligence, conscience, and memory each of us possesses. Many of us have
heard the phrase "there's no one quite like you." So far as our souls are
concerned, this phrase could not express the truth more completely. We
are all unique, according to God's sovereign plan and design. There was
no one quite like Adam and Eve, and there never will be. The same is
true of us, their descendants.

Sometimes we need to remember who we are and who God created
us to be. Each of us is a beloved child of the Creator—someone precious
and unique—a vital part of the great cosmic story that God has been
writing throughout all time. Thus our lives are filled with profound
meaning and significance. We are not solitary travelers left to our own
devices, at the mercy of mere impersonal chance. God has written each
one of us into His story. We are, most truly, part of His plan. It is as
the psalmist has written: "You formed my inward parts; You covered
me in my mother's womb. . . . Your eyes saw my substance, being yet
unformed. And in Your book they all were written, the days fashioned
for me, when as yet there were none of them" (Ps. 139:13, 16).

The second great statement that Dr. Graham made on the nature
of the soul is that "the human soul longs for peace, contentment and
happiness."[8] This was a theme taken up also by Graham's distinguished
evangelistic predecessor, D. L. Moody, who described the longing for
peace that all humans share:

You know the world is after peace; that's the cry of the world. That is what the world wants. Probe the human heart, and you'll find down in its depths a [need], a cry for rest. Where can rest be found? Here it is, right here. Put your trust in the living God, with all your heart, mind, soul, and strength, and you'll have peace.[9]

Lastly, Dr. Graham noted that, above all, "the soul has an appetite for God—a yearning to . . . have fellowship with Him forever."[10]

Think of that. Consider as well that there was a time when no humans were present on the earth. This is deeply important, for, as Oxford scholar John C. Lennox noted, Genesis 1 and 2 are not chapters that speak of God revealing Himself to humans who already existed. Rather, they explain how human beings came to exist in the first place. These chapters do not describe "the calling of existing human beings into fellowship with God," but state "how God physically created human beings from the dust of the earth in order to have fellowship with him."[11]

Do we ever stop to consider this? God created humanity because He desired fellowship with men and women—beings who could freely choose to love Him and, in gratitude for the gift of their existence, live their lives in communion with Him. Moreover, as Dr. Lennox has noted, this gift of fellowship was instantaneous. "The Genesis narrative," he wrote, "makes it evident that Adam and Eve did not need to be called into fellowship with God at the beginning: they were in fellowship with God from the start."[12] Each day God walked in the garden of Eden, and each day He walked with Adam and Eve. Oh, the wonder of what this must have been like!

And yet, tragically, horribly, it was not to last. It was the sin of Adam and Eve, Dr. Lennox wrote, "that broke that fellowship."[13] Sin sundered the fellowship God intended from the very creation of the world. The wonder of walking with God was to be no more. Could there ever have been a loss more grievous?

But—and herein lies the road to another miracle—when Adam and

Eve were most lost and in need of rescue, God gave a promise that all would at last be put right. How Adam and Eve were lost, and how God came with news of blessed hope, will be taken up in the next chapter.

3 ✦ God's Declaration: The Miracle of Our Promised Redemption

"You come of the Lord Adam and the Lady Eve," said Aslan. "And that is both honour enough to erect the head of the poorest beggar, and shame enough to bow the shoulders of the greatest emperor on earth."

—C. S. Lewis[1]

It was the cataclysm that forever altered the world—the world God intended. "Life in God's garden" is the heading the New King James Version of the Bible gives Genesis 2—the place where Adam and Eve's life in fellowship with God is described. Can we picture the most verdant and breathtaking place we've ever seen? It was nothing like God's garden. No mountain vista, no prospect of the sea, no jewel of the natural world that we know was ever like it.

But all this was just the setting.

Life in God's garden.

God was the Life of His garden! Adam and Eve knew Him! They could walk with Him, talk with Him, receive gifts from Him—as Adam had received Eve as a gift from the Lord. We can have no idea of the felicity, the sheer weight of blessing and happiness that Adam and Eve knew. They spent every day with their Maker! Every evening He walked with them in the cool of the garden. Was there ever anything like this, anything so wonderful?

And yet it all proved a fragile thing that could be broken by a tragic choice. The poet John Milton described it all in just two words—the title of his epic masterpiece in verse—*Paradise Lost*. There is no more heartbreaking account in all of Scripture than what takes place in Genesis 3:1–13.

> Now the serpent was more cunning than any beast of the field which the LORD God had made. And he said to the woman, "Has God indeed said, 'You shall not eat of every tree of the garden'?"
>
> And the woman said to the serpent, "We may eat the fruit of the trees of the garden; but of the fruit of the tree which is in the midst of the garden, God has said, 'You shall not eat it, nor shall you touch it, lest you die.'"
>
> Then the serpent said to the woman, "You will not surely die. For God knows that in the day you eat of it your eyes will be opened, and you will be like God, knowing good and evil."
>
> So when the woman saw that the tree was good for food, that it was pleasant to the eyes, and a tree desirable to make one wise, she took of its fruit and ate. She also gave to her husband with her, and he ate.
>
> Then the eyes of both of them were opened, and they knew that they were naked; and they sewed fig leaves together and made themselves coverings.
>
> And they heard the sound of the LORD God walking in the garden in the cool of the day, and Adam and his wife hid themselves from the presence of the LORD God among the trees of the garden.
>
> Then the LORD God called to Adam and said to him, "Where are you?"

So he said, "I heard Your voice in the garden, and I was afraid because I was naked; and I hid myself."

And He said, "Who told you that you were naked? Have you eaten from the tree of which I commanded you that you should not eat?"

Then the man said, "The woman whom You gave to be with me, she gave me of the tree, and I ate."

And the LORD God said to the woman, "What is this you have done?"

The woman said, "The serpent deceived me, and I ate."

~

What was lost when Adam and Eve fell into sin? According to biblical commentator John Stott, the Bible tells us that in creation God established for human beings three essential relationships: the first was to Himself, for He made humanity in His own image; the second was that of humans to one another, for the human race was plural from the beginning; and the third relationship was to the earth and the creatures over which God gave Adam and Eve dominion.[2]

Furthermore, the number three is a number of great significance in Scripture. In establishing three essential relationships for human beings, God was placing the sign of His majestic blessing upon the world that our first parents knew. As biblical scholar J. E. Hartill wrote, "With the number three we come to the number of union, approval, approbation, coordination, completeness, and perfection. It is the number of the Trinity, three Persons in One God—three members of divine perfection."[3] In the garden of Eden, therefore, God had established things that made for a true paradise.

It goes far beyond any notion we have of the word *tragic* to say that all three of the relationships established by God were sundered by Adam and Eve's fall into sin. They were horribly broken, and the fallout was both instantaneous and catastrophic. As Stott wrote: "All three relationships were skewed by the fall. [First] Adam and Eve were banished from the presence of the Lord God in the garden, [second] they blamed each other for what had happened, and [third] the good earth was cursed on account of their disobedience."[4]

Commentator Matthew Henry has also described what unfolded when the fall took place. We are separated by nearly three hundred years from his time, but no writer has surpassed the tragic eloquence of his words. He wrote,

> The eyes of their consciences were opened; their hearts smote them for what they had done. Now, when it was too late, they saw the folly of eating forbidden fruit. They saw the happiness they had fallen from, and the misery they were fallen into. They saw a loving God provoked, his grace and favour forfeited. . . . They were deprived of all the honours and joys of their paradise state, and exposed to all the miseries that might justly be expected from an angry God. They were disarmed, their defence was departed from them.[5]

Then, in one brief but devastating passage, Henry described the ravages of sin. "What a dishonour and disquietment sin is. It [causes injury] wherever it is admitted, sets men against themselves, disturbs their peace, and destroys all their comforts."[6]

We cannot imagine the overwhelming sense of grief that descended upon Adam and Eve. Once, they could see so many wondrous things, and now a terrible blindness had fallen on them. All that they had known was gone. "Before they had sinned," Henry wrote, "if they had heard the voice of the Lord God coming toward them, they would have run to meet Him." Now, He had become a terror to them. They had become a terror to themselves, and full of confusion. Consumed by fear, they fled from His presence.[7]

~

Yet, when all was most dire, God did something beyond anything Adam and Eve could have asked or imagined. True enough, a cosmic battle had been joined between the forces of darkness—represented by the serpent that had led Adam and Eve into sin—and God Himself. But in the wake of Adam and Eve's searing despair, God came bearing a promise strong with hope, beautiful as the rise of the sun on the wings of the morning. Scholars call this promise the *protevangelium*, or *first gospel*. This matchless promise confirmed that God would win this cosmic battle; indeed, the issue would *never* be in doubt. God revealed Himself to Adam and Eve as their almighty deliverer, and established that truth for all time.

"After the Fall," scholars tell us, "God purposed human redemption. There was a foregleam of this purpose in the protevangelium."[8] According to it, judgment was first pronounced upon the serpent, that is, upon Satan, the great deceiver. "Because you have done this," God said to the serpent, "you are cursed more than all cattle, and more than every beast of the field; on your belly you shall go, and you shall eat dust all the days of your life" (Gen. 3:14).

Then, God said that though there would henceforth be conflict between the seed of the serpent and the seed of the woman, one born of woman would ultimately triumph. "He shall bruise your head, and you shall bruise His heel" (Gen. 3:15). This Son who was to come would be wounded, but would have the final and complete victory.

God's mighty promise looked to the atoning work of Christ. Word was given that *the Word* would come and be made flesh—the Word who would dwell among us. Assurance was given that we would behold His glory, "the glory as of the only begotten of the Father, full of grace and truth" (John 1:14 KJV). The Word would become our redeemer—the one who would rescue us from the curse and death sentence of sin. The Word who would be "the way, the truth, and the life" (John 14:6 KJV).

In the protevangelium, God the Father gave us the first, most precious glimpse that all would at last be put right. All that had seemingly been broken beyond repair would at last be mended. Our mourning would someday be turned to everlasting joy.

~

Matthew Henry concluded,

> Here was the dawning of the gospel-day, no sooner was the wound given, than the remedy was provided and revealed. Here, in the beginning of the Bible, it is written of Christ. By faith in this promise, we have reason to think our first parents, and the patriarchs before the flood, were justified and saved. To this promise, and the benefit of it, [by] serving God day and night, they hoped to come.[9]

And so, while the word *protevangelium* might seem to many a cumbersome, hard-to-pronounce term of theology, it hearkens to the first—and many would say most beautiful—promise of grace found in Scripture. The hymn writer John Newton, who gave the world the timeless song "Amazing Grace," was deeply moved by the promise of redemption that God gave to Adam and Eve. He cast his thoughts in verse, the basis for one of his many fine hymns. It is a most fitting way to close this chapter.

> *On man, in his own image made,*
> *How much did God bestow!*
> *The whole creation homage paid,*
> *And own'd him Lord below.*
> *He dwelt in Eden's garden, stor'd*
> *With sweets for every sense;*
> *And there, with his descending Lord*

He walk'd in confidence.
But oh! by sin how quickly chang'd!
His honour forfeited.
His heart from God and truth estrang'd,
His conscience fill'd with dread!
But grace, unask'd, his heart subdu'd,
And all his guilt forgave;
By faith the promis'd Seed he view'd,
And felt his power to save.[10]

4 ✦ Noah and the Flood: Miracles of Deliverance

In the day of wrath, when the flood swept away a guilty race, the chosen family were secured in the resting-place of the ark, which floated them from the old condemned world into the new earth of the rainbow and the covenant. . . . [So it is with us,] we rest in the promises of our faithful God, knowing that His words are full of truth and power.

—C. H. Spurgeon[1]

T he story of Noah is a wondrous story, though set amidst dire circumstances. The first word written of him in Genesis 6 is that he "found grace in the eyes of the Lord" (v. 8). We learn next that he "was a just man," and "walked with God" (v. 9). His life and conduct were beacons in a dark time of human history.

Tragically, all others who lived then were corrupt and violent—so much so that scripture tells us "the earth was filled with violence" (v. 11). All save Noah and his family had forsaken God—their Maker and the Creator of the world. "The wickedness of man was great," we read, and "every intent of the thoughts of his heart was only evil continually" (v. 5).

In the space of only a few pages following the creation of Adam and Eve, our first parents, we read words that are shocking and cataclysmic: "And the LORD was sorry that He had made man on the earth, and He was grieved in His heart. So the LORD said, 'I will destroy man whom I have created . . .'" (vv. 6–7). Man and beast alike were to be annihilated. A death knell had sounded over the very creation in which God had once rejoiced, and once called good.

But Noah, whose very name reads like hope in the annals of history, would be saved. He who was just and had found grace would not be subjected to the dire sentence God would mete out to mankind. He and his family would be saved.

God commanded Noah to build an ark, a vessel to carry him, his family, and two of every living creature safely through the flood that God would bring upon the earth to destroy it. And even as God issued this command to His faithful servant, He spoke the first of His confirmatory miracles: "I will establish My covenant with you" (v. 18). Noah, his family, and the creatures that would be housed in the ark would be kept alive.

The ark was a literal means of salvation for Noah and his family, but it was also a symbol of God's grace and mercy amid the terrible judgment that mankind had brought upon itself. Following the preservation of Noah, his family, and all the creatures housed within the ark, God wrought a further miracle and sign of blessing: one that came in the form of a promise.

The story unfolds in Genesis 8. Beginning in verse 20, we read that with gratitude beyond words for all that God had done, Noah built an altar to the Lord and there offered sacrifices to Him. With this, the Lord was well pleased, and He said, "I will never again curse the ground for man's sake . . . nor will I again destroy every living thing as I have done" (v. 21). Then the Lord confirmed His word with a beautiful poem of promise:

While the earth remains,
Seedtime and harvest,
Cold and heat,
Winter and summer,
And day and night
Shall not cease. (v. 22)

Grace and mercy then flowed further, taking the form of a sacred and inviolable covenant. To Noah and his sons, God said,

And as for Me, behold, I establish My covenant with you and with your descendants after you, and with every living creature. . . . Never again shall all flesh be cut off by the waters of the flood; never again shall there be a flood to destroy the earth. (Gen. 9:9–11)

Last of all, God sealed the covenant of His promise with a sign of peace. We know it as the rainbow. God said,

This is the sign of the covenant which I make between Me and you, and every living creature that is with you, for perpetual generations: I set My rainbow in the cloud, and it shall be for the sign of the covenant between Me and the earth. It shall be, when I bring a cloud over the earth, that the rainbow shall be seen in the cloud. . . . And I will look on it to remember the everlasting covenant between God and every living creature. (vv. 12–16)

Matthew Henry wrote that the story of Noah was the story of "the return of [God's] mercy to mankind." God's call to Noah, Henry continued, "is very kind, like that of a tender father to his children to come indoors when he sees night or a storm coming."[2]

The storm had indeed come. The flood had overwhelmed the earth and destroyed all that had been. When Noah emerged from the ark, a new earth awaited him and his family. Setting foot on dry land once more, his thoughts might have run to many things, not least the building of some kind of shelter, for none as yet existed. Henry captured that moment, and what Noah actually did, in words that still stir the soul:

> Noah was now gone out into a desolate world, where, one might have thought, his first care would have been to build a house for himself, but he begins with an altar for God. He begins well, that begins with God. Though Noah's stock of cattle was small . . . saved at great care and pains, he did not grudge to serve God out of it. Serving God with our little is the way to make it more; we must never think that is wasted with which God is honoured. The first thing done [by Noah] in the new world was an act of worship.[3]

There was a very great lesson to be discerned in the miracles God wrought in the life of Noah. This the writer of Proverbs knew well: "Trust in the LORD with all your heart, and lean not on your own understanding; in all your ways acknowledge Him, and He shall direct your paths" (3:5–6).

Henry closed his commentary on Noah with a kindred thought: "What we do in obedience to the command of God, and in faith, we ourselves shall certainly have the comfort of, first or last."[4]

∿

Other biblical scholars, like Dr. Walter Kaiser, have noted that there are echoes of the fall of Adam and Eve in Noah's story. Stating that the fall of humanity was "earth's first greatest time of need," Kaiser wrote that the story of the flood unfolded during the period of "earth's second greatest time of need." Then, as with Adam and Eve, "an enactment of the salvation of God" was needed. Once again, wickedness had forced the hand of God. Judgment would come, a sentence upon the wickedness of humanity would have to be passed. But the family of Noah, righteous and faithfully obedient, would be saved.[5]

There is another parallel between the stories of Adam and Noah. Even as God had once said to Adam, "Be fruitful and multiply" (Gen. 1:28), the same phrase was also spoken by God to Noah in Genesis 9:1: "So God blessed Noah and his sons, and said to them: 'Be fruitful and multiply, and fill the earth.'"[6]

Last of all, Dr. Kaiser wrote, "God added His special covenant with nature" to the story of his dealings with Noah after the floodwaters had receded. He would maintain "seedtime and harvest, cold and heat, winter and summer, and day and night" without interruption as long as the earth remained (Gen. 8:22). This promise would be confirmed each time a rainbow appeared in the sky. And God also promised that He would "never again curse the ground for man's sake" (Gen. 8:21). In Adam's time, God had cursed the ground (Gen. 3:17). For Noah and all to come after him, such a curse would never be levied. Such points of connection and commonality lend richness and context to Noah's story. Despite the persistent wickedness of humanity, God's redemptive purposes remained.

Many had taken to calling themselves "sons of God," or kings after the fashion of the ancient Near Eastern world. Noah would only acknowledge God as his sovereign. All but a few in Noah's time would reject God, thinking to usurp His place. But God would save those whom He could.[7]

∼

Apart from the points in common between Adam and Noah, it is important to note that several kinds of miracles are associated with Noah's story. All fit within the framework of five kinds of miracles described in chapter 1 of this book. God's decision to save Noah and his family was a *confirmatory* miracle, which is a miracle "through which God shows his choice and support of certain individuals or groups."[8] The destruction of the world by the great flood was a miracle of *judgment*, as was meted out in "the plagues God visited on the Egyptians because they refused to obey the commands of God spoken to them by Moses."[9]

The preservation of Noah and his family in the ark was also a miracle of *mercy* that anticipated the miracles of healing performed through the prophet Elisha later in the Old Testament.[10] Furthermore, the saving of Noah and his family constituted a miracle of *deliverance* in that it resembled "the preservation of Daniel in the lions' den or the saving of his friends from death in the fiery furnace."[11]

Lastly, the story of Noah embodied the fifth type of miracle described in the Old Testament: that of *divine vision*. God spoke to Noah in a miraculous way, warning him of the judgment that was to come upon the wickedness of humanity. He told Noah how to construct the ark, how to save the animals that were to be placed in it, and how to save his family. Miracles of *divine vision*, as stated above, are acts that "reveal God's purpose for his people, or achieve some form of deliverance or punishment in behalf of individuals."[12]

Noah was delivered, for he had found grace in the eyes of the Lord. Two hundred years ago, the miracle of that deliverance spoke powerfully to John Newton, a man whom God had carried safely though many storms—"many dangers, toils and snares." So it was that he took pen in hand to remember Noah's story:

> *When the sun, with cheerful beams,*
> *Smiles upon a low'ring sky,*
> *Soon its aspect soften'd seems,*
> *And a rainbow meets the eye . . .*

Thus the Lord's supporting power
Brightest to his saints appears,
When affliction's threat'ning hour
Fills the sky with clouds and fears,
He can wonders then perform,
Paint a rainbow on the storm.
All their graces doubly shine,
When their troubles press them sore;
And the promises divine
Give them joys unknown before:
As the colours of the bow
To the cloud their brightness owe.[13]

5 + Abraham: Miracles and the Friend of God

But Isaac spoke to Abraham his father and said, . . . "Look, the fire and the wood, but where is the lamb for a burnt offering?"

And Abraham said, "My son, God will provide for Himself the lamb for a burnt offering." . . .

Then they came to the place of which God had told him. And Abraham built an altar there and placed the wood in order; and he bound Isaac his son, and laid him on the altar, upon the wood.

And Abraham stretched out his hand and took the knife to slay his son.

But the Angel of the LORD *called to him from heaven and said, "Abraham, Abraham!" So he said, "Here I am."*

And He said, "Do not lay your hand on the lad, . . . for now I know that you fear God, since you have not withheld your son, your only son, from Me."

—GENESIS 22:7–12

There are many who have found this story from Genesis deeply troubling, even horrific. How could any father contemplate the slaying of his son? How on earth could a loving God command such a thing?

These are not easy questions, but they need to be asked. Scripture does have an answer for them, and therein lies the basis for a miracle of *divine vision*, *deliverance*, and *mercy* at Mount Moriah—when God appeared to Abraham, and Isaac was spared. What unfolded at Mount Moriah was, from God's perspective, profoundly necessary and the reason why Abraham was so greatly beloved and called "the friend of God" (James 2:23).

Billy Graham is one of those who have reflected at length about this trying chapter in Abraham's life. "God tested the reality of Abraham's faith," Graham has said, telling him he had to sacrifice his beloved son Isaac. We cannot know the anguish that surely must have haunted and hurt the heart of Abraham through the long night as he wondered what this supreme sacrifice meant and what would be required of him. He had nothing to go on but God's word. But such was the strength of his faith that he resolved to call Isaac to him and do what God had asked. "The Bible," Graham wrote, "records no greater act of faith."[1]

We know nothing of what Abraham's feelings were when he walked with his son to the place where the altar would be built. He knew the awful mission God had appointed for him; Isaac knew nothing of what lay ahead. As they walked along, and Abraham looked at his son, how could he have found the strength to take another step in fulfilling this task?

And what did Isaac say? Was he mute as his father bound him? Did he not once say, "Father, what are you doing? . . . Why?" Here, Scripture is silent. But to ask such questions is to begin, perhaps, to glimpse something of the dread and pain father and son must have felt in that awful moment. Young as he was, Isaac knew what sacrifices were. He had seen animals ritually slain in this way. What was he feeling? And what of his father? We can only guess.

But in the terse language of the Genesis account, we do know that Isaac somehow submitted when his father bound him. He was then placed on the altar. His father unsheathed his knife, prepared to strike.

Then God intervened. At the last moment, the Angel of the Lord called to Abraham out of heaven, and said, "Abraham, Abraham! . . . Do not lay your hand on the lad, or do anything to him; for now I know that you fear God, since you have not withheld your son, your only son, from Me" (Gen. 22:11–12).

Old Testament scholar Douglas Stuart wrote that "within ancient Semitic culture, calling someone by saying his or her name twice was a way of expressing endearment, that is, great affection and friendship." Thus Abraham "would have understood immediately that he was being addressed by someone who loved and was concerned about him."[2]

Building further on this, Billy Graham has written of how many scholars believe, as he does, that the angel spoken of here was in reality a "theophany," or a miraculous Old Testament appearance of the Lord Jesus. *Theophany* is a term that denotes the manifestation of God on earth. Here, Christ assumed the role of an angel and thereby showed the principle of substitutionary atonement. God had demanded of Abraham the death of his son. That demand had to be met, and it was. But in place of Isaac, God the Father accepted the animal substitute of a ram through the Angel who was in reality His Son.[3]

Abraham heard the voice of God calling on him to spare his son. He also knew in the moment God said his name twice that the love of God was being poured out upon him and his son Isaac. The writer of the New Testament book of Hebrews tells us that Abraham reasoned "that God was able to raise him up, even from the dead, from which he also received him in a figurative sense" (11:19).

Abraham may have thought such things as he carried out God's command. But until he heard the voice of God calling to him in love, he didn't know with certainty that Isaac would be restored to him. Somehow, he was enabled to see with the eyes of faith. And when father and son heard that heavenly voice, the voice of mercy and love, how their hearts must have leapt!

But however awesome that moment must have been—a mixture of wonder, gratitude, and relief—Dr. Graham was surely right to ask, "How could God have asked for a human sacrifice? How could He have asked Abraham to slay Isaac when He had forbidden the killing of people (Gen. 9:6)? Is this not inconsistent with the nature of God?"[4]

The answer to these questions can be found in Paul's epistle to the Romans. There we read, "He who did not spare His own Son, but delivered Him up for us all, how shall He not with Him also freely give us all things?" (Rom. 8:32). God could ask Abraham to slay Isaac because He Himself had let His own Son die. God had not asked Abraham to do anything more than what He had in fact done with His only begotten Son.[5]

What is more—and this is crucial—Graham wrote,

> Neither Abraham nor Isaac had to drink the cup God presented. Isaac did not die, and Abraham did not slay him. But when we come to another cup in the Garden of Gethsemane, the picture is startlingly different. Jesus has now come; as the guiltless one for the guilty, as the sinless one for sinners, He was willing to accept the condemnation of God for the world's guilt, identifying Himself with it through His own death on Calvary.[6]

In pointing to the person of Christ to say what needs to be said about the story of Abraham, Isaac, and Mount Moriah, Dr. Graham has identified something vitally significant: Abraham was especially favored by God and allowed to see Christ in theophanic form.

To build on this key insight, it is important to ask one all-important question: what was the nature of Abraham's prior encounters with God? To explore the answers to this question is to be given a profoundly rich context in which to view what unfolded on Mount Moriah.

In Genesis 12, we read that God first spoke to Abraham. We are not sure how this happened; perhaps it was in a dream or vision. But we do know that it was the first of eleven times that Abraham either heard the voice of the Lord or called upon Him. Well before the events of Genesis 22, there was already a long-standing relationship between Abraham and his God.

What was the nature of each specific encounter with God? The first, described in Genesis 12:1–3, was a moment when God said to Abraham (then called Abram):

> *Get out of your country,*
> *From your family*
> *And from your father's house,*
> *To a land that I will show you.*
> *I will make you a great nation;*
> *I will bless you*
> *And make your name great;*
> *And you shall be a blessing.*
> *I will bless those who bless you,*
> *And I will curse him who curses you;*
> *And in you all the families of the earth shall be blessed.*

This was a *confirmatory* miracle, one in which God called Abraham and set him apart as a person upon whom special favor had been conferred. It also appears to have been a miracle of *divine vision*, wherein he learned that his descendants, to his complete astonishment, would become "a great nation." But more than this, he was told that in him "all the families of the earth [would] be blessed." It was an utterly extraordinary first encounter with God.

Still later, in Genesis 12:7, the Lord appeared to Abram a second time. He had by this time journeyed to the land of Canaan, as God had directed him to. Now that he had arrived there, specifically in the place called Shechem, the Lord told him, "To your descendants I will give this land." And so Abram built an altar there "to the LORD, who had appeared to him." From Shechem, Abram moved to the mountain east of Bethel. Pitching his tent there, he built a second altar to the Lord and called on His name.

In Genesis 13, Abram, having spent some time in Egypt, returned to Bethel. There, at the altar he had made, he once again called on the name of the Lord. By this time, Abram had become wealthy, possessing large numbers of "flocks and herds and tents" (v. 5). So, too, had Abram's nephew Lot; indeed, their combined possessions and holdings were so great that "the land was not able to support them, that they might dwell together" (v. 6). Strife inevitably arose between the herdsmen of uncle and nephew, and so it was decided that they should settle in different regions of the land before them. Lot went to the east, pitching his tent near the cities of the plain of Jordan, "even as far as Sodom" (v. 12). Abram, meanwhile, heard from the Lord once again, who said to him:

Lift your eyes now and look from the place where you are—northward, southward, eastward, and westward; for all the land which you see I give to you and your descendants forever. And I will make your descendants as the dust of the earth; so that if a man could number the dust of the earth, then your descendants also could be numbered. Arise, walk in the land through its length and its width, for I give it to you. (Gen. 13:14–17)

Following this, Abram moved his tent, and went and dwelt by the terebinth trees of Mamre, which were in Hebron. There he built a third altar to the Lord.

Abram had therefore heard the word of the Lord, or called upon Him, several times before; as we learn in Genesis 14, he met "Melchizedek king of Salem," and "priest of God Most High" (v. 18).

Melchizedek is an extraordinary figure. As we learn from the seventh chapter of the book of Hebrews, his name means "king of righteousness." He was also king of Salem, which means "king of peace." The writer of Hebrews went on to say that Melchizedek was "without father, without mother, without genealogy, having neither beginning of days nor end of life, but made like the Son of God, remains a priest continually" (7:2–3).

Any reader of these words would be justified in asking, "Who was Melchizedek?!" Commentator Warren Wiersbe wrote that "Melchizedek was not an angel or some superhuman creature; nor was he an Old Testament appearance of Jesus Christ. He was a real man, a real king, and real priest in a real city."[7] Yet it is fascinating to note, as Wiersbe did, that so far as the biblical record is concerned, Melchizedek "was not born, nor did he die."[8] Somehow, and in ways known only to God, Melchizedek is still serving as a priest and king. And in this, his priestly ministry during Abram's time points to the eternal high priestly ministry of Christ.[9]

Having now established who Melchizedek was, we can discuss what his meeting with Abram was like. The *Life Application Bible Commentary* tells us that this meeting took place just after Abram had won a great battle against a combined force of several ancient Near Eastern kings. Abram, Barton noted, now commanded the greatest military power in the region. What did he do? He "took a tenth of all he had won in the battle and gave it to Melchizedek, because Melchizedek was a priest of God Most High."[10]

In doing this, Abram was giving a gift to God's representative. Abram and Melchizedek had only recently met, but they both worshipped and served the one God who "made heaven and earth." What is more, Melchizedek was as wise as he was reverent. During the moment of Abram's great triumph—he had just defeated an army and freed a large group of captives—Melchizedek rightly reminded Abram who had gained the victory. "Blessed be God Most High," Melchizedek declared, "who has delivered your enemies into your hand" (Gen. 14:20).[11]

After this profoundly important meeting with Melchizedek, we learn in Genesis 15 that "the word of the LORD came to Abram in a vision." The first thing the Lord said in this incredible encounter was, "Do not be afraid, Abram. I am your shield, your exceedingly great reward" (v. 1).

The remaining verses of Genesis 15, in their entirety, are taken up with what God said and promised to do for Abram. The revelation he received was epic in scale, including prophecies for the future, and a Moses-and-the-burning-bush-like manifestation of God's presence.

But while all this was true, Abram's encounter with God at this time did not seem to begin in the way one might expect. For, as soon as God had said, "Do not be afraid, Abram. I am your shield, your exceedingly great reward," Abram's reply was, "Lord GOD, *what* will You give me, seeing I go childless, and the heir of my house is Eliezer of Damascus? . . . You have given me no offspring" (vv. 2–3, emphasis added).

Abram could not see *how* God could be his "exceedingly great reward" since he had no son. In reply, the Lord said that Eliezer of Damascus "shall not be your heir, but one who will come from your own body shall be your heir" (v. 4). This was followed by an astounding passage in the Genesis account. For in Genesis 15:5–6 we read:

Then He [God] brought him [Abram] outside and said, "Look now toward heaven, and count the stars if you are able to number them." And He said to him, "So shall your descendants be." And he believed in the LORD, and He accounted it to him for righteousness.

We are not sure just how God brought Abram outside. The most likely explanation would seem to be that God prompted him to do so, rather than physically appear, then take him by the hand, so that they could go outside together. But however it did happen, it was a transcendent moment for this man who lived a nomadic lifestyle and dwelt in tents. God, who, Melchizedek had told him, "made heaven and earth," was bidding Abram to look to heaven and the stars God made, saying, "I can make *you* the father of numberless descendants." What an altogether extraordinary thing!

But God was not yet done. "I am the LORD," he told Abram, "who brought you out of Ur of the Chaldeans, to give you this land to inherit it" (Gen. 15:7). One would have thought that Abram had heard more than enough to take God at His word. He was, after all, in the midst of a miracle in which God was speaking to him. Still, Abram's reply to this statement from God was a questioning one. "Lord God," he said, "how shall I know that I will inherit it?" (v. 8).

God's reply came in the form of a directive command. "Bring Me a three-year-old heifer, a three-year-old female goat, a three-year-old ram, a turtledove, and a young pigeon." Abram did as he was bidden, bringing all these kinds of animals together, slaughtering them, and cutting them in two, down the middle, and placing each piece opposite the other. But the birds, however, he did not cut in two (vv. 9–10).

After this, some time seems to have gone by, for "When the vultures came down on the carcasses, Abram drove them away" (v. 11). The account continues:

> Now when the sun was going down, a deep sleep fell upon Abram; and behold, horror and great darkness fell upon him. Then He said to Abram: "Know certainly that your descendants will be strangers in a land that is not theirs, and will serve them, and they will afflict them

four hundred years. And also the nation whom they serve I will judge; afterward they shall come out with great possessions. Now as for you, you shall go to your fathers in peace; you shall be buried at a good old age. But in the fourth generation they shall return here, for the iniquity of the Amorites is not yet complete." (vv. 12–16)

This was a great word of prophecy that looked to the time when Abram's descendants, who would later become the nation of Israel, would be enslaved for a time in Egypt. Still, there was more that God had to tell Abram, for as we read in Genesis 15:17–21:

And it came to pass, when the sun went down and it was dark, that behold, there appeared a smoking oven and a burning torch that passed between those pieces [of animal sacrifice that Abram had prepared]. On the same day the LORD made a covenant with Abram, saying: "To your descendants I have given this land, from the river of Egypt to the great river, the River Euphrates—the Kenites, the Kenezzites, the Kadmonites, the Hittites, the Perizzites, the Rephaim, the Amorites, the Canaanites, the Girgashites, and the Jebusites."

~

Following this theophanic manifestation of God's presence with the "smoking oven and a burning torch" of Genesis 15, Abram experienced five more miraculous experiences of God before the events that took place with him and his son Isaac on Mount Moriah. The first of these took place in Genesis 17:

The LORD appeared to Abram and said to him, "I am Almighty God; walk before Me and be blameless. And I will make My covenant between Me and you, and will multiply you exceedingly." Then Abram fell on his face, and God talked with him, saying: "As for Me, behold, My covenant is with you, and you shall be a father of many nations. No longer shall your name be called Abram, but your name shall be Abraham; for I have made you a father of many nations." (vv. 1–5)

The change of name from Abram to Abraham is highly significant and fraught with great meaning in an ancient Near Eastern culture. The name *Abram* means "exalted father." *Abraham* means "father of many nations." This name change sealed the covenant God was establishing with Abraham, as confirmed by what God said to him in Genesis 17:6–7:

I will make you exceedingly fruitful; and I will make nations of you, and kings shall come from you. And I will establish My covenant between Me and you and your descendants after you in their generations, for *an everlasting covenant*, to be God to you and your descendants after you. (emphasis added)

The change in name Abraham had been given was a confirmation of God's everlasting intent for him and the children of promise that would follow.

In Genesis 18, the remarkable account of Abraham's intercession with God for the people of Sodom takes place. Concerning this incident, Warren Wiersbe has offered many important insights. "An intercessor," he wrote, "must know the Lord personally and be obedient to His will. He must be close enough to the Lord to learn His 'secrets' and know what to pray about."[12] Further more, Abraham's prayer on behalf of Sodom was based not on the mercy of God but on the justice of God. As Genesis 18:25 declares, "Shall not the Judge of all the earth do right?" God is just and holy. He could not destroy righteous believers with wicked unbelievers. This is vitally important, for Lot was a believer (as we read in 2 Peter 2:6–9), even though his actions and words seemed to belie the fact.[13]

Abraham couldn't bear to see all those people die (wicked or not) and be lost forever. So he became one of the great intercessors of the Old Testament, prompted by a deep concern for the salvation of the lost, no matter what their sins were.[14]

It is crucial as well to see that Abraham did not argue with the Lord. He was very humble as he presented his case (which is described in Genesis 18:27, and verses 30–32). He believed that there were at least ten believers in the city.[15] In fact, there proved not to be. But that takes nothing away from the beauty of Abraham's intercessory act. It was a grace-filled thing.

Aside from this incident, there was the moment when Abraham prayed to God to heal King Abimelech and his court, as recorded in Genesis 20:17. God heard and answered Abraham's prayer. Then, just one chapter later in Genesis 21:12, God reassured Abraham that it was through Isaac, and not Ishmael (his son with the slave woman Hagar), that his offspring would be reckoned.

Twenty-one verses later, in Genesis 21:33, Abraham performed an act of commemoration following the establishment of his covenant with King Abimelech. He "planted a tamarisk tree in Beersheba, and there called on the name of the LORD, the Everlasting God." Truly, he had come a very long way in his sojourn of faith. God had proved Himself to Abraham time and time again in miraculous ways, and in planting a tree, Abraham wished to acknowledge that truth in a way that would live on. The tree was a sign of living faith.

～

And so, well before encountering the person of Christ in the theophany on Mount Moriah, Abraham had already "met" God in many profound ways and had already begun to understand a great deal concerning His miraculous purposes and divine character. This lends a remarkable context to what unfolded on Mount Moriah in Genesis 22, specifically *why* the writer of the book of Hebrews would tell us that "Abraham reasoned that God could even raise the dead" (Heb. 11:19 niv). If Abraham had already had so many miraculous meetings with God, the reasons for his great faith in the face of having to sacrifice Isaac are easier to understand. This does not mean that the pain he felt over the searing prospect of this sacrifice was in any way less. But it does help us understand why Abraham could have trusted God so implicitly and completely. The back story, if one might call it that, to what took place on Mount Moriah was extraordinary and without precedent anywhere else in the history of the world.

6 ✦ Moses:
Miracles of the Exodus

It is when the hour is darkest, when sorrow is heaviest, [and] hope is dying . . . then He interferes to whom Time is not, save as the setting wherein He has been pleased to place His work.

—Samuel Wilberforce[1]

Moses, the leader of Israel from the thrall of slavery. Moses, the one through whom God parted the Red Sea. Moses, the bringer of the Ten Commandments.

Moses, the murderer? That is where his story must begin, for God took this man who had taken another's life and made of him a sterling model of mercy and redemption.

He had from birth been set apart as a deliverer of his people. But at the moment when he killed a man and hid his body in the sand (as we read in Exodus 2), he himself stood in need of deliverance.

This murder, strange as it may seem, sprang from a misguided attempt to aid the cause of his people, the ancient Hebrews. It was not an auspicious beginning. We read,

> Now it came to pass in those days, when Moses was grown, that he went out to his brethren and looked at their burdens. And he saw an

Egyptian beating a Hebrew, one of his brethren. So he looked this way and that way, and when he saw no one, he killed the Egyptian and hid him in the sand. And when he went out the second day, behold, two Hebrew men were fighting, and he said to the one who did the wrong, "Why are you striking your companion?"

Then he said, "Who made you a prince and a judge over us? Do you intend to kill me as you killed the Egyptian?"

So Moses feared and said, "Surely this thing is known!" When Pharaoh heard of this matter, he sought to kill Moses. But Moses fled from the face of Pharaoh and dwelt in the land of Midian. (Ex. 2:11–15)

Biblical commentator M. D. Dunnam has described Moses, the boy whose life was preserved when he was hidden in the bulrushes, as a "miracle child."[2] This is certainly so, but sometimes a "miracle child" may go awry. When Moses committed murder, he had horribly lost his way. How could God use someone like this? A man who had to flee for his life—leaving Egypt, where his people were in bondage—to dwell as a refugee in the land of Midian?

Moses could not have been farther from God. Or was he? True, he spent the next forty years in Midian, but God hadn't forgotten him. Nor were God's purposes being thwarted when Moses was absent from Egypt. God's purposes *were* being accomplished during Moses' long sojourn in Midian. Once a prince in Egypt, Moses was now a shepherd. Can God use a shepherd? He would later call a young man named David from tending his flocks to become the future king of Israel. The sovereign Lord who could do all that was at work centuries before in Moses' life.

M. D. Dunnam has also written with great insight about the way God made Himself known to Moses during his time as a shepherd on "the high grassy slopes" of the Sinai wilderness.[3] "Life as a shepherd had become routine," Dr. Dunnam wrote, "and on this day [Moses was] leading the flock 'to the back of the desert.'"[4] Then, it happened. As we read in Exodus 3:2, "The Angel of the LORD appeared to [Moses] in a flame of fire from the midst of a bush."[5] It was a miracle. God suspended the laws of nature so that a bush could be illumined with fire and yet not be consumed. But there was more. Moses, drawing closer, heard the voice of the Lord "from the midst of the bush," calling his name, "Moses, Moses!" (v. 4).

It was a theophany, a scholarly word that means "an appearance of God." Fire, Dr. Dunnam said,

> was and continues to be associated with God's presence. Throughout Scripture, fire is the emblem of deity. . . . When God entered into His covenant with Abraham, the lamp of fire denoted God's presence. . . . So the burning bush does symbolize God's presence. And what symbolism is there in its not being consumed? It is that we can know God's presence eternally.[6]

God can find us wherever we are and make of us whomever He will. His intervention in Moses' life stands testament to this. Sometimes, Dunnam wrote, "there are miracles leaning against lampposts right on our own corners."[7] God appeared to Moses in the ordinariness of his life, but there was nothing ordinary about the call of God upon him. Tested and refined during his wilderness sojourn, Moses was now a man God could begin to use.

What else can we learn about this theophany and God's call to Moses? Old Testament scholar Douglas Stuart, cited earlier in the chapter on Abraham, wrote that "God then began to reveal Himself from within the theophanic fire by addressing Moses through a speech pattern ('Moses! Moses!') that may be called a 'repetition of endearment.'"[8]

How wonderful this is! Moses, the murderer, was no less Moses,

beloved of God. Humbled and broken, he was now ready to be transformed by the love that called to him from the burning bush. He
might have given up on himself, but God had never given up on him.
Learned as he was in the ways of Egypt, steeped in its culture, powerful as he once was as a prince—there were lessons yet that he had to
learn, and a power to reckon with that was unlike anything to be found
in Egypt. The transformation that now began to unfold in Moses' life
has been movingly described by Samuel Wilberforce, a bishop in nineteenth-century Britain. "The everlasting, self-existent, Almighty God,"
Wilberforce said, "stood beside [Moses]; called him by his name; stood
beside him . . . manifested Himself by words of wonder, by signs of
power, by revealed purposes of love."[9]

This revelation brought about a profound transformation. Bishop
Wilberforce continued,

> Moses passed through that awful crisis, and was another man. The sage
> learned in all Egyptian lore; the great soul mighty in word and deed;
> the deep philosophic intellect furnished with all transmitted wisdom,
> trained in all school subtleties, practised [in] great affairs, [had been]
> ripened into mellowness by solitude, nature, and self converse—these
> remained. But on them all had passed a mighty change . . . as there
> settles down upon the mountain's brow the wreath of the morning
> mist, investing every peak and pinnacle and crag with glory.[10]

~

Before going further with Moses' story, it is important to take a few
moments to understand the miracles that had taken place to this point in
his life. In the saving of Moses' infant life from Pharaoh's terrible death
sentence against the infants born to the children of Israel, God worked
two kinds of miracles from the list that has been used throughout earlier

chapters of this book. On the one hand, it was a *confirmatory* miracle, which, it will be remembered, is a miracle "through which God shows his choice and support of certain individuals or groups."[11] The child Moses had been set apart by God for great things. On the other hand, the saving of Moses' life was also a miracle of *deliverance*.[12] His life was preserved, when so many young lives were lost.

Lastly, the appearance of God to Moses in the burning bush was a miracle of *divine vision*. Even as God had spoken to Noah in a miraculous way, warning him of the judgment that was to be visited upon the wickedness of humanity, God also spoke to Moses, revealing things that were to come.[13]

Other kinds of miracles were yet to come: primarily miracles of judgment. The promised deliverance of Israel would not take place without a struggle. Egypt would pay a terrible price because of the hardness of her ruler's heart. Moses would be at the center of that struggle. The issue would never be in doubt, but much had to unfold before it was finally decided.

~

Ten plagues were the means by which Egypt and her king were bowed and conquered. They began, Bishop Wilberforce wrote, "as all God's judgments do . . . in the muttered and distant thunder of the voice of warning." From this, "they passed next into the crash and peal of instant sentence." The onslaught of the ten plagues "closed in blackness and desolation upon the very heart of Egypt."[14]

This great and terrible drama plays itself out in the book of Exodus. Within the chapters of this book, as pastor John Piper has written,

God began to shape the corporate life of his chosen people. For the rest of her existence Israel looked back to the Exodus as the key event in her history. So in the Exodus we can see what God is up to in choosing a people for himself. In Exodus 9:16 God speaks to Pharaoh a word that lets him (and us) know why God is multiplying his mighty acts into ten plagues, instead of making short work of Egypt's stubbornness in one swift catastrophe. This text is so crucial that the apostle Paul quotes it in Romans 9:17 to sum up God's purpose in the Exodus. God says to Pharaoh, "But for this purpose I have caused you to stand [or 'appointed you'], to show you my power, *so that my name may be glorified throughout all the earth.*"[15]

"So the point of the Exodus was to make a worldwide reputation for God,"[16] and in the accomplishment of that stupendous task, Moses was to be God's chosen instrument—His emissary and spokesperson.

The point of the ten plagues and miraculous Red Sea crossing was to demonstrate the astonishing power of God on behalf of his freely chosen people, with the aim that this reputation, this name, would be declared throughout the whole world.[17]

As recorded in Scripture, the ten plagues were: (1) the plague of the turning of the waters of Egypt to blood, (2) the plague of the frogs, (3) the plague of lice, (4) the plague of flies, (5) the plague of God's killing Egypt's cattle, (6) the plague of boils, (7) the plague of thunder and hail, (8) the plague of locusts, (9) the plague of darkness, and (10) the plague of the killing of Egypt's firstborn children.

Of these plagues several things may be noted. First of all, as biblical scholar Peter Enns noted,

the deliverance of Israel from Egypt is entirely God's doing and under His complete control. The impending Exodus is a play in which God is author, producer, director and principal actor. The purpose [here] is not to introduce some abstract philosophical notion of God's sovereignty. Rather, [what unfolds] is further confirmation . . . that God is with Moses and with Israel. Now we begin to see how pervasive His presence truly is. . . . Not only is Israel's fate in God's hands, but Egypt's as well.[18]

Dr. Graham Scroggie has also used the metaphor of epic drama to convey what God did through Moses in delivering Israel. He saw the context of these plagues as "a drama . . . the parties of which are God, Egypt and Israel. The object of this drama is three-fold: to reveal the power of God over his enemies; to demonstrate that Israel belonged to God and not to Pharaoh; and to establish the faith of Israel in God."[19]

Within this drama, Scroggie detected three distinct movements. One is *exploratory*, the next *evidential*, and the third *executive*. Under the exploratory movement, Moses appears before Israel and Pharaoh. These encounters are chronicled in Exodus 4:29–6:8 and Exodus 6:9–7:13.

The first two encounters in Exodus set the stage. In the closing verses of Exodus 4, Moses and his brother Aaron appear before the children of Israel. Miracles are performed through Moses, and the people believe that he is their promised agent of deliverance. We read,

> Then Moses and Aaron went and gathered together all the elders of the children of Israel. And Aaron spoke all the words which the LORD had spoken to Moses. Then he did the signs in the sight of the people. So the people believed; and when they heard that the LORD had visited the children of Israel and that He had looked on their affliction, then they bowed their heads and worshiped. (vv. 29–31)

In the opening verses of Exodus 5, Moses and Aaron's meeting with Pharaoh is described. Moses pleads for the release of the Israelites, and in response Pharaoh defies any notion of the Lord God of the Hebrews.

"Afterward," it is stated there, "Moses and Aaron went in and told Pharaoh, 'Thus says the LORD God of Israel: "Let My people go, that they may hold a feast to Me in the wilderness"'" (v. 1).

"And Pharaoh said, 'Who is the LORD, that I should obey His voice to let Israel go? I do not know the LORD, nor will I let Israel go'" (Ex. 5:1–2).

Under the second movement, the evidential movement, the ten plagues are unleashed upon Egypt. These were described by Scroggie as "a clash between two powers, one Divine, and one human; a conflict between two religions, one true, and one false; [and] a struggle for the supremacy of heaven, or of earth." The struggle, Scroggie continued, "was protracted and the battle swayed to and fro, but the devil was defeated by the Deliverer."[20]

At the same time, more was at work in this dramatic contest than "devices to reduce Pharaoh's power of resistance." The ten plagues "were attacks upon the religion of the Egyptians, and upon their many gods." Further, the plagues unfolded in "a trinity of triplets, with a final movement which is both a curse and a blessing, and plague and a Passover."[21]

The third movement, the executive movement, should be viewed as set apart from those that had preceded it. The death of the firstborn, Scroggie wrote, was "vastly more than a plague on Egypt, [it was also] the first institution of the people now about to become a nation." The most important thing to note about this tenth and last plague, Scroggie wrote, "the central fact and feature of the Passover," was the slain lamb. For that lamb pointed forward to the Messiah who was to come, "the shedding of whose precious blood was to make atonement for sin."[22]

~

In the New Testament, when Jesus was transfigured, Moses appeared with Him, along with Elijah. Many things can and have been said about this extraordinary miracle—chief among them that it was a glimpse of what heaven will be like.

Yet in some respects, one of the most remarkable things about this event can be seen from the perspective of redemptive history. Who could have predicted that Moses, a one-time murderer, would ever have been called of God and used by God as he was in the Exodus account? Wonder of wonders—and here lies the greatest miracle where Moses was concerned—who could have predicted that a one-time murderer would play so signal a part in the history of redemption, helping point the way to the promised Messiah?

7 ✦ Elisha: Miracles in the Time of the Prophets

All the praying souls upon earth, all the saints in glory, all the angels of the Lord, and the Lord of angels himself, are with you. If the veil were withdrawn, if you could see with the eyes of Elisha's servant or [those] of Stephen, you would see that there are many more for you than against you.

—JOHN NEWTON[1]

His name means "My God is salvation," and his is a fascinating story. From it, the English language has gained at least one enduring proverbial phrase: "the passing of the mantle." One event in his life, involving the prophet Elijah and the chariot of fire, inspired classic verse from the poet William Blake. It also lent a title to the Academy Award-winning film *Chariots of Fire.*

When we think of Elijah and the chariot of fire, we think of the power and majesty of God. And it is only right to do so. But prior to its appearance and the carrying of Elijah in that chariot to heaven, Elisha made what would seem to many to be a strange request. "What may I do for you, before I am taken from you?" Elijah had asked. In response, Elisha said, "Please let a double portion of your spirit be upon me."

"You have asked a hard thing," Elijah replied. "Nevertheless, if you see me when I am taken from you, it shall be so for you; but if not, it shall not be so" (2 Kings 2:9–10).

What, one may well wonder, was going on here? For answers, we may turn with profit to the writings of Dr. Herbert Lockyer. He stated that after Elijah and Elisha had crossed the Jordan River, "Elijah was desirous of bestowing a departing, spiritual benediction upon his spiritual son."[2] When Elisha made his astounding request, Elijah quite rightly replied that his spiritual protégé had asked a hard thing. The reason, Dr. Lockyer explained, was this: "The granting of such a petition was not in Elijah's own power, but in God's." Only if he were to see Elijah's translation into heaven, that is, witness the outpouring of God in this way, would "Elisha be blessed with the boon that he asked for."[3]

This is straightforward enough, but what about asking for a double portion of Elijah's spirit? This sounds like a very obscure, if not strange, thing. But what Elisha was asking for was not "a gift of the miraculous or a gift of the spirit of prophecy twice as large as [that which] Elijah possessed."[4] Instead, Elisha was making a spiritual request that had everything to do with the rights of firstborn sons in ancient Near Eastern culture. By law, firstborn sons inherited two parts of their father's property, as stated in Deuteronomy 21:17. Elisha's request was that he be treated as the firstborn among the "sons of the prophets," and so receive twice as great a share of "the spirit and power" of his master and teacher.[5] In short, Elisha wished to have conferred upon himself the status of the firstborn among Elijah's spiritual sons.[6]

We know from Scripture how this story ended. Elisha did indeed see the sudden translation of Elijah into heaven on the chariot of fire drawn by horses of fire. And so he was granted the boon he had asked of his spiritual mentor. Central to our purposes here, it is important to note that what Elisha had witnessed was a miracle of *divine vision*. He had glimpsed the glory and power of God. Henceforth, Elisha was to be the firstborn among the sons of the prophets who were left in Israel following Elijah's departure.

Many associate Elisha's prophetic ministry with the miracles of healing that God performed through him. They are a vital part of what God did in and through him. As such they were miracles of *mercy*. But it is startling to note that one of the first miracles that God worked through Elisha was a very severe miracle of *judgment*.

Shortly after Elijah was carried away into heaven, Elisha set out for Bethel. As he walked upon the road, a mob-like crowd of young people came out from the city and mocked him, saying, "Go up, you baldhead! Go up, you baldhead!"

At this, Elisha turned and looked at them and cursed them in the name of the Lord. Within moments, two female bears came out of a nearby wood and mauled forty-two of the abusive young toughs (2 Kings 2:23–24).

But however abusive this crowd of toughs was in their use of language, to be mauled by bears seems a terrible fate. So it was—but there is a context to be borne in mind.

To explore that context we may turn to Charles Simeon, the great British pastor and teacher from the nineteenth century. The name of "bald head," he wrote, was intended as a reproach, and that of the very worst kind. Scornful language unjustly heaped upon anyone is sinful. But, as Simeon rightly noted, the reproach used on this occasion "was an insult to God himself," for Elisha was a prophet of the Most High.[7]

Crucially, the use of the phrase "Go up, go up" by these young toughs seems to have referred "to the recent exaltation of Elijah in the fiery chariot." Their scorn indicated that they regarded the event either as a fiction to be disbelieved or to be despised.[8]

Profane contempt was what these young men were guilty of.[9] It was a sin not unlike that of blaspheming the Holy Spirit, as described in the New Testament. "Such reproaches," Simeon wrote, "strike at God himself, who [judges] them by a very different standard from that which we use. We view them as a [mocking] exposure of folly; but he views them as [acts of] impious contempt."[10]

Nor was the judgment meted out to the gang of toughs inflicted by Elisha, Simeon wrote. He was no more under the influence of revenge than Peter was when he passed sentence of death on Ananias and Sapphira; or than Paul was when he declared that Elymas, the sorcerer, should be struck blind. He was merely the means whereby God pronounced a curse against them. The bears that came upon them out of the wood were "like the whole creation, animate and inanimate"—ready to execute the vengeance of God.[11]

In all this, the justice of God was uppermost. "What greater dishonour could be done to the God of heaven and earth," Simeon asked, "than to make the most stupendous efforts of his goodness a subject of reproach?" Looking to the New Testament, Simeon recalled the dire judgment pronounced against those who blaspheme the Holy Spirit. Such a grievous sin, Christ had declared, "will not be forgiven."[12]

~

From such a grim event, it is a welcome change to consider the miracles of healing and provision that God performed through Elisha. For our purposes here, consideration will be given to two: the purification of the lime-laden water and the miracle of the widow's oil.

The miracle relating to the cleansing of the lime-laden water is one that doesn't receive a lot of attention among the many wondrous things God did through Elisha, but it is a beautiful event rich in meaning and symbol.

This tainted water, which flowed out of a mountain spring, was a blight upon the lives of the people who lived near it. It caused trees to shed their fruit prematurely and cattle to give birth too soon, resulting in the death of their young. To make matters worse, the water was unfit for human consumption. A miracle was needed to put things right and bring healing to the land, its flora, fauna, and people.[13]

This, God did through Elisha. Asking to be given an earthenware pot and a measure of salt, Elisha went to the tainted spring and cast the salt upon it. This was a moving symbol of grace. God alone could purify the water, but he used Elisha and the salt as the medium through which this mighty act was done. Water that had formerly been a curse now became a source of blessing.[14]

The miracle of the widow's oil is one that has long been celebrated in literature. It is one of those proverbial stories that was known to everyone only two or three generations ago. Children in those years were commonly taught Bible stories, and this one was a perennial favorite—not least because it showed how God cared deeply for the plight of the poor and destitute.

The story unfolds in 2 Kings 4. There, beginning in verse 1, we read,

A certain woman of the wives of the sons of the prophets cried out to Elisha, saying, "Your servant my husband is dead, and you know that your servant feared the LORD. And the creditor is coming to take my two sons to be his slaves."

So Elisha said to her, "What shall I do for you? Tell me, what do you have in the house?" And she said, "Your maidservant has nothing in the house but a jar of oil."

Then he said, "Go, borrow vessels from everywhere, from all your neighbors—empty vessels; do not gather just a few. And when you have come in, you shall shut the door behind you and your sons; then pour it into all those vessels, and set aside the full ones."

So she went from him and shut the door behind her and her sons, who brought the vessels to her; and she poured it out. Now it came to pass, when the vessels were full, that she said to her son, "Bring me another vessel."

And he said to her, "There is not another vessel." So the oil ceased. Then she came and told the man of God. And he said, "Go, sell the oil and pay your debt; and you and your sons live on the rest." (vv. 1–7)

There is about this story, Herbert Lockyer has observed, "a spirit of gracious, soothing, holy beneficence."[15] The miracle depicted here was, according to the criteria we have been using heretofore, both a miracle of *mercy* and *deliverance*. This widow and her two sons, wrote Matthew Henry, "were all amazed to find their pot, like a fountain of living water, always flowing, and yet always full; they see not the spring that supplies it, but believe it to be in Him in *whom all our springs are*."[16] Henry then closed with this moving reflection:

> We are never straitened [or impoverished] in God, and in his power and bounty, and the riches of his grace. All our straitness [or poverty] is in ourselves. It is our faith that fails, not his promise. He gives above what we ask: were there more vessels, there is enough in God to fill them; enough for all, enough for each.[17]

Truer words were never spoken.

~

War, or the prospect of war, is a horrendous thing to contemplate. One miracle of divine vision during the ministry of Elisha took place amid the dread specter of war. The setting was this: The king of Syria wished to make war on Israel. By divine intervention, Elisha received words of knowledge about the plans and intentions of the Syrian monarch. Thus informed by God, Elisha sent warning to the king of Israel.

The king of Syria thought he had a traitor in his midst, someone who was relaying information as a spy to the king of Israel. Calling his retainers and servants, he demanded, "Will you not show me which of us is [secretly] for the king of Israel?"

"None, my lord, O king," one of his courtiers replied, "but Elisha, the prophet who is in Israel, tells the king of Israel the words that you speak in your bedroom." That was more than enough for the Syrian king. He instantly sent horses and chariots and a great army to capture Elisha at the city of Dothan (2 Kings 6:11–14).

The scene that met the eyes of Elisha's servant the following morning was a staggering one. Stepping outside the building where they were staying, the servant saw to his horror and dismay that the entire city was surrounded with horses and chariots. It was a great and awesome host of mortal enemies.

Returning at once to Elisha, the servant arrived breathless and said, "Alas, my master! What shall we do?" (v. 15). The two stepped outside, probably so that Elisha could confirm what he had been told. Seeing the great host before them, he did something quite unexpected. He may well have placed his hand on the servant's shoulder. But whether or not this was so, we do know the words that he spoke. "Do not fear," he said, "for those who are with us are more than those who are with them" (v. 16).

And then Elisha prayed, saying, "LORD, I pray, open his eyes that he may see." Immediately, the young man was granted miraculous sight. Any thought of the hosts of the Syrian king was instantly banished. What had been fear was now transformed into holy awe. For with the sight God bestowed upon him, the servant saw that the nearby mountain "was full of horses and chariots of fire" (v. 17). The Lord of Hosts was encamped around the enemies of Israel. There was no reason to fear.

When the Syrian host came down to seize Elisha, the prophet prayed, and the Lord struck them with blindness. Pretending to offer to lead them to "the man whom you seek," Elisha deceived them. He took them all the way to Samaria and delivered them into the hand of the

the king of Israel. Once the Syrian host was all gathered in Samaria, Elisha prayed once more that the Lord would open their eyes. To their utter astonishment and fear, they found themselves in the hands of the Israelite monarch (vv. 19–20).

The king of Israel thought to slay them on the spot, but Elisha said no. "Set food and water before them," he directed, "that they may eat and drink and go to their master." And so a great feast was prepared, where mercy reigned. Afterward, the Syrian army departed and returned to their king. The story of what had happened must have made an incredible impression, for "the bands of Syrian raiders came no more into the land of Israel" (vv. 21–23).

Reflecting on this passage from 2 Kings 6, Charles Simeon came away with this telling insight: "Thus are all the saints watched over by an Almighty Power; and under his protection they are safe."[18] It may be, he continued,

> that God sees fit to let the enemies of his people prevail over them: but their success is only for a moment: the time is near at hand when the apparent inequality of these dispensations will be rectified; when God, as "a righteous Judge, will recompense tribulation to those who trouble us; and to us who are troubled, rest."[19]

Simeon stated,

> [God] narrowly inspects, not the actions only, but the dispositions also, of men, in order to render unto them according to their works. In due time, "he will rain upon [the wicked] snares, fire and brimstone, and an horrible tempest," and they "shall drink it to the very dregs."[20]

On the other hand, God loves "the righteous, and beholds them with delight." He reserves for them "a weight of glory proportioned to all that they have done and suffered for him." If a believer is persuaded of this, of whom does he have to be afraid? No weapon formed against him can prevail, unless God in His infinite wisdom has ordained that it should. And no evil can come upon him that will not be recompensed a hundredfold even in this life. How much more, Simeon concluded, shall evil be recompensed "in that world where God himself will be the unalienable portion of all his people."[21]

Christians all through the centuries have been comforted with the same kind of thoughts, and often they draw the mind to that matchless passage from the apostle Paul in chapter 8 of the New Testament book of Romans: "What then shall we say to these things?" Paul asked.

If God is for us, who can be against us? He who did not spare His own Son, but delivered Him up for us all, how shall He not with Him also freely give us all things? Who shall bring a charge against God's elect? It is God who justifies. Who is he who condemns? It is Christ who died, and furthermore is also risen, who is even at the right hand of God, who also makes intercession for us. Who shall separate us from the love of Christ? Shall tribulation, or distress, or persecution, or famine, or nakedness, or peril, or sword? . . .

Yet, in all these things we are more than conquerors through Him who loved us. For I am persuaded that neither death nor life, nor angels nor principalities nor powers, nor things present nor things to come, nor height nor depth, nor any other created thing, shall be able to separate us from the love of God which is in Christ Jesus our Lord. (vv. 31–39)

~

One would have thought that the many miracles God wrought through Elisha would cease with his passing. But it is one of the strangest stories in Scripture that one more miracle associated with Elisha took place after his death. It was, ultimately, a miracle of *mercy*. But nothing like it before or since is related in the Bible.

The story is told in 2 Kings 13. Beginning in verse 20, we read:

> [After] Elisha died . . . they buried him. And the raiding bands from Moab invaded the land in the spring of the year. So it was, as they were burying a man, that suddenly they spied a band of raiders; and they [quickly] put the man in the tomb of Elisha; and when the man was let down and touched the bones of Elisha, he revived and stood on his feet. (vv. 20–21)

Just two verses, and so much that is utterly astounding! It was, Herbert Lockyer wrote, "a post-mortem corroboration of [Elisha's] undying influence."[22] In life, so many of the miracles God had performed through him

> were manifestations of a life-power or resurrection-energy overcoming death. Now, after his death, his bones continue and conclude Elisha's quickening ministry. . . . This last miracle in connection with Elisha was a sign to Israel that the God of Elisha still lived and was ready to do wonders for them as before, if they would but seek and trust in Him.[23]

Lockyer concludes by saying that this miracle is a beautiful anticipation of the life-giving power of Christ's death. Thus Elisha's last miracle looks "unto Jesus the author and finisher of our faith" (Heb. 12:2 KJV).

8 ✦ The Promise of His Coming: The Miracle of the Incarnation

And more to mark the grace of Heaven,
This Son by miracle was given.

—Hannah More[1]

The central miracle asserted by Christians is the Incarnation. They
say that God became Man. Every other miracle prepares the way for
this, or results from this.

—C. S. Lewis[2]

B ut our peace is put in impossible things . . . round an incredible star."[3] These are lines from G. K. Chesterton's classic poem, "The House of Christmas."

And most truly, the Christian faith *is* faith in impossible things. God moved a piece of the heavens so that His Son could come down from heaven to dwell among men and be their redeemer. A star scribed its course across the night sky so that three royal seekers could find the hope of all ages—the one who was Himself "the bright and morning star."[4]

Then there is the miracle of the incarnation itself, of God becoming man. The eternal second person of the Trinity taking on humanity in the person of Jesus.[5] It was a moment when the holy purposes of God were accomplished through the courageous belief of a young woman of beautiful faith. In the gospel of Luke, this matchless story is told. We read,

> Now in the sixth month the angel Gabriel was sent by God to a city of Galilee named Nazareth, to a virgin betrothed to a man whose name was Joseph, of the house of David. The virgin's name was Mary. And having come in, the angel said to her, "Rejoice, highly favored one, the LORD is with you; blessed are you among women!"
>
> But when she saw him, she was troubled at his saying, and considered what manner of greeting this was. Then the angel said to her, "Do not be afraid, Mary, for you have found favor with God. And behold, you will conceive in your womb and bring forth a Son, and shall call His name JESUS. He will be great, and will be called the Son of the Highest; and the Lord God will give Him the throne of His father David. And He will reign over the house of Jacob forever, and of His kingdom there will be no end."
>
> Then Mary said to the angel, "How can this be, since I do not know a man?"
>
> And the angel answered and said to her, "The Holy Spirit will come upon you, and the power of the Highest will overshadow you; therefore, also, that Holy One who is to be born will be called the Son of God. . . . For with God nothing will be impossible."
>
> Then Mary said, "Behold the maidservant of the Lord! Let it be to me according to your word." (Luke 1:26–35, 37–38)

Aside from Mary's courageous belief in the word of the Lord, as given to her by the angel Gabriel, there are several things about her that we ought to remember always when it comes to the incarnation. Theologian Timothy George wrote that "Mary stands, along with John the Baptist, at a unique intersection between the old and new covenants. Mary's role points backward. In the gospels, she is the culmination of a prophetic lineage of pious mothers—Sarah, Rachel, [and] Hannah."[6] The exception is that Mary gave birth to *the* child of promise, while these other praiseworthy mothers gave birth to important children of promise.

Consistent with this idea, as Dr. George noted, "Evangelicals can and should join with other Christians in celebrating the virgin Mary as *theotokos*: or as historian Dr. Jaroslav Pelikan translated the classic theological word, as 'the one who gave birth to the one who is God.'"[7]

These are indeed special distinctions to be noted about Mary—deeply important reasons to thank God for her life and her sterling faith. But other aspects of her courageous belief should also be remembered and celebrated. She was to have a child that, to all conventional appearances of her day, was out of wedlock. This meant many things. For one, Joseph, Mary's betrothed and the man who would eventually marry her, would be Jesus' stepfather.[8] But more immediately, and more worryingly, Mary's future could have been one of disgrace had not God intervened miraculously in Joseph's life.[9] Why this could have been so, and was not, is described in Matthew 1:18–25. We read,

> Now the birth of Jesus Christ was as follows: when His mother Mary had been betrothed to Joseph, before they came together she was found to be with child by the Holy Spirit. And Joseph her husband, being a righteous man and not wanting to disgrace her, planned to send her away secretly.

But when he had considered this, behold, an angel of the Lord appeared to him in a dream, saying, "Joseph, son of David, do not be afraid to take Mary as your wife; for the Child who has been conceived in her is of the Holy Spirit. She will bear a Son; and you shall call His name Jesus, for He will save His people from their sins."

Now all this took place to fulfill what was spoken by the Lord through the prophet: "Behold, the virgin shall be with child and shall bear a son, and they shall call his name Immanuel," which translated means, "God with us."

And Joseph awoke from his sleep and did as the angel of the Lord commanded him, and took Mary as his wife, but kept her a virgin [that is, he did not sleep with her] until she gave birth to a Son; and he called His name Jesus. (NASB)

~

Christians rightly stand in awe of the miracles that surround the birth of Jesus, but as Dr. George pointed out, if we think only of these things we might miss something very important about the role that Mary played in Jesus' life as He grew to manhood. "Mary," George wrote, "was not merely the point of Christ's entrance into the world—the channel through which he passed as water flows through a pipe."[10] No, more than this, she was a mother who cared for Jesus' physical needs as a boy. She nursed Him, nurtured Him, and taught Him the ways of the Lord. She would also have taught Him to memorize the Psalms and to pray, thus contributing in a very vital way to His growth "in wisdom and stature, and in favor" with God and others (Luke 2:52).[11]

Aside from the loving guidance that was the hallmark of Mary's parenting, great reformers of the Protestant tradition have also expressed their gratitude for her role in the life of Jesus. John Calvin referred to her as "the treasurer of grace," the one who kept faith as a deposit. Through her, Calvin wrote, we have received this precious gift from God. "She deserves to be called blessed, for God has accorded her a singular distinction, to prepare his son for the world, in whom she was spiritually reborn." At the same time, Martin Luther, when sequestered in Wartburg Castle in 1521, prepared for press his *Commentary on the Magnificat*. At this time, he wrote that Mary is the embodiment of God's unmerited grace.[12]

In the context of the deep and abiding appreciation that these reformers had for Mary, Dr. George himself observed that "she is called blessed not because of her virginity or even her humility, but because she was chosen as the person and place where God's glory would enter most deeply into the human story." As the poet T. S. Eliot, in an echo of Chesterton's poem "The House of Christmas," wrote in his own poem, "The Four Quartets," Mary is "the place of impossible union where past and future are conquered and reconciled in incarnation."[13]

Supremely, the great reformers recognized Mary "as the one who hears the Word of God and responds in faith, and thus is justified by faith alone." It might sound strange, but it is true that "Mary was a disciple of Christ before she was his mother, for had she not believed, she would not have conceived." And as far as her faith is concerned, the reformers saw it "not [as] the achievement of merit, but the gift of divine grace." In concert with this, Dr. George wrote: "This means that when we praise and love Mary, it is God whom we praise for his gracious favor to his chosen handmaid."[14]

Of course, what Scripture itself tells us of Mary is of most compelling and primary importance. In the New Testament, Mary is shown to be "among the last at the cross, and among the first in the Upper Room. She bridges not only the Old and New Testaments at Jesus' birth, but also the close of his earthly ministry and the birth of the church." And, as Dr. George noted, "It is significant that in Eastern iconography, Mary is never depicted alone, but always with Christ, the apostles, and the saints."[15]

Mary's sterling courage and ardent, persevering faith showed again when, at the moment that "all of the disciples (including Peter!) had fled in fear" after the arrest and crucifixion of Jesus, "Mary remained true to Christ and his word. Her fidelity unto the Cross showed that the true faith could be preserved in one sole individual, and thus Mary became the mother of the (true remnant) church." This, Dr. George concluded, "is why the Reformers honored Mary."[16]

~

And what of Jesus Himself?

For Christians, Jesus is known by many names in Scripture. One of them is the name Immanuel. In Matthew 1:23, we learn that the giving of this name was tied to a promise from the Old Testament book of Isaiah: " 'Behold, the virgin shall be with child, and bear a Son, and they shall call His name Immanuel,' which is translated, 'God with us.' "

Only by Christ's coming to earth, taking upon Himself a human nature, could the promise of our redemption and salvation be fulfilled. Jesus' coming into the world was both deeply necessary and a source of untold blessing. This was captured very beautifully by G. K. Chesterton, who wrote that "the place the shepherds found . . . was a place of dreams come true."[17] Each Christmas we pause and remember anew the stupendous meaning of the Christ child's name: "You shall call His name JESUS, for He will save His people from their sins" (Matt. 1:21).

This is one very helpful way to begin to understand what is meant by what scholars call the incarnation. That is to say, the way in which Jesus was conceived.

Here, we may turn to theologian J. I. Packer, who has written very helpfully on what the incarnation means. For a start, he wrote, the word *incarnation* means "enfleshing." It is what was meant when the apostle John declared in his gospel that "the Word became flesh" (John 1:14).

The concept in view here is "not that the Son [of God] put on a human body as one puts on an overcoat," nor is it "that a human being and a divine person lived together under one skin," nor yet "that a divine person came to possess two sets of powers (or natures)."

Rather, Packer wrote, "the Son lives life through the mind-body complex that constitutes humanity. . . . Without diminishing His divinity, He added to it all that is involved in being human."[18] Fully divine and fully human, He grew within Mary's womb, lived His life on earth, and now reigns eternally in heaven.[19]

Packer has also written about how the doctrine and miracle of the incarnation unites Christians—whatever faith tradition within the church they may align themselves with. When Jesus, Packer wrote, is hailed as "one person in two natures," as He is according to the Council of Chalcedon of AD 451, what is meant is that through the incarnation, the Son became more than He was before, for a human element was integral to the ongoing life of the Triune God. Being fully human and fully divine was an indispensable part of the Son's identity, destiny, and glory. All Evangelicals, Orthodox, and Catholic believers unite in professing this.[20]

This exploration of what the incarnation is serves a very good purpose, and all Christians owe Dr. Packer a debt for his excellent overview. But to gain an abiding sense of the wonder that this most blessed of events should inspire in us, we can do no better than turn to the great seventeenth-century divine, Jeremy Taylor.

Taylor's prose often reads like poetry and stirs the heart with a profound sense of reverence. His words draw our hearts to God.

And so we read this prayer from Taylor, a prayer of thanks to God for the coming of Christ.

O eternal and almighty God, [Thou] didst send Thy holy angel in embassy to the blessed Virgin mother of our Lord, to manifest . . .

Thine eternal purpose [for] the redemption of mankind by the incarnation of Thine eternal Son.[21]

Taylor then described the incarnation as the "first beginnings of the work of our redemption." Such a thought prompted many more to follow: a doxology in its own way, a paean of praise to God and His eternal purpose. "That which shines brightest," Taylor wrote, "presents itself first to the eye; and the devout soul, in the chain of excellent and precious things which are represented in the counsel, design, and first beginnings of the work of our redemption."[22]

At times Taylor felt himself overwhelmed with the sense of how God's mercy, love, and grace infused the incarnation. It was, he wrote,

> out of mere and perfect charity and the [depths] of compassion God sent into the world His only Son, for remedy to human miseries, to ennoble our nature by an union with divinity, to sanctify it with His justice, to enrich it with His grace, to instruct it with His doctrine, to fortify it with His example, to rescue it from servitude, to assert it into the liberty of the sons of God, and at last to make it partaker of [His] resurrection.[23]

Jeremy Taylor was not alone among the great writers and scholars of Scripture who have mined the riches of spoken language to describe all that the incarnation means. Thomas Aquinas wrote,

> Of all the works of God, the mystery of the Incarnation most transcends reason. Nothing more astonishing could be imagined as done by God than that the true God and Son of God should become true man. To this chief of wonders, all other wonders are subordinate.[24]

~

In his classic text *The Cross of Christ*, John Stott wrote much about the nature of the incarnation and why it made our redemption possible. For example, he wrote that "the incarnation is indispensable to the atonement. In particular, it is essential to affirm that the love, the holiness and the will of the Father are identical with the love, holiness and the will of the Son. God was in Christ reconciling the world to himself."[25]

But there was also a cost implicit in the incarnation, that "of entering into our condition in order to reach us." Thus, we are told that when God sent His Son, He was "born under law, to redeem those under law" (Gal. 4:4–5).[26] And further, the incarnation involved great sacrifice, "since by becoming flesh the Son both 'emptied himself' and 'humbled himself'" (Phil. 2:7–8). Throughout His public ministry, Jesus demonstrated that He had come "not to be served but to serve." But, Stott observed, "according to his teaching and that of his apostles, the climax of his incarnation and ministry was his self-giving on the cross as a ransom for many" (Mark 10:45).[27]

Aside from this, Stott said that "only an incarnation can span these divides" between us and God. An incarnation refers to entering other people's worlds, their thought-worlds, and also the worlds of their alienation, loneliness, and pain. Still more, the incarnation led inexorably to the cross. Jesus first took on our humanity, then He bore our sin. In all of these ways, He entered our world to reach us. By comparison, our modest attempts to reach people appear amateurish and shallow.[28]

Most truly, therefore, we can say that there was nothing God would not do, not even giving His Son to die on the cross, to redeem us.

But all of this began with the word of the Lord to a young woman of great faith. The promise of impossible things. The place of the stable. Christmas. Wise men following a great star.

All these things have become synonymous with the incarnation and the birth of Christ. So we ought to kneel and offer grateful thanks as shepherds once did for the miracle of our Lord's coming to dwell among us.

He left His heavenly home so that we might find the way home—to the Jerusalem that abides forever. As the close of G. K. Chesterton's poem affirms so beautifully:

> To an open house in the evening
> Home shall men come,
> To an older place than Eden
> And a taller town than Rome.
> To the end of the way of the wandering star,
> To the things that cannot be and that are,
> To the place where God was homeless
> And all men are at home.[29]

9 ✦ Signs and Wonders:
The Miracles of Jesus

*He began to preach at the age of thirty. And having, for about three
years and a half, preached the Gospel, He taught us His Father's
will—revealing to us the secrets of eternal life . . . the mightiness of
His miracles, and the power of His doctrine.*

—JEREMY TAYLOR[1]

We mark history from the birth of Christ. For Christians,
He is both the author of history and its center. God
became man. Jesus lived a sinless life and was unjustly
subjected to a criminal's death. But death could not hold Him. He conquered death, and so secured our redemption. If ever a miracle unfolded
over the course of a lifetime, it was in the life of Christ.

The poet T. S. Eliot once wrote of "the still point of the turning
world."[2] So it was that within a stable in the ancient Near Eastern town
of Bethlehem, eternity stepped into time. God became a man, and so
began the unfolding of our redemption. The Source of all miracles was
a miracle in Himself.

"Because of who He was, Christ could not but perform miracles."[3]

So Herbert Lockyer stated in his now classic text, *All the Miracles of the Bible*—first published in 1961, and still an authoritative work on the subject.

Truer words were never written than those Lockyer used to describe the person of Jesus. And they are but an echo of Scripture itself, for as we read in the gospel of John: "Truly Jesus did many other signs [miracles] in the presence of His disciples, which are not written in this book; but these are written that you may believe that Jesus is the Christ, the Son of God, and that believing you may have life in His name" (20:30–31).

Lockyer wrote that one central aspect of the miracles Jesus performed is the way they mirrored His own character and naturally expressed His love and sympathy for humanity.[4] This thought recalls that beautiful passage from the Old Testament book of Isaiah, the very passage that the Lord read out in the synagogue in Nazareth on the day that He commenced His public ministry.[5] We read,

> The Spirit of the Lord GOD is upon me, because the LORD has anointed Me to preach good tidings to the poor; He has sent Me to heal the brokenhearted, to proclaim liberty to the captives, and the opening of the prison to those who are bound; to proclaim the acceptable year of the LORD, and the day of vengeance of our God; to comfort all who mourn, to console those who mourn in Zion, to give them beauty for ashes, the oil of joy for mourning, the garment of praise for the spirit of heaviness; that they may be called trees of righteousness, the planting of the LORD, that He may be glorified. (Isa. 61:1–3)

In Luke's gospel, we again see Jesus stating explicitly the credentials of His ministry, this time in response to a question put to Him by the two followers of John the Baptist: "Are You the Coming One, or do we look for another?" (Luke 7:20). To this Jesus gave an answer that forms a stirring counterpart to the prophecy given about Him in Isaiah long centuries before. "Go and tell John," Jesus said, "the things you have seen and heard: that the blind see, the lame walk, the lepers are cleansed, the deaf hear, the dead are raised, the poor have the gospel preached to them. And blessed is he who is not offended because of Me" (Luke 7:22–23).

Other passages from the Old Testament pointed to the nature of Jesus' ministry and the miracles that attended it. The prophet Isaiah, mentioned above, spoke elsewhere of what Christ's ministry would be like. From that ministry would issue streams of living water, one of the finest metaphors in Scripture. Those who placed their faith in Him would find the verdant land that is most truly the promised land:

> Then the eyes of the blind shall be opened, and the ears of the deaf shall be unstopped. Then the lame shall leap like a deer, and the tongue of the dumb sing. For waters shall burst forth in the wilderness, and streams in the desert. The parched ground shall become a pool, and the thirsty land springs of water. (Isa. 35:5–7)

Here, commentator John Stott introduced a very important distinction about how we ought to view the miracles of Christ. Their value, Stott wrote, "comes not so much from their supernatural character as from their spiritual significance." Christ's miracles are "signs" as well as "wonders." What kind of signs were they? Certainly, they "were never performed selfishly or senselessly," nor were they instances of "showing off," or acts intended "to force people into submission." Most of all, Christ's miracles "were not so much demonstrations of special power as illustrations of moral authority. They are in fact the acted parables of Jesus. They demonstrate his claims visually. The things he does dramatize the things he says."[6]

All of this is underscored clearly in the gospel of John. This book of the Bible was structured so as to highlight selected "signs" associated with the great "I am" declarations that Jesus made during the course of His ministry.[7]

The first of these signs is one that has given a common phrase to the English language: the changing of "water into wine" that took place during a wedding at Cana in Galilee.

Why did Jesus do this? Was it merely to ensure that the guests at this special occasion were well provided with wine? No, His true purpose was of far greater import. John tells what that purpose really was.

The water that Christ turned into wine had been gathered in stone jars typically used for ceremonial washing. This might seem like a strange detail to include in the story, but Dr. Stott noted that sometimes the true key to understanding a text lies in seemingly slight details. They are clues to unlocking the richness and meaning of a passage in Scripture.

So it is with the reference to stone jars for ceremonial washing in this account. The water that had been gathered in these jars was a symbol of the old religion, the religion of the law that the Hebrew people had known for centuries. The wine that Christ transformed the water into was a symbol of the new religion, Christianity, that Jesus would establish. Stott phrased it this way: "Just as he changed the water into wine, so [Christ's] gospel would supersede the law. The sign [or miracle] backed up the claim that Jesus was the one who would bring in this new order. He was the Messiah."[8]

When we turn to the story of the miracle called "the feeding of the five thousand," we also discover that there was far more at work than merely the satisfying of hunger, important though that was. This miracle, we learn, illustrated Christ's "claim to satisfy the hunger of the human heart." It is as He said in John 6:35, "I am the bread of life. He who comes to Me shall never hunger, and he who believes in Me shall never thirst."

Still later, in John 9:1–11, we read of Christ opening the eyes of a man born blind. Just one chapter earlier, in John 8:12, Jesus had said, "I am the light of the world. He who follows Me shall not walk in darkness, but have the light of life." The connection here is clear: if Christ "could restore sight to the blind, he can open people's eyes to see and know God."[9]

Nowhere is the interplay of miracle and purpose more beautifully seen than in the resurrection of Lazarus, described in John 11:38–44. The story related here is one incandescent with hope, and much else besides.

Then Jesus, again groaning in Himself, came to the tomb. It was a cave, and a stone lay against it. Jesus said, "Take away the stone."

Martha, the sister of him who was dead, said to Him, "Lord, by this time there is a stench, for he has been dead four days."

Jesus said to her, "Did I not say to you that if you would believe you would see the glory of God?"

Then they took away the stone from the place where the dead man was lying. And Jesus lifted up His eyes and said, "Father, I thank You that You have heard Me. And I know that You always hear Me, but because of the people who are standing by I said this, that they may believe that You sent Me."

Now when He had said these things, He cried with a loud voice, "Lazarus, come forth!" And he who had died came out bound hand and foot with graveclothes, and his face was wrapped with a cloth."

Jesus said to them, "Loose him, and let him go."

"That they may believe you sent me." Sent for what purpose? Here, the reflections of John Stott bring us to the heart of the matter. "Jesus," he said, "had resuscitated a dead man." It was a sign, for the life of the body symbolizes the life of the soul. The raising of Lazarus was as much as saying that Christ is to be the life of the believer before death and will be the resurrection of the believer after death. Further, a miracle such as this was a most powerful parable, illustrating the truth that "as human beings we are spiritually hungry, blind and dead, and that only Christ can satisfy our hunger, restore our sight and raise us to new life."[10]

Miracles attest the reality of all that Christ wishes to give us, if only we will believe.

~

As we consider the miracles of Christ, it is well worth considering what the great British preacher Charles Spurgeon once said in this context. "God will bless the earth for Christ's sake," Spurgeon said, "even as he once cursed it for man's sake." Commenting on this potent phrase, writer Randy Alcorn observed that "God has never given up on his original creation." Nevertheless, we often miss an entire biblical vocabulary that makes this point clear—as in the words *reconcile, redeem, restore, recover, return, renew, regenerate, and resurrect*. In view of this, Alcorn stated forcefully that "it's impossible to understand the ministry of Christ without the larger view of redemption's sweeping salvage plan."[11]

Have we ever stopped to consider this? The noted scholar Albert Wolters wrote that all of Jesus' miracles (save that of cursing the fig tree) "are miracles of restoration—restoration to health, restoration to life, [or] restoration to freedom from demonic possession." These miracles, Wolters concluded, "provide us with a sample of the meaning of redemption, a freeing of creation from the shackles of sin and evil, and a reinstatement of creaturely living as intended by God."[12]

As one might expect, Spurgeon had much more to say about the miracles of Christ than has been mentioned above. In a sermon given at the Metropolitan Tabernacle of London, Spurgeon spoke of the "witness" that miracles bear. "Our Lord," he said, "claimed that his miracles and life-work were a sufficient witness to his Messiahship. 'The works,' [said Jesus,] 'which the Father hath given me to finish, the same works that I do, bear witness of me, that the Father hath sent me.'"[13]

What conclusion did Spurgeon draw from this? For him the words of Christ spoke with crystalline clarity. He observed,

> There is perhaps no better evidence of the truth of our Saviour's mission than his character, life, and miracles. The truths which he revealed, the perfections which he displayed, and the wonders which he wrought—all went to show that he was, indeed, anointed of God, and sent to be the Saviour of men.[14]

$\sim$

Aside from the foregoing discussion of Christ's miracles, it is important as well to consider the words used in the New Testament in connection with miracles, and what each of these words has to teach us.

There are, we learn from Herbert Lockyer, three words in Greek used in the New Testament to denote miracles. *Terata*, which means "wonder"; *semeion*, which means "sign"; and *dunamis*, which means "power"—from which our word dynamite is derived.[15]

Why take time for a brief word study? Is it not a rather arcane academic exercise? Far from it. For Lockyer wrote that "no one term can possibly exhaust all the significance of a miracle." That is why "various terms are used of miracles"—"only . . . all these together [will afford] an adequate conception of that which we desire to understand."[16]

And so we come to the first of our three words, *terata*, or wonder. This word, Lockyer wrote, "indicates the state of mind produced on the eyewitnesses by the sight of miracles. Astonishment was excited in them. The extraordinary character of the miracle was observed and kept in the memory." More than this, *terata* is the word most frequently used to refer to miracles.[17]

At this point, Lockyer offered a word of caution. In places where the word *terata* is used, we are to bear certain things in mind. (1) True enough, he wrote, "such a display of power was contrary to previous expectation—opposite to any law with which [Jesus' eyewitnesses] were acquainted." (2) These miracles, however, were never "to be regarded merely as 'wonders,' producing a momentary amazement. Attention had to be given to their purpose."[18]

Here, a marvelous passage from the writings of the theologian Frédéric Godet captures just what Lockyer is trying to convey:

> The miracles of Jesus are not mere prodigies (*terata*) intended to strike the imagination. There is a close relation between these marvellous facts and the person of Him who does them. They are visible emblems of what He is and what He comes to do, images which spring as rays from the abiding miracle of the manifestation of Christ.[19]

Semeion, the Greek word meaning "sign," carries with it the connotation that, wrote Lockyer,

> miracles [were] seals by which God authenticated the miracle-worker himself. In *semeion*, the ethical purpose of the miracle is most prominent. A miracle was to be looked upon as a token and indication of the near presence and working of God and a proof of the genuineness of revelation.[20]

A "sign," he continued, "designates a proof or evidence furnished by one set of facts to the reality and genuineness of another." So far as the person of Christ was concerned, or an apostle like Paul, the "signs" they performed were acts that legitimized "the miracle-worker's claim to be accepted as God's representative." They were "seals of power," or, to think of it another way, divine stamps of approval. The New

International Version's rendering of Acts 14:3 is a prime example of this. There we read, "So Paul and Barnabas spent considerable time there, speaking boldly for the Lord, *who confirmed the message of his grace by enabling them to do miraculous signs and wonders*" (emphasis added).

Dunamis, the Greek word that means "power," has a fascinating context of meaning. As used in the Bible, miracles are "powers" in that "they manifest the mighty power of God which was inherent in Christ Himself." The plural of *dunamis*, "powers," is the same word translated in the King James Version of the Bible as "wonderful works," for example, in Matthew 7:22; or "mighty works," as in Matthew 11:20, Mark 6:14, and Luke 10:13. The plural of *dunamis* is also translated as "miracles" in Acts 2:22, Acts 19:11, 1 Corinthians 12:10 and 28, and Galatians 3:5.[21]

One verse of Scripture, Acts 2:22, is a place where each of the three Greek words we've been exploring are used in concert with one another. This verse reads: "Jesus the Nazarene, a man set forth by God to you by works of power [*dunamesin*], and wonders [*terasin*], and signs [*semeois*], which God wrought by Him in your midst."[22]

Such a passage carries in itself the richness of what we're meant to know and bear in mind when it comes to miracles. They are performed by an almighty God. They are meant to foster a sense of wonder in us and worship also—as we praise the One from whom such blessings flow. Lastly, they are signs (emblems or pledges) given in confirmation of the message of God's grace—as He enables His servants, such as Paul and Barnabas, to do miraculous signs and wonders (Acts 14:3).

~

Now as to Jesus Himself, John Laidlaw, the noted nineteenth-century Bible scholar, identified four types of miracles that Jesus performed: (1) nature-miracles, (2) healing-miracles, (3) raisings from the dead, and (4) a post-resurrection miracle.[23]

As identified by Laidlaw, *nature miracles* refer to those miracles that demonstrated Christ's power over nature. There were eight in all. The turning of water into wine is described in John 2. The story of the great catch of fish is told in Luke 5. The stilling of the storm appears at the close of Mark 4. The miracle of the loaves is found in Matthew 14, which is also the chapter detailing the scene where Christ walks on the water. Mark 8 is where we find the story of the second miraculous feeding. The close of Matthew 17 is the location of the story of the fish caught with the coin in its mouth. And the withering of the fruitless fig tree is described in Matthew 21.[24]

Laidlaw next identified twenty distinct *miracles of healing* that took place during Jesus' ministry. At the close of John 4, we read of the healing of the courtier's son. Luke 4:33—35 recounts the deliverance of a man possessed by a demon in the synagogue. The healing of Simon Peter's mother-in-law is described in Matthew 8. Luke 5 recounts the cleansing of a leper. Chapter 2 of Mark's gospel is where Christ healed a man stricken with palsy, by the word of His power. One chapter later, in the same book, Jesus healed a man with a withered hand. The healing of the servant of the centurion of great faith takes place in Luke 7.[25]

John 5 presents the story of how a man afflicted with infirmity for thirty-eight years was healed by Jesus at the pool of Bethesda. In Matthew 8, the Gadarene demoniacs were delivered by Christ, while the woman with an issue of blood was restored to health in chapter 8 of Luke's gospel. Matthew 9 is the place where two healings unfold at the hands of Christ: the healing of the two blind men and the man who was mute and demon-possessed. The deliverance of the demon-possessed daughter of a Syro-Phoenician woman unfolds in Matthew 15. Traveling to Decapolis, Jesus healed a deaf man with a speech impediment—a story recounted at the close of Mark 7. One chapter later, in Mark 8, the miracle of Jesus' healing of the blind man at Bethsaida takes place. Matthew 17 is the place where Christ's healing of an epileptic boy is found. In John 9, the healing of a man born blind is described, while the healing of a woman oppressed for eighteen years with "the spirit of infirmity" is related in Luke 13. Christ's healing of a man afflicted with dropsy takes place in Luke 14, the cleansing of ten lepers in Luke 17. And last of all, the blind beggar Bartimaeus was healed by the Lord in Mark 10.[26]

There were three instances when Christ *raised someone from the dead* in the Scriptures. In Mark 5:21–23, Jesus brought the daughter of a synagogue leader named Jairus back to life. Luke 7:11–17 is the place where the account of Jesus' raising of the widow's son from the city of Nain is given. The raising of Lazarus of Bethany from the dead, discussed earlier, is described in John's gospel, chapter 11.[27]

Last of all, Dr. Laidlaw drew attention to the one *post-resurrection miracle* performed by Christ. In John 21, Christ appeared to His disciples by the Sea of Galilee, and there told them where to cast their nets. As soon as they heeded Him, "they were not able to draw it in because of the multitude of fish" (John 21:6).

This was a wonderful miracle in substance and in symbol. In John 14, the Lord said, "Most assuredly, I say to you, he who believes in Me, the works that I do he will do also; and *greater works than these he will do, because I go to My Father*" (v. 12, emphasis added). The gathering of the vast multitude of fish was a harbinger of what Christ said when He would make His disciples "fishers of men." Great and wondrous would be the gathering of souls to their heavenly Father in the years to come. Great and wondrous, too, would be the miracles performed through disciples by the mighty power of God. Ever and always, these manifestations of grace would point to Christ.

10 ✦ The Crucifixion and Resurrection: The Miracles of Our Redemption

Then was Christian glad, and said: "He hath given me rest by his sorrow, and life by his death." Then he stood awhile to look and wonder, for that the sight of the Cross should thus ease him of his burden.

Now, as he stood looking, behold three shining ones came to him, and saluted him with "Peace be to thee;" and the first said to him, "Thy sins be forgiven."

—*The Pilgrim's Progress*[1]

passage from *The Ball and the Cross*, one of G. K. Chesterton's most famous novels, has often been quoted. The setting is this: two foes, swords drawn, were determined to fight a duel. James Turnbull, an atheist, pitted against Evan MacIan, a Roman Catholic.

But it was, however, a duel that went far beyond any physical form of mortal combat. Larger forces were at work, of which they were then only half aware. Cosmic forces, that had to do with matters of eternal moment. And so we come to a place in fiction that yielded one of Chesterton's finest lines ever about the cross. As the two foes were about to clash, Turnbull said in deadly earnest:

> "Courage, my friend, we have come to the country of honour."
>
> MacIan did not even notice the incongruous phrase "my friend," but nodding again and again, drew his sword and flung the scabbard far behind him in the road.
>
> "Yes," he cried, in a voice of thunder, "we will fight here and *He* shall look on at it."
>
> Turnbull glanced at the crucifix with a sort of scowling good-humour and then said: "He may look and see His cross defeated."
>
> "The cross cannot be defeated," said MacIan, "for it is Defeat."[2]

There were two levels of meaning woven into what Chesterton said here. On one level, all that the followers of Christ had placed in Him by way of hope had been crushed. When He was seized by the Roman authorities, His disciples fled in fear for their lives. They were scattered and completely devastated. Their master and teacher—one to whom they looked as a Savior—was now to die a criminal's death. The victory of Christ's triumphal entry into Jerusalem had become an utter rout. His defeat could not have been more total.

All this was part of the horrible prelude to Christ's crucifixion. But what was to come, and what Christians have cherished for two thousand years, was that the death of Jesus was not the end of the story. There was another chapter to be written—one in which death was swallowed up in a victory of cosmic totality. It was the miracle of the resurrection. Christ defeated death itself. As John Stott has so beautifully written, "Most men live and die: Christ died and lived!"[3] As the timeless and mighty old hymn has it:

Death cannot keep his prey—
Jesus, my Saviour!
He tore the bars away—
Jesus, my Lord!
Up from the grave he arose,
With a mighty triumph o'er his foes;
He arose a Victor from the dark domain,
And he lives for ever with his saints to reign.
He arose! He arose!
Hallelujah! Christ arose![4]

"His resurrection produced a total revolution in the condition of man," said the poet and playwright Hannah More. It is "the main hinge on which the whole of Christianity turns. . . . If this doctrine could be got rid of, it would subvert the whole fabric of Christianity."[5]

That the resurrection of Christ is the heart of Christianity has been a recurring theme from the writings of the apostle Paul to Billy Graham. Turn to chapter 15 of Paul's first letter to the Corinthians, where he stated explicitly in verse 14: "If Christ is not risen, then our preaching is empty and your faith is also empty." But—and this was Paul's anthem of victory—"Christ *is* risen from the dead" (v. 20, emphasis added). As the heading for this passage in the New King James Version of the Bible has stated so fittingly: "The risen Christ, faith's reality." And in concert with this thought, Paul wrote, "The last enemy that will be destroyed is death" (v. 26). This Christ has done. The risen Christ has become our incomparable hope, the eternal hope for all who will believe.[6]

This, Paul hastened to say, was not merely an admirable idea, a thought meant to comfort—along the lines of "He lives in our hearts." No, he insisted there was proof of Christ's resurrection. There were eyewitnesses to this transcendent truth, and they were still living when he put pen to paper.

"Christ died for our sins according to the Scriptures," Paul stated in 1 Corinthians 15. "He was buried, and . . . rose again the third day according to the Scriptures, and . . . He was seen by [Peter], then by the twelve. After that He was seen by over five hundred brethren at once, *of whom the greater part remain to the present.* . . . After that He was seen by James, then by all the apostles. . . . Last of all He was seen by me also, as by one born out of due time" (vv. 3–8, emphasis added). The resurrection was a miracle for which there was proof. As the King James Bible says so beautifully: Jesus "is able to save them to the uttermost that come unto God by him, seeing he ever liveth" (Heb. 7:25).

The Book of Common Prayer, for its part, has captured the Christian's hope as movingly as any treasured text ever has. It sounds praise to "Almighty God, who, through thine only-begotten Son, Jesus Christ, hast overcome death, and opened unto us the gate of everlasting life."[7]

Hannah More, a daughter of the Church of England, wrote movingly of those who gave their lives professing unshakable belief in this blessed hope. "Why did the apostle Paul, and so many other martyrs, expose their lives to perpetual peril?" she asked.

> Why, but from the firm persuasion, that as Christ was risen, they should rise also. Rob them of this sustaining confidence, strip them of this glorious prospect, and their zeal would lose its character of virtue, their piety its claim to wisdom. Their perseverance would be fatuity. Mighty then must be their motive, powerful indeed their assurance, clear and strong their conviction, that their brief sorrows were not worthy to be compared with the glories which were insured to them by the resurrection of Christ.[8]

Fast-forward to the recent past, and we find Billy Graham speaking this peerless truth to our historical moment. In an article published in *Time* magazine in June 2001, "The Message of Miracles," Dr. Graham was quoted stating that if he were an enemy of Christianity, he would "aim right at the Resurrection, because that's the heart of Christianity." The bodily resurrection of Christ is crucial, Graham said, for without it, "you'd have to throw out the Easter story." Jesus showed His disciples the nail prints in His hands. And if Christ didn't rise, as the apostle Paul tells us, "it all has no meaning."[9]

In the nineteenth century, A. R. Fausset, the canon of York, stated that the resurrection was the greatest miracle of all those to be found in Scripture or in history. The resurrection, he wrote, "is the central miracle toward which all the rest converge."[10]

It was this reality that sustained Saint Stephen as he faced his own impending death. His final words were a testimony that captured the beauty and sustaining power of this miracle—in all its facets. Stephen said,

Men of Israel, listen to this: Jesus of Nazareth was a man accredited by God to you by miracles, wonders and signs, which God did among you through him, as you yourselves know. This man was handed over to you by God's set purpose and foreknowledge; and you, with the help of wicked men, put him to death by nailing him to the cross. But God raised him from the dead, freeing him from the agony of death, because it was impossible for death to keep its hold on him.

David said about him:

"I saw the Lord always before me.

Because he is at my right hand,

I will not be shaken.

Therefore my heart is glad and my tongue rejoices;

my body also will live in hope." (Acts 2:22–26 NIV 1984)

Stephen lived and died in the assurance of this truth. For centuries since, countless others have as well. It has been the cornerstone of their beliefs, the strong anchor of their souls.

~

But before a watching and skeptical world, the doctrine of the resurrection seems the height of folly. "Whoever heard of a suffering God?" the Oxford scholar Alister McGrath wrote. "The idea is plain daft. God is up in heaven, and there he will stay." Then, following a brief pause, McGrath continued, "But wouldn't it be wonderful if it were true? If God came to visit us, like a great king visiting his subjects? Or, even better, if he came among us."[11]

This was but an echo of words written by the apostle Paul twenty centuries before, for as he conceded, "The message of the cross is foolishness to those who are perishing." But, and here was the heart of the matter, "to us who are being saved it is the power of God" (1 Cor. 1:18).

Few have written more aptly or more memorably about the resurrection than John Stott, the former rector of All Souls Church, Langham Place, London. He had a matchless gift for commending the teachings of Christianity to those who were unchurched, or to seekers curious about the truth claims of the faith. His reflections on the resurrection, as given in his book *Basic Christianity*, were no exception. He could unpack the ancient-world context in which the resurrection took place, while also drawing connections to our own era, when skepticism about this teaching is no less prevalent.

"If the resurrection is true," Stott wrote, "it has great significance." What makes Him unique, above all others, is not the question of His spiritual survival, nor that of His physical resuscitation. No, it is Christ's conquest of death and His resurrection that hold the key—for they ushered in a new plane of existence altogether. No one else, in all human history, has had this experience. This is why modern people are as scornful of Christianity as the Athenian philosophers were who heard Paul preach on the Areopagus twenty centuries ago. They mocked, as many people do today, any notion of the resurrection of the dead.[12]

The argument here is not that Christ's resurrection establishes His deity. No, the earth-shattering thing is that the resurrection is consistent with His deity. Think about it for a moment. Is it not to be expected that a supernatural person should come to our planet and leave it in a supernatural way? It should therefore come as no surprise that this is, in fact, what the New Testament teaches. It is, in consequence, what the Christian church has always believed. Christ's birth was natural, but His conception was supernatural. His death was natural, but His resurrection was supernatural. His miraculous conception and resurrection do not prove His deity. Rather, they are in keeping with it.[13]

This brings us to the question of miracles itself. Christ was a supernatural person. Miracles are consistent with His identity. The writer George MacDonald understood this profound truth and all its implications. He framed a contrast that put the matter in its proper light. "I do not wonder at most of those to whom the miracles are a stumbling-block," he stated. "I do a little wonder at those *who can believe in Christ* and yet find them a stumbling-block."[14]

Why does the resurrection matter? Or, to consider the question as MacDonald phrased it, why was this miracle needful? It was, he said, "the best hope that might be given of a life beyond the grave." Then followed an exploration of all that flowed from such a belief. He declared,

If Christ be risen, then is the grave of humanity itself empty. [If, as Christians] we have risen with Him . . . death has henceforth no dominion over us. Of every dead man and woman it may be said: he—she—is not here, but is risen and gone before us. . . . The Lord lay down in the tomb, and behold it was but a couch whence He arose refreshed. . . . [Thus] we may say of every brother: he is not dead but sleepeth. He too is alive and shall arise from his sleep.[15]

~

In the story about the death of Lazarus, his sister Martha—about whom we know so little—spoke a sentence that prompted a response from Jesus for which Christians have been thankful for millennia. She spoke from the place of grief and sorrow, saying, "I know that [my brother] will rise again in the resurrection at the last day" (John 11:24). She thought her brother dead, and that she would never see him again on earth.

In reply, Jesus spoke from the place of everlasting solace and hope: "I am the resurrection and the life," the Lord declared. "He who believes in Me, though he may die, he shall live. And whoever lives and believes in Me shall never die. Do you believe this?" (vv. 25–26).

It was the gospel complete in thirty-three words. Words of prophecy and confirmation—words of reassurance and transcendent hope. "I am the resurrection and the life." It was the promise that came true, and the promise given to all who would believe.

"The cross cannot be defeated," Chesterton wrote, "for it is Defeat." What did he mean? His countryman Charles Spurgeon knew. And in words that still stir the soul more than one hundred years after they were written, he declared that we ought to dwell upon the resurrection more and more,

for there lies your hope. Hear this! Our Lord "was delivered for our offences." God gave Him up to justice, as if he had said, "Condemn Him, scourge Him, crucify Him; for He is made a curse for my people. I have delivered Him up, I have left Him, and forsaken Him."

See the soldiers lead Him through the streets of Jerusalem! See, they fasten His hands and feet with nails to the cruel cross! Behold Him lifted up to die in agony. . . . [Then] they take down those precious limbs, wrap them in white linen, and place them in the sepulchre. He is delivered unto the grave for our offences. There went all my sin, and the sins of all believers. He made an end of sin in His death. The wrath of God was spent upon Him . . . and now those sins are gone for ever! How do we know? We know because our Surety is set free.[16]

11 ✦ A Light from Heaven:
The Miracle of Paul's Conversion

You know, I can't explain to you, really, how He does it. But He proved Himself to me in such a holy way, such a complete way, that I'd die for that faith and I'd die for that belief, because it's more than a belief—He lives in my heart. . . .

Those people that knew me before, didn't know that I could believe something so strong. The gospel is simply this: Jesus will forgive all your sins, if you'll come to Him humbly, lay down at His feet, and say, "You're the Lord, and I'll follow you the rest of my life on earth, so that I can have the rest of eternity with you—and the glory of your Father."

—KEITH GREEN[1]

The story of the first miracle associated with Paul of Tarsus is that of his conversion.

Few stories in Scripture are more famous, and this account from the life of Paul has become proverbial. One phrase describing what happened to him has entered the language. Many, if not most, have heard of the phrase "a-road-to-Damascus experience." Commonly understood, it refers to having an epiphany or sudden flash of insight that is far-reaching in its consequences.

The conversion of Paul on the road to Damascus was so far-reaching as to nearly defy description. It led to a chain of events that changed the destiny of nations—indeed nations that did not exist in his time—and continents that neither he nor any of his contemporaries knew existed. Paul, the great missionary of the early Christian church, was largely responsible for the gospel coming to Europe. From Europe, in the centuries to come, Christianity would eventually spread, as it now has, to every corner of the world. Billions of people today call themselves Christians, and all faith traditions across the Christian landscape can trace their spiritual lineage to Paul and his great missionary journeys.

And it was a miracle that ushered in the history-changing transformation of Paul—a man who once fought God at every turn and who was an agent of terrible persecution against the faith he would one day embrace.

There is no better guide to understanding the nature and import of this miracle than John Stott, who wrote about it at length in his book *Why I Am a Christian*.[2] He began by describing a common experience. Many of us have heard people say, "I've had no road-to-Damascus experience—no sudden flash of insight or change in thinking." People say this, Stott wrote, because they think that Paul's conversion was sudden in nature.

But they are mistaken. Paul's road-to-Damascus experience was instead the climax of a whole series of experiences that had taken place earlier in his life. For a long time, Paul had been resisting the call of God to his heart. The miracle of his road-to-Damascus experience proved the final catalyst to his embracing of faith.

To begin to explore the context of this series of experiences, we must begin with the passage we find in Acts 26. At this time, Paul was called Saul. In recounting the story of his conversion, he remembered,

As I journeyed to Damascus . . . at midday . . . along the road I saw a
light from heaven, brighter than the sun, shining around me and those
who journeyed with me. And when we all had fallen to the ground,
I heard a voice speaking to me and saying in the Hebrew language,
"Saul, Saul, why are you persecuting Me? It is hard for you to kick
against the goads." (vv. 12–14)

The key word in this passage is the word *goad*. What is a goad? It
has its origin in the Greek word *kentron*, which can be translated "spur,"
"whip," or "goad." Classical writers, like Aeschylus, used this word meta-
phorically, but for our purposes, its usage in the Old Testament book of
Proverbs is most telling: "A whip for the horse, a bridle for the donkey,
and a rod for the fool's back!" (26:3).

Bearing this in mind, we can now see that when Jesus spoke to Paul
in his miraculous road-to-Damascus vision, He was saying that He was
much like a farmer trying to train a young colt who was fighting Him
all the way. Jesus had been continually prodding Paul in his conscience,
but he was stubbornly resisting God's relentless, steadfast pursuit of love.
Paul refused to yield his heart to God, and was finding it "painful, even
futile, for him to kick against the goads."[3]

But what were these goads? How had Jesus been pursuing and
prodding Paul? We can piece together the evidence from passages given
in the book of Acts and also from autobiographical flashes in Paul's
letters.[4]

Here we learn first that Jesus was goading Paul—or Saul, as he was
then called—in his mind. A brilliant man, trained under the great Rabbi
Gamaliel, Saul was steeped in all the collective wisdom of the Jewish
faith. Morally, he lived a life of great probity and was incredibly zealous in terms of his commitment to his faith. As he would later write in
Philippians 3:5–6, he was "circumcised the eighth day, of the stock of
Israel, of the tribe of Benjamin, a Hebrew of the Hebrews; concerning

the law, a Pharisee; concerning zeal, persecuting the church; concerning the righteousness which is in the law, blameless."

All that Saul had heard of Jesus of Nazareth was a blasphemous affront to what he knew and cherished. He couldn't possibly be the promised Messiah spoken of in the Old Testament. Had He not died a criminal's death by crucifixion? And didn't the book of Deuteronomy teach that "he who is hanged is accursed of God" (Deut. 21:23)? Surely Christ had been the very worst kind of impostor and deserved the punishment that had been meted out to Him. And as for the so-called followers of Christ, did they not deserve the same fate?

All this was uppermost in Saul's conscious mind. But subconsciously, perhaps, things weren't at all the same. Yes, all the things Saul had heard about the scandalous death of Jesus were true—but what about the unsettling rumors he had been hearing?—rumors of the beauty and authority of Jesus' teaching, or the meekness, gentleness, and sterling quality of His character. Still other rumors spoke of His compassionate service to the poor and mighty works of healing. One rumor above all others was especially troubling. People were saying that death had not been the end of Jesus. Many claimed to have seen Him, touched Him, and spoken with Him *after* His death.[5] If there was any truth to these rumors, any truth at all, Saul's perception of things might have to change. There might be a different set of considerations to reckon with. There was only one problem: he refused to do so.

～

Second, Jesus was goading Saul in his memory. As we read in the book of Acts, Saul had been present at the stoning of the martyr Stephen. He had seen Stephen's face shining like "the face of an angel" (Acts 6:15). He had heard Stephen say in the face of death that he could see "Jesus standing at the right hand of God" (Acts 7:55). And he was there when

Stephen cried at the last, "Lord Jesus, receive my spirit. . . . Lord, do not charge them with this sin" (Acts 7:59–60). All these things were etched on Saul's memory. He had been complicit in Stephen's death. How could he not be troubled by thoughts of a brave man willing to die for his convictions—a brave man he had helped put to death?[6]

Third, Jesus was goading Saul in his conscience. As we saw earlier, Saul considered himself righteous beyond reproach in terms of conformity to the teachings of the Mosaic law. "Blameless" was how he described himself.

But what about now? How did he see himself after his role in the death of Stephen? Had he helped to commit murder? And did not the Ten Commandments declare, "Thou shalt not murder"?

Moreover, as he later confessed in Romans 7, he had known "every kind of covetous desire" (v. 8 NIV 1984). This was deeply troubling, for the Ten Commandments also declared, "Thou shalt not covet."

And yet he had—constantly throughout his life. Covetousness, Stott wrote, is "an insatiable lust."[7] Saul knew he was guilty of this sin, and Stott likened what Saul must have felt over this realization to a passage from the writings of C. S. Lewis. "For the first time," Lewis recalled in his autobiography, *Surprised by Joy*, "I examined myself with a seriously practical purpose. And there I found what appalled me; a zoo of lusts, a bedlam of ambitions, a nursery of fears, and harem of fondled hatreds. My name was legion."[8]

Saul, in later life, had written of himself in much the same unsparing language that Lewis had used.

> I would not have known sin except through the law. For I would not have known covetousness unless the law had said, "You shall not covet." *But sin . . . produced in me all manner of evil desire. . . .* [And] when the commandment came, sin revived and I died. (Rom. 7:7–9, emphasis added)

Last of all, Jesus was goading Saul in his spirit. In this, Stott said he was referring "to that part of the human makeup which is aware of the transcendent reality of God."[9] As a Hebrew, zealous for his faith, Saul of course believed in God. But, in view of what has been said already of what he knew to be true about the deeply sinful nature of his heart, he faced a profoundly troubling problem. Sin, he had been taught from his youth, separated people from God. Those guilty of sin were alienated from God in the most heinous of ways, for God hated sin. If he was sinful, as he knew himself to be at heart, he was lost to God and without hope.

It all made for a perfect storm of disquiet and unacknowledged pain. Jesus had been prodding Saul in his mind, filling it with doubts as to whether Jesus was an impostor or not. Jesus had been stirring Saul's memory with recurring images of Stephen's face—his words, his great dignity, and his courageous death. Jesus had been prodding Saul in the depths of his conscience, convicting him of evil desires that warred within his heart. And Jesus had been convicting Saul in his spirit. It had become for him a "vast, empty vacuum of alienation." For years, such things had been taking place. Jesus had been hurting Saul that he might, at the last, find a place of true healing. Had not the very fanaticism with which Saul sought to persecute Christians betrayed a deep vein of inner turmoil?[10]

All this, taken together, meant that when Jesus appeared to Saul on the Damascus road, a miracle unfolded that led to the place of final surrender. Jesus revealed Himself to Saul, and Saul fell to the ground, calling Him Lord. His was an incredible conversion experience—so profound that his very name was changed from Saul to Paul. He was a completely different man, a new man, a Christian.[11]

~

It runs against conventional wisdom to think that some miracles take time, or that they are the climax to a whole series of life experiences. Somehow the word *miracle* seems to convey a sense of rapid transformation or something that unfolds in a crowded hour.

The conversion of Paul runs counter to this perception. God's patience in drawing this man to faith is instead the hallmark of what took place. Such a thought is well captured in a phrase penned centuries ago. "A gracious hand," it has been said, "leads us in ways we know not, and blesses us not only without, but even against, our own plans and inclinations."[12]

Christendom would never have come into being in the way that it did, were it not for this tremendous and transformative truth. Paul became the great missionary to what we now know as Europe. His letters, as given in the New Testament, established and set forth many of the central doctrinal tenets of the faith. Further, as the apostle Peter noted in Scripture, Paul made the intellectual case for Christianity—becoming its first, and some would say its greatest, apologist.[13] All this was made possible by what happened on the road to Damascus: a miracle that has reverberated throughout all subsequent history.

PART II

Miracles in the Lives of God's People

W e now move from a survey of miracles presented in Scripture to a series of key moments and stories of God's work in the lives of His people throughout church history and the modern era. The hymn writer Isaac Watts once wrote of "God, our help in ages past, our hope for years to come."[1] Miracles are not only events that fall within the province of ancient times. They grace our modern historical moment as well.

It is profoundly important for us to realize that the annals of the church, and the days of the more recent past, are filled with instances of God's miraculous dealings. For two thousand years the hope of heaven has called to people in ways that are extraordinary. When we stop to consider their stories, God's voice calls to us as well. Should we take the time to listen, our faith can be deepened and immeasurably enriched.

12 ✦ Perpetua: Miracles in the Life and Death of a Martyr

Much of the current interest in "spirituality" suffers from a kind of amnesia—forgetful or oblivious that there is indeed a centuries-long well to draw from, full of an inheritance which can enrich our lives. . . . God works beyond our own small personal experiences, and beyond our own lifetime.

—Leighton Ford[1]

The time of Perpetua is separated from ours by nearly two thousand years. In the early third century, the Roman Empire held sway over much of the known world and over everyone's lives within the provinces of its empire. Run afoul of the authorities, and your life was forfeit. For Christians who lived in this era, martyrdom was an ever-present possibility.

From the early church father Tertullian we learn something of the violent, poisonous prejudice that characterized the ancient Roman Empire when it came to Christians. "Of every military defeat," Tertullian stated, "of every popular distress, the Christians are supposed to be the cause. If the Tiber riseth or the Nile doth not rise, if the heavens stand fast or the earth moveth, if there be famine or pestilence, it is always '[Throw] the Christians to the lions!'"[2]

This prejudice was widely shared by the Roman military. They were accustomed to making and unmaking sovereigns and would not bear with subjects who not only asserted but also exercised independence.[3]

Warning signs of the violence to come could be seen in the case of Apollonius, a Roman senator arrested during the reign of the Emperor Commodus on the charge of being a Christian. Brought before the Senate, he refused to renounce his faith and voiced a lengthy defense. He was therefore condemned to die, and this sentence served as the rationale not long afterward for an edict issued by the Emperor Severus forbidding any further conversions to Christianity.[4]

Among the first to suffer martyrdom under this order were five young converts at Carthage. Two of the five were women. One, of noble birth, was named Perpetua.[5]

When she was arrested, Perpetua was about twenty-two years old and still nursing her infant son. She was said to be "of excellent family and education."[6]

Posterity is especially fortunate in that Perpetua dictated her own account of all that she suffered up to the point of her martyrdom. The following pages draw on that surviving document, in order to re-create as much of her own story as possible. Her words deserve to live again, that her faith may speak to those living now.

"From the time," Perpetua told us, "that I joined my companions in professing Christ, my father not only wished to turn me from my purpose with arguments, but also persisted in trying to break down my faith."

"Father," she said one day, "do you see this vessel lying here—a jug, or whatever it is?"

He nodded. "I see it," he said.

"Well then," said she, "can one call anything by any other name than what it is?"

"No."

"So," Perpetua said with quiet determination, "neither can I call myself anything else but what I am—a Christian."

Greatly angered, her father seized her as though he were bent on violence. But, his anger subsiding a little, he only shook her. He then stormed from her house and did not return for several days.

Not long afterward, Perpetua was baptized. Then the Holy Spirit intimated to her that she was soon to experience suffering as a result. A few days later, she was taken to prison. "O awful day!" she recalled, "with such fearful anger arising from the crowd and the jostling of the soldiers! [Worst of all] I was racked with anxiety for my baby."

Still, during her time of greatest need, Perpetua was solaced by the kindness of friends. "Then Tertius and Pomponius," she said, "blessed deacons who were ministering to us, arranged by bribery for us to go forth for a few hours and gain refreshment in a better part of the prison." This done, she had a brief and modest measure of freedom during which she was able to nurse her baby. It was this for which she was most grateful, since her little boy had already grown weak from hunger.

During this time, Perpetua spoke to her mother and entrusted her son to her. On one level she was relieved. But separated as she was from her family, particularly her little boy, she grew increasingly worried. For many days, she knew this kind of distress.

Then a small mercy was accorded her. She obtained permission for her child to come stay with her in the prison. Immediately upon this news, she began to gain strength. Reunited with her son, she recalled, "My prison suddenly became to me a palace, so that I preferred to be there rather than anywhere else."

It was at this time that Perpetua was granted the miracle of a vision. Her brother in the faith and fellow prisoner Saturus came to her and said, "Sister, thou art already in such a position that thou mayest ask God for a vision, and that it may be shown thee whether we are to suffer or to be released."

Something about this admonition spoke to Perpetua and resonated with her spirit. She believed what Saturus had told her. "To-morrow," she told him, "I will tell thee what the Lord tells me."

So saying, she went to prayer. And as she petitioned the Lord, she was granted a miraculous vision. "I saw," she remembered, "a brazen ladder of wondrous size reaching up to heaven; narrow, however, so that only one could go up it at once, and on its sides I saw every kind of iron instrument fixed—swords, lances, hooks, daggers—so that if one went up carelessly, or not fixing one's attention upwards one would be torn, and pieces of one's flesh would be left on the iron implements."

She saw other things in the course of her vision as well. "There was also," she said, "lying under the ladder a dragon of wondrous size, which laid snares for those climbing it, and frightened them from attempting to climb it." As she looked on in her vision, her friend Saturus went up first to the ladder. He had, she remembered, "given himself up voluntarily after our arrest on our account, because he had taught us the faith."

In her vision, as Saturus got to the top of the ladder, he turned and said, "Perpetua, I am waiting for you; but take care that that dragon does not bite you."

To this she replied, "In the name of Jesus Christ he shall not hurt me."

At this, her vision changed. The dragon, as if afraid of her, slowly thrust his head underneath the ladder itself; and she trod upon his head as if she were treading on the first step.

As Perpetua neared the top of the ladder, she saw a large space of garden, and in the midst, a man with white hair sitting, in the garb of a shepherd, tall, milking sheep; and a white-robed host standing round him.

As she approached, he lifted his head and saw her, and said, "Welcome, child." He then called to her and gave her a piece of the cheese he was making. Receiving it with joined hands, in the manner of communion, she ate what she had been given, following which all those around her said, "Amen."

At the sound of this word she awoke, still tasting something sweet.

The following day Perpetua went to Saturus and told of her vision. Both agreed that it meant they were about to suffer martyrdom.

Not long after this, they received word that their case was to be heard by the Roman authorities. At the same time, Perpetua's father came up from the city of Carthage. Wearied and disgusted with her behavior, his errand once again was to break down her faith.

In so doing, he spoke with great pathos. "Daughter," he said, "pity my grey hairs; pity your father, if I am worthy to be called father by you, do not make me disgraced before men. Think of your brothers; think of your mother and your aunt. Look at your son, who cannot live without you. Set aside this faith: do not cut us off entirely."

All this her father said with great affection, kissing her hands and throwing himself at her feet, and with tears called her not "daughter," but "lady."

This was a source of great distress to Perpetua. For he alone, of all her relatives, "would not rejoice at my martyrdom." So she sought to comfort him, saying, "This will be done on that stage which God has willed. For I know that we have not been placed in our own power but in God's." Upon hearing this, her father left her with great sorrow.

Not many days had passed before Perpetua and her fellow believers were suddenly carried off to their trial and taken to the forum. The rumor of it immediately went around the neighborhood, and an immense crowd gathered. One by one, each of Perpetua's fellow prisoners was placed in the dock and questioned. Each confessed their faith in Christ.

At last, Perpetua's turn came. During her time of questioning, her father appeared on the spot with her little son, and drew her down from the step of the dock, saying to her, "Pity thy child."

At this the presiding Roman official said, "Spare thy father's grey hairs; spare thy infant boy. Offer a simple sacrifice for the safety of the Emperor."

Perpetua's heart must have been rent over the choice set before her, yet she would not recant her faith.

Summoning her strength, she told the procurator with quiet courage, "I do not sacrifice."

"Art thou a Christian?" the procurator asked.

"I am," she said.

Seeing this, Perpetua's father began to plead with her to renounce her faith. Angered by this disruption of the proceedings, the procurator ordered that he be beaten with a rod. "I felt it as keenly as though I had been struck myself," Perpetua recalled, "and I was sorry for his miserable old age."

Following this, the procurator pronounced his sentence, condemning Perpetua and her fellow prisoners to be thrown to the beasts in the arena.

Now knowing her fate, Perpetua requested that she be allowed to nurse her child one last time. She sent word to her father to bring her little boy to her, but her father refused to give him up.

Several more days passed, during which time Pudens, the adjutant, or governor of the prison, began to show some measure of humanity, allowing people in to see Perpetua and her fellow prisoners.

As the day of her time in the arena drew near, her father came again to see her, and worn out with despair, he began to tear out his beard and throw it on the ground. He threw himself to the ground, pleading with her on account of his age and misery. Deeply touched, Perpetua grieved to see him in such a state.

One day before she was to be forced to fight in the arena, Perpetua experienced another vision. In it she saw Pomponius, a deacon she knew, coming to the door of her prison and knocking forcefully. She went to the door and opened it for him. There he stood, clothed in a loose white robe.

And he said to her, "Perpetua, we are waiting for you; come."

He then took her hand, and they began to traverse rough and winding passages. At last, with difficulty, they arrived panting at the amphitheater, and he led her into the middle of the arena, saying to her, "Fear not: I will be here with thee, and will assist thee." Then he departed.

As her vision continued, Perpetua beheld a vast crowd eagerly watching all that went on in the arena. Knowing she was to be given to the beasts, she wondered why the beasts were not sent to fight with her.

Then she described a certain Egyptian of terrible aspect coming forth against her along with his assistants, ready to fight with her. She was then readied for combat according to custom.

But before she was sent to fight, a certain man came forth, of wondrous size, whose height was greater than the amphitheater, wearing a loose, purple robe with two broad stripes over the middle of his breast and embroidered shoes wrought of gold and silver. He carried a rod like a fencing-master, and a green branch on which were golden apples. Calling for silence, he said, "This Ægyptian, if he conquer her, shall kill her with the sword, but if she conquer him she shall receive this branch."

Then this man of wondrous size departed for a time, and Perpetua went to face her Egyptian foe. They began to exchange blows. He tried to catch her by the feet, but she struck his face with her heels. Borne aloft in the air, she began to strike him as though she were not treading upon the ground. She then joined her hands and interlocked her fingers. Then she caught him by the head, and he fell on his face and she trampled on his head.

At this, the spectators in Perpetua's vision began to shout and sing psalms. She then left the place of combat and walked to the man of wondrous size. From him she received the branch, which seemed to have symbolized peace. He gave her a kiss, and said, "Daughter, peace be with thee."

Then Perpetua began to walk with glory to the gate Sanavivaria, the gate reserved for combatants who had survived the contests in the arena. After this, she awoke.

~

Here, Perpetua's narrative ended, and the account of her martyrdom was given by the chronicler mentioned in the opening of this chapter, the early church father Tertullian.

Perpetua and her fellow prisoners, he wrote, "went forth from the prison into the amphitheatre as if to heaven—joyful, and with radiant countenances, trembling, if at all, with joy, not with fear."

When they were brought to the gate, where they would normally have been compelled to put on costumes, the priests of Saturn and the women devotees of Ceres told Perpetua and her companions, "We have pledged our life that we will not make you do this." So it was that the tribune allowed them to be led to the arena in whatever attire they were already wearing.

Perpetua, for her part, sang a psalm. Her fellow believers, Revocatus, Saturninus, and Saturus, admonished the spectators of the intended combat, and when they caught sight of the procurator, they said to him, "You may judge us, but God will judge you."

Upon hearing these things, the spectators became infuriated and demanded that these men be punished with scourges in front of the line of beast-fighters. When this had been decided, Revocatus, Saturninus, and Saturus rejoiced that they were to share in something like the sufferings of Christ.

In the days leading up to their combat in the arena, each of these men had spoken of the kind of death he desired to face. Saturninus had said he wished to be thrown to all the beasts, so that he might obtain a more glorious crown. So it proved to be. At the beginning of the contest, he was set against a leopard. Then, still alive, he was placed upon a platform and mauled by a bear.

Saturus, for his part, feared being killed by a bear more than anything but thought that he might die more quickly if killed by a leopard. His death, in the event, proved more trying and drawn out. He was made to face a wild boar, but the professional fighter who had tied him to the beast was pierced instead and died soon after the show was over. Saturus was only dragged about by the beast. Next, when he was tied up to the bear on the bridge, the bear refused to come out of his cell. So it was that Saturus was called back a second time unhurt.

The young women, of whom Perpetua was one, were set to face a mad cow, tormented and driven to rage for that very purpose. So it was that when the beast had been prepared, they were brought forth, stripped, and clothed only in nets.

At this, the crowd shuddered, seeing one, a delicate girl, and another, just come from nursing her child. In such plight they were called back and clothed with loose garments. Perpetua was tossed first by the horns of the cow and fell on her loins. Somehow she managed to sit up and draw back her tunic, which had been torn from her side.

Then she stood, and seeing that Felicitas, the young girl, had been tossed as well, she went to her, extended her hand, and lifted her up. Both stood equally firm, and, the cruelty of the crowd being conquered, they were called back to the gate Sanavivaria—which, it will be recalled, was the gate reserved for combatants who had survived the contests in the arena.

Once there, Perpetua was received by a certain catechumen named Rusticus, who had attached himself to her, and, as if awaking out of sleep (so completely was she in the Spirit and in an ecstasy), she began to look round and, to the utter astonishment of everyone, said, "I wonder when we are going to be led forth to that cow."

When told that it had already happened she did not at first believe it, until she saw some marks of the tossing on her body and her dress. Then, having sent for her brother, she addressed him and the catechumen, saying, "Stand fast in the faith and let all love each other; and let not our sufferings be a stumbling-block to you."

Likewise Saturus, who stood at another gate, was exhorting Pudens the adjutant (who had become a believer), saying, "In a word, as I expected and foretold, I have up to now absolutely escaped every one of the beasts. Now, do thou believe with thy whole heart. Lo, I am about to come forth thither, and by one bite of the leopard I will die."

So it was that at the end of the contest in the arena, when a leopard was let loose, Saturus was bitten and poured forth so great a quantity of blood that the people shouted out to him in bitter scorn, mocking the Christian rite of baptism by saying, "Well washed; well washed!"

Saturus, badly injured, took a small ring from his finger, and having dipped it in his wound, gave it to Pudens as a pledge and memorial of his sufferings. As he died, he said to Pudens, "Farewell: remember me and my faith; and let not these things trouble you, but strengthen you." Then faint, or nearly so, he was laid along with the others in the accustomed place for the throat cutting.

After this, when the arena spectators demanded that Perpetua and the remaining captives should be brought into their midst in order that they might look upon the sight of the sword piercing their bodies, Perpetua and her friends voluntarily rose up and walked to where the crowd wished.

Before during so, they had mutually exchanged the kiss of peace spoken of in Scripture. Others, unable to move and so take leave of their friends in this way, were put to the sword in silence.

Saturus was the first to die. This done, Perpetua took the hand of the gladiator told to kill her. He seemed to have become unnerved by what he was being forced to do, and his hand was unsteady. In an act of great courage, she guided his hand and the sword he held to her own throat. A few moments later, she was dead.

No words seem adequate to describe what Perpetua and her fellow believers endured. Tertullian's tribute, brief though it was, is perhaps the only thing that could be said. He wrote, "O most brave and blessed martyrs!"[7]

13 + Augustine: Miracles in the Life of a Philosopher

Like Dante, Augustine moves simultaneously both outward, exploring the revelation of God, and inward, letting the revelation affect and alter him.

—GARRY WILLS[1]

The Confessions speaks for itself. The earliest of autobiographies, it remains unsurpassed as a sincere and intimate record of a great and pious soul laid bare before God.

—CHARLES W. ELIOT, PRESIDENT OF HARVARD[2]

It was late summer, AD 386. Thirty-three-year-old Augustine of Milan was in the throes of a spiritual crisis. Highly ambitious, he greatly desired all that the world had to offer. He longed for status and had won highly sought-after laurels of intellectual attainment. He was no less wedded to the pursuit of pleasure and sex. One woman had already borne him an illegitimate son.

And yet he found himself inexplicably drawn to the things Christians had shared with him of the life they had embraced. He felt himself torn and unable to find peace. He faced his own Rubicon, a spiritual one, and did not know which way to turn.

It was then, in September 386, that his life was forever changed by the miracle that has come to be called "a grand stroke of grace."[3] It was a miracle that drove him to his knees and raised him up to walk the path that became the way of a saint.

Augustine recorded all that brought this great transformation in his life. His recollections of this time form the centerpiece of a book that has become a classic of world literature: *The Confessions of St. Augustine*. In its pages, the miracles that God wrought in his life shine with a light that sixteen centuries haven't dimmed. We begin first with his account of the spiritual crisis that threatened to overwhelm him.

One day, in company with his friend Alypius, Augustine's long-standing, agonizing concern over his spiritual condition threatened to overwhelm him. Try as he might and search though he had done, he could find no sense of peace about matters of eternal destiny. He and Alypius had been talking together in a beautiful garden, but Augustine could take no solace from his pleasant surroundings, derive no comfort from his friend's company. Getting to his feet, he said that he needed to be alone for a while. As he stepped away, tears came. He felt as lost as he ever had at any time of his life. He seated himself beneath a fig tree, and the full tide of sadness washed over him.

But it was then, while feeling a most bitter contrition of heart, that he seemed to hear from a neighboring house a voice, as of a boy or a girl—he wasn't sure—chanting and often repeating the words, "Take up and read; Take up and read."

Instantly, his tears were checked; he began to consider most intently whether children ever did such things while at play, but he could not remember ever having heard that they did. He got to his feet and walked over to where he had set down his copy of the writings of Saint Paul. Taking it up, he began to read the first chapter that he found there.

The first passage he saw contained these words: "Let us walk properly, as in the day, not in revelry and drunkenness, not in lewdness and lust, not in strife and envy. But put on the Lord Jesus Christ, and make no provision for the flesh, to fulfill its lusts" (Romans 13:13–14). He stopped there, "nor did I need to read further," he would later recall. "For instantly at the end of this sentence a light, as it were, of serenity flooded into my heart, all the darkness of doubt vanished away."[4]

~

Through hearing and heeding a miraculous voice, Augustine had set out on the road to becoming the man Christians through the centuries would come to revere, the man whose writings so many would cherish: Saint Augustine of Hippo.

Augustine bequeathed many things to the literature and history of the Western world. Among them was the gift of autobiography. Rarely, if ever, before his time, had anyone crafted a book written entirely in the first person. With his use of the word *I* in writing his celebrated *Confessions*, he changed the course of literature for all time to come. His was the first, and still is one of the greatest works of autobiography.

~

It is fascinating, given the miraculous nature of Augustine's conversion, that he thought—as he did in his younger years as a bishop—that "spectacular proofs," or miracles, were no longer needed to bring people to faith.[5] Yet that is what one distinguished biographer, Peter Brown, wrote.

Over time, however, Augustine's understanding of miracles changed and grew, as did his view of their place in our lives. As an older man, he came to see that "the human race had remained much the same, always frail, always in need of compelling authority. 'The God of our fathers,' he would write, 'is our God also'. . . . God could fully determine, for Himself . . . how often miracles should or should not occur."[6]

This view of God's sovereignty deeply enriched Augustine's understanding of miracles. "God," he stated in a sermon from his later years, "never stops bearing witness; and He knows the right way to bring His miracles to our notice. He knows how to act, so that they may be famous; He knows how to act, so that they don't become commonplace."[7]

Other facets of the nature of miracles flow from this central truth. Augustine lived in an age not unlike our own, when people often thought "to consult the stars" to try and discern the meaning of their lives or what the future might hold. Against such a pervasive backdrop of astrology, Augustine penned this striking reflection about that star that heralded the birth of Christ.

[Some] suppose that Christ was born under the control of the stars, just because the Magi saw a star in the East when he was born. . . . [Yet] Christ was not born under [the star's] control, but rather appeared as its controller. It did not keep to the starry tracks in the heavens, but [rather it] pointed . . . the men who were looking for Christ . . . to the very place where He was born. So it wasn't the star that caused Christ wonderfully to live, but Christ that caused the star wonderfully to appear; nor was it the star that controlled Christ's miracles, but Christ that revealed the star as one of His miracles. He, you see, when born of His mother, presented the earth with a new star from the sky, just as when born of the Father He fashioned the earth and the sky.[8]

Elsewhere in his sermons, Augustine wrote richly about the reasons that miracles marked the earthly ministry of Jesus. He wrote,

The reason, our Lord Jesus Christ performed miracles was to signify something by these miracles, so that in addition to the fact that they were wonderful, and tremendous, and divine, we should also learn something from them.[9]

Building upon this idea, he stated,

Our Lord Jesus Christ, you see, wanted the things He did materially to be also understood spiritually. . . . He wasn't just performing miracles for the sake of miracles; He did them so that what He did should be marvelous to those who saw them, true to those who understood them.[10]

Such reflections on the nature of miracles prompted a still greater flow of ideas. Dipping his stylus in the inkwell, Augustine continued to write. Miracles, he stated, are something of a mystery to most people, rather like seeing the letters in a beautifully written codex, which they are unable to read. True enough, such people are full of praise for the penmanship and beauty of the letters. Still, they haven't the slightest idea what those letters mean, or what they have to say. But there are others, a fortunate few, who can appreciate the scribe's artistry and also grasp the meaning of what he has written.

In the same way, Augustine reasoned, some people in the time of Christ beheld His miracles, but didn't understand what they meant. But there were some who were both astonished at the things that happened and enriched by understanding what they meant. "That's the group we should belong to," Augustine stated, "those to be found in the school of Christ."[11] His prayer was that God would open the eyes of people's understanding. He longed for everyone to be numbered among the students in God's school.

~

For many, it is difficult to choose between Augustine's *Confessions* and his other great work, *The City of God*. Happily, we do not here have to choose a favorite between the two. Rather, we can say that for the purpose of seeing what Augustine believed about miracles, *The City of God* is also a work rich in such reflections.

In this book, he laid down some basic principles concerning the nature of miracles. "We cannot but believe," he wrote, "that all miracles, whether wrought by angels or by other means . . . are done so as to commend the worship and religion of the One God in whom alone is blessedness."[12]

At the same time, Augustine wanted his readers to understand that the gift of existence itself, and the world in which we live, are ever-present miracles. "Whatever marvel happens in this world," he stated, "it is certainly less marvelous than this world itself,—I mean the sky and the earth, and all that is in them,—and these God certainly made."[13]

Why does God choose to work miracles among us? Augustine wondered. As an answer, he stated that miracles occur in large part because God wishes to draw us to Himself, even as Augustine had once been drawn to God through the voice that told him to "take up and read." The same God who made "the visible heaven and earth," he wrote, "does not disdain to work visible miracles in heaven or earth, that He may thereby awaken the soul . . . to worship Himself, the Invisible."[14]

Augustine moved next to considering the credibility of miracles. Here, his thoughts bring to mind how C. S. Lewis so often referenced pagan ideas and beliefs as a context from which to make a cogent point. "Will some one say," Augustine asked,

that [all] miracles are false, that they never happened, and that the records of them are lies? Whoever says so, and asserts that in such matters no records whatsoever can be credited, [must] also say that there are no gods [according to any religion] who care for human affairs. For [as the pagans believe, the gods] have induced men to worship them only by means of [so-called] miraculous works, [with] which the heathen histories testify, and by which the gods have made a display of their own power.[15]

In essence, according to Augustine, if one rejects the idea of any miracle as false, one is not at liberty to make exceptions if it suits one, or the worldview to which one subscribes. One must be logically consistent.

However, this digression, interesting though it is, was not Augustine's main purpose. He presupposed that miracles occur, and his central theme was to explore what miracles tell us about God the Father and the Lord Jesus Christ.

And so Augustine began with a description of God the Father, saying that He is "the invisible and unchangeable Founder of this visible and changing world." Supremely, God is "the truest bestower of the blessed life which resides, not in things created, but in Himself."[16] The upshot here was that miracles are by definition "things created," but they are never an end in themselves. The blessed life, it bears repeating, resides in God Himself—to whom miracles point and of whom they testify.

Augustine turned next to the Psalms, particularly Psalm 73:28, which states, "It is good for me to draw near to God." Among philosophers, Augustine declared, "it is a question: what is that end and good to the attainment of which all our duties are to have a relation?" In the verse cited above, the psalmist, Augustine stated, did not say it is good to have great wealth or to wear imperial insignia—the purple, a scepter, or a diadem. No, the greatest good has nothing to do with wealth of this kind. The greatest good is to possess spiritual strength. For had not the psalmist also said: "It is good for me to draw near to God"? [17]

The psalmist had discerned this, Augustine concluded, because he possessed a right understanding of miracles. He could say, "It is good for me to draw near to God" because "he had learned from Him whom the holy angels, *with the accompanying witness of miracles*, presented as the sole object of worship."[18]

~

The idea that miracles were so often bestowed as a confirmation of true faith was a recurring and favorite theme for Augustine. He loved to ponder the Old Testament and what might be called his "hall of faith," even as the writer of the New Testament book of Hebrews did. His sense of wonder over the reality that miracles promoted genuine faith and pointed to it was always great, as demonstrated in one long and very revealing passage.

"It might seem tedious," he wrote, "were I to recount all the ancient miracles, which were wrought to attest the promise God made to Abraham thousands of years ago—that in his seed all the nations of the earth should be blessed."[19] Yet what could anyone do other than marvel that Abraham's barren wife, Sarah, should have given birth to a son at so great an age? What could anyone do other than marvel that when Abraham offered a sacrifice, a flame from heaven moved between the divided parts?

Still more, Augustine stated, Abraham had hospitably entertained angels in human form—divine emissaries who had renewed God's promise that Abraham would be given a son. These same angels also predicted the destruction of Sodom by fire from heaven and promised that Abraham's nephew Lot would be rescued from Sodom as the fire was just descending to destroy the city. Then, too, there was the miracle of judgment that had come upon Lot's wife, who, disobeying the divine command, had looked back toward Sodom as they fled and was immediately turned into salt. It was a tragic fate, Augustine reckoned, but her story stood "as a sacred beacon, warning us that no one who is being saved should long for what he is leaving."[20]

Augustine turned next to "the wonders done by Moses to rescue God's people from the yoke of slavery in Egypt, when the magi of the Pharaoh, that is, the king of Egypt, who tyrannized over this people, were permitted to do some wonderful things that they might be vanquished all the more signally!" They did these things, he said, by the magical arts and incantations in service to Satan; while Moses, having much greater power—as he had right on his side, and the aid of angels—"easily conquered them in the name of the Lord who made heaven and earth."[21]

As he stepped away from his "hall of faith" and the miracles enshrined there, Augustine penned a conclusion that rings true and still inspires seventeen centuries after his time. All these miracles, he marveled, and others in Scripture that were too numerous to mention, "were wrought for the purpose of commending the worship of the one true God, and prohibiting the worship of a multitude of false gods."[22] God was in them declaring His uniqueness and our unique privilege to kneel before Him in grateful acknowledgment of His almighty power and purpose.

One more word remained. All these miracles, Augustine stated, "were wrought by simple faith and godly confidence."[23]

Simple faith and godly confidence. Such should be our Christian profession: childlike faith—entire confidence in the One most worthy of trust. Augustine's conclusion is an ancient word that is ever new and just one of the reasons why posterity is profoundly indebted to him.

14 + Julian of Norwich: Miracles in the Visionary Realm

In 1393 Lady Julian, the ankeress here, was a strict recluse, and had two servants to attend her in her old age. This woman was in these days esteemed one of the greatest holiness.

—Blomefield's *History of Norfolk*[1]

In lumine Tuo videbimus lumen.
In Thy light we shall see light.

—from an ancient Latin proverb[2]

J ulian of Norwich was born in 1342 and died sometime after 1416— the precise date of her death is not known. But what we do know of her life is extraordinary. She bequeathed to the church the record of what she believed was a series of miraculous visions God had given her. On the 8th day of May, 1373, a "Revelation of Love was shewed to her, 'a simple creature, unlettered,' who had before this time made certain special prayers from out of her longing after more love to God and her trouble over the sight of man's sin and sorrow."[3] One morning, over a period of five hours, she stated that she received fifteen "shewings" from God—the following night still another, for a total of sixteen visions in all.

In the centuries since her book, *Revelations of Divine Love, Recorded by Julian, Anchoress at Norwich*, first appeared, it has stirred both controversy and admiration. Julian believed that her shewings "taught, among other things, that God is our mother as well as our father, that he cannot be angry with us and that no Christian will be damned—doctrines which [she] had great difficulty in reconciling with the Church's teachings."[4]

Notwithstanding these unorthodox elements, and they are not to be lightly dismissed, there are other aspects of Julian's book for which many in Christendom have been grateful. The Nobel Prize–winning poet T. S. Eliot is among them.[5] He was deeply drawn to the beauty of language and imagery found in Julian's *Revelations*, going so far as to place passages from them directly into the text of his celebrated poem *The Four Quartets*. One section of the poem, "Little Gidding," bears these lines:

> *Whatever we inherit from the fortunate*
> *We have taken from the defeated*
> *What they had to leave us—a symbol:*
> *A symbol perfected in death.*
> *And all shall be well and*
> *All manner of thing shall be well*
> *By the purification of the motive*
> *In the ground of our beseeching.*[6]

The line "all shall be well, and all manner of thing shall be well" is taken directly from Julian (revelation 13), as is the line "the ground of our beseeching"—a slight paraphrase of a line from revelation 14—"I am Ground of thy beseeching."[7] The simply wrought beauty of such lines recall passages from a work like *The Pilgrim's Progress*, the immortal allegory by John Bunyan that begins, "As I walk'd through the wilderness of this world, I lighted on a certain place, where was a Denn; and I laid me down in that place to sleep: and as I slept I dreamed a dream."[8] Both writers have imparted an abiding source of richness to the English language, and for that we are indebted to them both.

Other stirring and beautiful phrases fall within the pages of Julian's book. In its opening pages, for example, she wrote that she "conceived a mighty desire to receive three wounds in my life: that is to say, the wound of very contrition, the wound of kind compassion, and the wound of steadfast longing toward God."[9]

Other passages from the *Revelations* speak of the Godhead, such as this reflection on the Trinity: "For the Trinity is God—God is the Trinity; the Trinity is our Maker and Keeper, the Trinity is our everlasting joy and bliss, by our Lord Jesus Christ."[10] The love of God is another recurring theme, as shown in the line, "He is to us everything that is good and comfortable for us—He is our clothing that for love . . . encloseth us for tender love, that He may never leave us; being to us all-thing that is good."[11]

The idea of spiritual rest, of a heart finding its home in God, is another source of meaningful reflection for Julian. She wrote, "Our Lord God shewed that it is full great pleasance to Him that a helpless soul come to Him simply and plainly and homely."[12] Rest and the goodness of God are for Julian kindred sources of comfort for the Christian. "For He is the endlessness," she wrote, "and He hath made us only to Himself, and restored us by His blessed Passion, and keepeth us in His blessed love; and all this of His goodness."[13]

To read this beautifully rendered line is to be reminded at once of the immortal passage from the opening of *The Confessions of St. Augustine*:

Great art Thou, O Lord, and greatly to be praised; great is Thy power, and of Thy wisdom there is no end. And man, being a part of Thy creation, desires to praise Thee,—man, who bears about with him his mortality, the witness of his sin, even the witness that Thou "resistest the proud,"—yet man, this part of Thy creation, desires to praise Thee. Thou movest us to delight in praising Thee; for Thou hast formed us for Thyself, and our hearts are restless till they find rest in Thee.[14]

Touching on this passage from Saint Augustine in connection with Julian is an apt reminder that the *Revelations*, though a unique work in itself, is also part of a tradition of spiritual autobiography that began with Augustine's use of the pronoun *I*. We are indebted to Julian for the gift of her book, as she is "the first writer in English who can be certainly identified as a woman."[15] The window she opened on the world of medieval spirituality is unlike any other, particularly from a woman's perspective. Hers is a voice that helps bring that world to life, and without it our understanding of this period of history and literature would be greatly diminished.

That the joy of the Lord is our strength was a reality in which Julian exulted. "Marvellous joy shall be shewn us all then we see Him," she wrote.

And this willeth our Lord that we seek for and trust to, joy and delight in, comforting us and solacing us—as we may with His grace and with His help—unto the time that we see it verily. For the most fulness of joy that we shall have, as to my sight, is the marvellous courtesy and homeliness of our Father, that is our Maker, in our Lord Jesus Christ that is our Brother and our Saviour.[16]

At other times, Julian showed herself a master of the concise, deeply meaningful line. Echoing the words of the apostle Paul in 1 Corinthians 13, she placed her own stamp on the things that matter most: "For in faith, with hope and charity, our life is grounded."[17] Elsewhere, Julian's description of grace as an undeserved favor is one that lingers in the memory: "For we are so blind and unwise that we never seek God till He of His goodness shew Himself to us."[18]

There are also moments in the *Revelations* when the cross of Christ and the atonement purchased for us there take center stage. The message of redemption has seldom been so movingly expressed as in that passage where Julian wrote,

> We know in our Faith, and believe by the teaching and preaching of Holy Church, that the blessed Trinity made Mankind to His image and to His likeness. In the same manner-wise we know that when man fell so deep and so wretchedly by sin, there was none other help to restore man but through Him that made man. And He that made man for love, by the same love He would restore man.[19]

The vision that Julian had of "our Lady Saint Mary" in revelation 11 conjures stirring images of the nativity, the crucifixion, and the promise of heaven. Christmas in the stable of Bethlehem, the cross and Golgotha, and the felicities of paradise—where the shadowlands fall away—all these shone through in the three glimpses Julian had of Mary. "The first," Julian remembered, "was she was with Child; the second was she was in her sorrows under the Cross; the third is as she is now in pleasing, worship and joy."[20]

"I learned that our soul shall never have rest till it cometh to Him," Julian stated in the opening of revelation 12. "It is I that thou longest for, I that thou desirest." It was in this moment, she felt, "our Lord shewed Himself more glorified, as to my sight, that I [ever] saw Him before."[21] In her thirteenth revelation, Julian's words took the color and cadence of a doxology, and her brief hymn of praise reads as follows: "Christ Jesus is both God and man. . . . He is Himself highest bliss, and was, from without beginning, and shall be, without end."[22] And further in the same revelation, there was an encore. Speaking once again of Christ, Julian stated, "He is the Ground, He is the Substance, He is the Teaching, He is the Teacher, He is the End, He is the Meed for which every soul travaileth."[23]

Fullness of joy was a theme to which Julian returned in revelation 13. Wrapped up in this were thoughts of God's sovereignty, particularly as Ruler and Creator of the universe, and the consummation of all things in the kingdom that endures forever. "Fulness of joy," she said, "is to behold God in *all*: for by the same blessed Might, Wisdom, and Love, that He made all-thing, to the same end our good Lord leadeth it continually, and thereto Himself shall bring it; when it is time we shall see it."[24]

Julian also believed she had been gifted with a definition of mercy that lingered in her mind. Love and grace were its attendants. "Mercy," she stated, "is a working that cometh of the goodness of God, and it shall last in working all along, as sin is suffered to pursue rightful souls. And when sin hath no longer leave to pursue, then shall the working of mercy cease, and then shall all be brought to rightfulness and therein stand without end."[25] For those who have fallen, there was also an abiding word of consolation; redemption, restoration, renovation—these were its hallmarks: "And by His sufferance we fall . . . in His blissful Love with His Might and His Wisdom we are kept; and by mercy and grace we are raised to manifold more joys."[26]

Our lives, Julian felt she'd come to understand, are a gift—a time wherein we might come to know God and so prepare for eternity. "And as long as we are in this life," she said, "what time that we by our folly turn . . . our Lord God toucheth us and calleth us, saying in our soul: *Turn thee to me—I am enough to thee—and take joy in thy Saviour and in thy salvation.*"[27]

~

That is as good a word upon which to close this chapter as can be thought of, as fine a vision of what can be as could be conceived—when we make the glad surrender to Christ. Such a surrender Julian had made, the source of her everlasting gratitude and wonder. In a time of dire extremity, when she felt herself to be near death, she believed she had been gifted with glimpses of God on this side of eternity. Her life was spared, and she gave us the gift of beautiful language that has drawn the hearts of many nearer to God. When she departed from this life, words that are beacon for us all in 1 Corinthians 13 became the light of her reality in heaven: "For now we see in a mirror, dimly, but then face to face. Now I know in part, but then I shall know just as I also am known" (v. 12).

15 + Martin Luther: Miracles and the Dawn of the Reformation

Miracles are recorded for us . . . We learn and believe by them that in Christ we have a gracious, meek, loving, beneficent Lord, who is able and knows how to help us.

—MARTIN LUTHER[1]

He was born a peasant's son at Eisleben, Germany, on November 10, 1483. Yet Martin Luther would become, as one eminent church historian has written, "the greatest religious genius which the 16th century produced."[2]

It came as a surprise to no one that Luther, a greatly gifted student, earned his academic degrees "in an unusually brief time." He secured his bachelor's degree in one year, and his master's degree three years later. His father, justifiably proud, made it plain that he wished his son to become a lawyer. But Luther had decided to pursue another course. Plagued by the onset of religious doubts, he suddenly resolved to enter the Erfurt Convent of the Augustinian Eremites. He quickly completed his novitiate there and became a monk.[3]

Within the convent at Erfurt, so it is said, "Luther set himself to find salvation." The means he initially took, however, brought him no peace. They did, in fact, deepen his sense of anguish. He sought the path of the ascetic. He fasted and scourged himself, doing all the things he'd been taught he should do, but they purchased no relief from the misery he felt.[4]

At this time, Luther believed that God was "an implacable judge, threatening punishment for breaking a law which it was impossible to keep." In moments of troubling honesty, he admitted to himself that he often felt hatred toward "this arbitrary Will," which he knew, or thought he knew, as God.[5]

Not knowing where to turn, but seeking solace wherever he might find it, Luther "wearied his superiors with his attendance at the confessional." They were perplexed as to why peace of mind seemed so elusive to their prize student. Other friends and colleagues seemed to consider him "a young saint, and his reputation extended throughout the convents of his order." Why couldn't he see himself as they saw him?[6]

For two interminable years, Luther endured his dark night of the soul, "no nearer the pardon of God" than he was at the outset. But then, his elders in the order hit upon the source of his real difficulty. With their guidance, and based upon what they urged him to read in the Scriptures, Luther came to see that "God's pardon was to be won by trusting to His promises."[7]

It was his mentor, Johannes Staupitz, who came alongside young Luther at a crucial moment during this crisis of faith. As he would later remember, "Through Staupitz, the Lord Jesus repeatedly uplifted and strengthened me in the most wonderful way."[8]

"Attach yourself to Christ," Staupitz told his young friend. "Then everything will turn for the good." Words that Staupitz had taken for a personal motto may well have been among those he shared with Luther. They spoke of a glad surrender to Christ, and of trust in God's mercy:

"I am Thine, save me." The tormented could look to Christ. There, they could find safety, and much else besides. It was promised to them.[9]

∽

This realization and acceptance of grace, noted church historian T. M. Lindsay, "gave Luther a sense of freedom, and the feeling that life was given by God to be enjoyed." It was a source of inward peace that was to stay with him the length of his days.[10]

Soon after he had found peace, Luther was ordained. He also continued his studies in theology, devoting himself to the more experiential portions of Saint Augustine's works. He also read widely in the writings of the French twelfth-century abbot Bernard of Clairvaux, known widely for his stirring writings on the love of God.[11]

From this time forward, Luther rapidly advanced in his monastic order. In 1512, he was sent by Staupitz, his superior as vicar-general, to Erfurt to receive further education in theology. Once finished, the intent was that he would eventually succeed Staupitz as professor of theology at the newly founded University of Wittenberg. Luther took to his studies in earnest and graduated with the degree of doctor of the Holy Scripture. He then "took the Wittenberg doctor's oath to defend the evangelical truth vigorously, and became a member of the Wittenberg Senate." Three weeks later, he succeeded Staupitz as professor of theology.[12]

From the first, scholars have noted, "Luther's lectures in theology differed from those ordinarily given at the time." He differed from many of his contemporaries and colleagues "because he looked at theology in a more practical way." Many relished discussing the fine points and niceties of this field of study; Luther believed theology "ought to be made useful to guide men to the grace of God and to tell them how to persevere in a life of joyous obedience to God and His commandments." He began offering lectures that were really commentaries on the Psalms and on the epistles of Saint Paul.[13]

Within a few years, Luther began to find himself at variance with proponents of scholastic theology—declaring that it was, in fact, heretical, and "repudiated Augustinian doctrines of grace." Further, scholastic theology neglected to teach the supreme value of that faith "which throws itself upon God." Luther, who was a gifted speaker, had a rare gift for commending the intellectual heart of faith to his students. His lectures, and the teaching they contained, "soon made a great impression." Students began to flock to the small, obscure University of Wittenberg, and it rapidly became famous.[14]

So it was that by 1517, the stage was set for what would become a history-changing confrontation. But scarcely anyone, least of all Luther himself, knew how it would all unfold.

∼

Luther had been troubled for some time about the sale of indulgences and the corruption it symbolized (namely, swelling the coffers of an avaricious pope in Rome). "Love," he believed, "covers a multitude of sins, and is better than all the pardons of Jerusalem and Rome."[15]

Taking pen in hand, he cast his concerns in writing. They became what history now knows as his *Ninety-Five Theses*. Luther's intent was to debate these concerns among his colleagues at Wittenberg. So, in keeping with common practice, he posted a copy in Latin on the door of the Castle Church—the proverbial Wittenberg Door.[16]

Luther little knew that in posting his *Ninety-Five Theses* he would inaugurate what has come to be known as the Reformation. Yet that is indeed what happened. He wished for welcome changes in the policies and teachings of Rome, but they were not forthcoming. Luther was excommunicated and became a fugitive, fearing for his life. He did not ultimately become a martyr, but the chain of consequences that flowed from this turn of events led, inexorably, to the birth of Protestantism. Luther's act of conscience and his courageous stand on principle were primary catalysts.

~

Given Luther's stature as one of the great reformers of history and as a subsequent translator of the Bible, his reflections on the nature of miracles in Scripture are necessarily of great value. His views on subjects like this did much to shape the newly burgeoning Protestant movement and its growth in the years following his death. And while a full discussion of Luther's understanding of miracles cannot be given here, some representative examples of his thinking can be explored.

At the outset, it is interesting to note that Luther greatly admired the story of the centurion as recorded in Matthew 8:5–13. Therein lay threads of the miraculous, about which Luther wrote at length. The story from Scripture is as follows.

> Now when Jesus had entered Capernaum, a centurion came to Him, pleading with Him, saying, "Lord, my servant is lying at home paralyzed, dreadfully tormented."
>
> And Jesus said to him, "I will come and heal him." The centurion answered and said, "Lord, I am not worthy that You should come under my roof. But only speak a word, and my servant will be healed. For I also am a man under authority, having soldiers under me. And I say to this one, 'Go,' and he goes; and to another, 'Come,' and he comes; and to my servant, 'Do this,' and he does it."
>
> When Jesus heard it, He marveled, and said to those who followed, "Assuredly, I say to you, I have not found such great faith, not even in Israel!" . . .

Then Jesus said to the centurion, "Go your way; and as you have
believed, so let it be done for you." And his servant was healed that
same hour.

In this story, Luther believed, there "is a twofold miracle: one
performed by Christ, the other through the centurion." We can readily understand what is meant by the miracle wrought by Christ, but
why would Luther speak as he did of the Roman officer? As Luther
read his Bible, "Jesus himself marvelled at [the centurion's] very strong
faith." Based on that, he drew the conclusion that "what Christ regards
and praises as a miracle, that we also should reasonably regard as a
miracle."[17]

On the other side of the spectrum, Luther firmly believed in miracles
of judgment, that is to say, "miracles performed for the chastisement of
those who disregard the truth [those who reject the faith]."[18] Further,
he went on to say, "God sometimes permits genuine miracles to be performed by bad men."[19] And here, he marshaled biblical examples to
support his view, citing the prophecy of Caiaphas "that Jesus would die
for the nation, and not for that nation only, but also that He would gather
together in one the children of God who were scattered abroad" (John
11:51–52). He pointed also to the Old Testament account of Balaam,
whose prophetic message in Numbers 24 read in part:

> The oracle of Balaam son of Beor,
> the oracle of one whose eye sees clearly,
> the oracle of one who hears the words of God,
> who sees a vision from the Almighty . . . (vv. 3–4 NIV 1984)

Turning next to the eighth chapter of Matthew, Luther observed
that there were two miracles recorded in this portion of Scripture, "that
first [Christ] should preach, and afterwards confirm his preaching by

miracles, in order that every one should more readily believe."[20] Luther followed this by saying something that comes as something of a shock. "Thank God," he wrote, "we do not *need* miracles now, for the doctrine is already so well confirmed by miracles, that no one needs to doubt."[21] While he thought this was true, he admitted that miracles played a very important role in the Christian economy. He continued,

> And yet it seems necessary, that all Christians, and especially those who preach the Gospel, should not only be able to *speak* as Christians, but also to *live* as Christians, and confirm their teachings by their works. For the kingdom of God is not in word only, but also in power.[22]

This can be seen in Luther's reflections on the miracle of the feeding of the five thousand, as told beginning in Matthew 15:34: "Jesus said to them, 'How many loaves do you have?' And they said, 'Seven, and a few little fish.'" Here, Luther observed that Christ asked the disciples a second time for advice, in order that the magnitude and certainty of the miracle might become known. "If one had suspected that there might have been more loaves, the glory of the miracle would have been destroyed or darkened, just as at the present day all the creations and arrangement of the whole creation become unappreciated, which are equal or still greater miracles than this one was because they take place year in and year out."[23]

Luther went on to make a vital distinction based upon this. He said,

> But when the majesty of God's works is to be understood, one must imagine: *what if they did not exist?* If, for instance, we would form an idea of the majesty of the sun, we should ask ourselves, what would be the case if there were no sun, but for a single day? Christ now reminded the disciples, that of the work which he was about to perform, there was now nothing yet in existence.[24]

In this case, Luther believed that part of why this great miracle was performed was to provide a sense of eternal perspective. Christ's disciples, though in the presence of the Messiah, had an earthly perspective. In their eyes, Luther wrote, "everything was impossible." Why else would they have said, "Send the multitude away"? Had they never stopped to consider, Luther wondered, "that even provisions which they [might have bought] would not be in existence if they had not also grown up out of the earth in a wonderful way and had been preserved by God?"[25] The disciples needed to shift their gaze from "present things," to look on the things of eternity. The Son of God Himself was among them; they were constantly witnesses to miracles of all kinds. Could they not see that nothing was impossible with God?

Luther also wrote at length about the New Testament account of John the Baptist sending two of his followers to Jesus, asking, "Are you He who is to come?" By way of an answer, Luther observed, Christ said "neither yes nor no, but pointed them to the open testimony of his works." There were, Luther believed, two reasons for this. "First, neither John nor any one else had ever done such works. Second, these works had been previously foretold by the prophets."[26] To support this view, he referred his readers to Matthew 11:4–6, which states:

Jesus answered and said to them, "Go and tell John the things which you hear and see: the blind see and the lame walk; the lepers are cleansed and the deaf hear; the dead are raised up and the poor have the gospel preached to them. And blessed is he who is not offended because of Me."

He pointed also to Isaiah 35:4–6, which reads in part:

Say to those who are fearful-hearted, "Be strong, do not fear! Behold, your God will come. . . . Then the eyes of the blind shall be opened, and the ears of the deaf shall be unstopped. Then the lame shall leap like a deer, and the tongue of the dumb sing. For waters shall burst forth in the wilderness, and streams in the desert."

What was crucial about this account of John's inquiry, Luther believed, was that "Christ appeals to his works, and wishes to have the tree known by its fruit, in order to forestall all false teachers, who come in his name, and say, We are Christians; for here we have the truth. Where there are no works, there is also no Christ."[27]

For those who marveled that Christ spoke in Matthew 11 of "the dead being raised," Luther acknowledged the stupendous nature of such a thing. But then he went on to say that something else mattered far more. "To raise the dead is a great miracle," he said, "but [another] miracle is much greater and more glorious . . . namely, that God from eternity has ordained his Son to be a king of poor sinners, and that he should preach the gospel to them; therefore [Christ] places it as the very last and best of his works."[28] Here, Luther was harkening back to Matthew 11:5, the close of which read, "The dead are raised up and the poor have the gospel preached to them."

∼

Perhaps the finest series of reflections Luther ever offered on the subject of miracles are those that close out this chapter. He was powerfully impressed with the words of Christ in John 14:12: "Most assuredly, I say to you, he who believes in Me, the works that I do he will do also; and greater works than these he will do, because I go to My Father."

The first thing Luther noticed here were the words of consolation that Christ gave to the disciples. They should not be troubled, Luther observed, because He would be leaving them to go to the Father. Rather, they should consider what a great benefit would stem from this, namely, "that they shall do the same works which he had done, and even greater."[29]

This was truly a staggering thought. To stress its importance, Luther posed a question to his readers. "But what shall we think of this, that Christ says this *not only of the apostles, but of all those who believe on him?* What kind of works could these be, which shall be greater than those of Christ?"[30]

In framing the answers he had gleaned from his reading of Scripture, Luther's words assumed the reverent, wonder-filled tone of a doxology—not unlike passages he had read in the writings of the apostle Paul. "In the first place," Luther stated, "these believers who are to come have the Gospel, Baptism and The Lord's Supper," three things that had never before existed, and that were of imperishable worth.[31]

What flowed from these three gifts? Through them could come "the conversion of others, the rescue of souls from the devil, and the snatching of them from hell and death." But there was more as well. Through these gifts given by Christ, the prospect of an eternity with God was held out as a blessed hope, one whereby Christians might "comfort distressed consciences." Thus, those who have placed their faith in Christ might "teach all men in all conditions," offering instruction and counsel as to how "they can live a Christian life and die a happy death."[32]

If Christ had come to fulfill the promises of centuries past and perform miracles that were a testimony to the truth of who He was as Savior and Messiah, those who would place their faith in Him were offered a host of privileges that would flow from what Christ had done. But these privileges could only be imparted once He had ascended to the Father. Within the divine economy, great privileges indeed would be given to all who became Christians, and hence ambassadors of Christ. It was as the apostle Paul had written in the third chapter of his letter to the Ephesians: "To me, who am less than the least of all the saints, this grace was given, that I should preach among the Gentiles the unsearchable riches of Christ" (v. 8).

16 ✦ Gilbert Burnet: Miracles and the Church of England

If facts, that are plainly supernatural, are proved to have been really done, then here is another clear and full argument, to prove a Being superior to nature . . .

—GILBERT BURNET[1]

T he American Civil War general Ulysses S. Grant was once memorably described as "a reasonable man in an unreasonable time."[2] Gilbert Burnet, bishop of Salisbury, also lived in a tempestuous age. Born in 1643, during the period of the English Civil Wars, he too was in many ways "a reasonable man in an unreasonable time." Regicide, revolution, and violent religious strife: he saw all of these baleful things in his lifetime.

A self-described "lover of peace," Burnet was a stalwart ally of Robert Leighton, archbishop of Glasgow, in his efforts to bring about "a compromise between the Episcopal and Presbyterian communions."[3] In 1669, he published a manifesto calling for a rapprochement between these two kindred faith traditions, *A Modest and Free Conference Between a Conformist and a Nonconformist.* In the same spirit, he devoted five years of his life to crafting a book many consider one of his best: *An Exposition of the Thirty-Nine Articles of the Church of England,* first published in 1699. Through his life, and as expressed in his writings, Burnet "hoped for a comprehensive scheme which might include non-conformists in the English Church."[4] These hopes were never realized, but that in no way detracts from the compelling nature of the mere Christianity he championed.

Burnet's hopes for a conformist/nonconformist reunion remained unfulfilled, but the gift of his book about *The Thirty-Nine Articles* is one that posterity has had occasion to cherish. Reprinted many times during the 150 years after its initial publication, it became a widely acknowledged classic. And it is for that reason, and in light of the mere Christianity that it championed, that its teachings on the subject of miracles are well worth exploring. The richness of Anglican orthodoxy is on full display in its pages, a perspective that was warmly appreciated by another ornament of the Church of England—his great friend John Tillotson, the archbishop of Canterbury. In one moving letter, Tillotson closed with offering "a prayer that Burnet might long be spared to do . . . service to the Church."[5] So, indeed, Burnet's book has done, and contin-ues to do to this day.

~

"The essence of God is one perfect thought, in which He both views and wills all things."[6] Here, at the outset of Burnet's book, we have a beautiful affirmation of the perfection of God, as well as His sovereignty and transcendence. God is perfect, He rules all things, and, beyond the sphere of what we know as time, He sees all. Past, present, and future—all that is to be known in these realms of time is known to Him.

Building upon these thoughts, Burnet stated that God's "transient acts," that is, those things that He does once only, and in a specific time and place, "are done in a succession of time." This is to say that they unfold in history as we know it. Among God's transient acts are the creation of the world, moments when His providence is clearly at work, and miracles.

Miracles, according to Burnet, may be defined as instances when "nature has been put out of its course," and words or signs occur that are clearly wrought "by a power superior to the course of nature."[7] God is the only one who can bring about such things, and thus miracles speak in various ways of the reality of who He is.

Article I of *The Thirty-Nine Articles* declares,

There is but one living and true God, everlasting, without bodie [*sic*], parts or passions, of infinite power, wisdom and goodness, the maker and preserver of all things both visible and invisible; and in the unity of this Godhead there be three Persons of one substance, power, and eternity, the Father, the Son, and the Holy Ghost.

From this first article, Burnet deduced several important things. He began by reflecting on God's omnipotence, or His infinite power. "The Supreme Mind," Burnet wrote, "can by a thought set matter into what motions it will."[8] All matter, he continued, is "constantly subject to such impressions as the acts of the Divine Mind give it. This absolute dominion over all matter makes it to move, and shapes it according to the acts of that Mind."

This, Burnet concluded,

gives us a distinct idea of miracles, [for even] as the acts of the Eternal Mind gave matter its first motion, and put it into that course that we do now call the course of nature; so another act of the same Mind can either suspend, stop, or change that course at pleasure, as he who throws a bowl may stop it in its course, or throw it back if he will; this being only the altering that impulse which [He] himself gave: so if one act of the infinite Mind puts things in a regular course, another act interposed may change that at pleasure.

And thus with relation to God, miracles are no more difficult than any other act of Providence: they are only more amazing to us, because they are less ordinary, and go out of the common and regular course of things. [All these things] may carry us to form livelier and clearer thoughts of God.[9]

Burnet's description of God's transcendence of the natural order—He created it, and therefore can alter it as best suits His purposes and pleasure—recalls a summary from mathematician John Lennox of how a similar line of argument from C. S. Lewis helped him see the flaws in philosopher David Hume's "oft-cited arguments against miracles in general, and the resurrection of Christ in particular." As Lennox wrote,

Against the prevalent notion that miracles "break the laws of nature," Lewis argued that the laws of nature are not causes but, rather, are our descriptions of what normally happens, so that the Creator, who is ultimately responsible for the regularities in the cosmos, is not a prisoner of those regularities. He is perfectly free to feed something new into the system. It is therefore absurd to suggest that science has shown that God could not encode himself into human life ["the Word becoming flesh," as described in John 1:14].[10]

It is amazing that Burnet set out arguments so closely resembling those of Lewis, though he was writing some two and half centuries *before* Lewis put pen to paper. What is more, both men were clearly onto something of eternal moment. God is the Lord of the cosmic dance. He can alter those steps (what we perceive to be the "immutable laws of nature") whenever He chooses. He is over and above the created order. To return to Burnet's line of thought, moments of the miraculous "are only more amazing to us, because they are less ordinary, and go out of the common and regular course of things." Taken together, the insights of Burnet and Lewis are great gifts to the church, and they "carry us to form livelier and clearer thoughts of God."[11] And at the same time, what Lewis and Burnet have stated call to mind lines of verse from G. K. Chesterton. They are taken from his poem "Gloria in Profundis":

> *There has fallen on earth for a token*
> *A God too great for the sky.*
> *He has burst out of all things and broken*
> *The bounds of eternity:*
> *Into time and the terminal land*
> *He has strayed like a thief or a lover,*
> *For the wine of the world brims over,*
> *Its splendour is spilt on the sand.*[12]

~

Burnet's discussion of article IV of the Church of England considers how the resurrection and ascension of Christ speak to the heart of Christianity. This article states, "Christ did truly rise again from death, and took again his body, with flesh, bones, and all things appertaining to the perfection of man's nature, wherewith he ascended into heaven, and there sitteth, until he return to judge all men at the last day."

Building out from this statement of faith, Burnet declared that "among all Christians the article of the resurrection and ascension of Christ was always looked on as *the capital one, upon which all the rest depended.*"[13] From the reality of these two events came the inauguration of the Christian Church, in support of which more wonders were yet to follow. They were, Burnet stated, "gathered together in a book, and published in the very time in which they were transacted: the *Acts of the Apostles*."[14]

What were these wonders? Among them were the many instances when the early Christians saw Christ after His resurrection and spoke with Him. Second, following His ascension, His disciples "received extraordinary powers from him to work miracles in his name, and to speak in diverse languages. This last was a most amazing character of a supernatural power lodged with them."[15] Burnet called this "the effusion of the Holy Ghost,"[16] and in this instance, it was a beautiful way of confirming the word of Christ in John 15:26: "But when the Helper comes, whom I shall send to you from the Father, the Spirit of truth, who proceeds from the Father, He will testify of Me."

This naturally leads into a discussion of article V, which states that "the Holy Ghost proceeding from the Father and the Son, is of one substance, majesty, and glory with the Father and the Son, very and eternal God."

Burnet marveled over the promised coming of the Holy Spirit as spoken of in Scripture. "The Holy Spirit," he wrote, "is in the Scripture proposed to us as a Person, under Whose economy [are] all the various gifts, administrations, and operations that are in the church."[17] What did the church receive with the miraculous advent of the Holy Spirit? Burnet loved to cite the words of the Savior: "He shall abide with you: He shall guide you into all truth; and shew you things to come. He shall bring all things into your remembrance: He shall convince the world of sin, of righteousness, and of judgment." But here was not an end to what the Spirit would do, for according to the apostle Paul, "The Spirit searches all things, and intercedes for us." In the New Testament, Burnet concluded, the word we translate as the Holy Spirit "stands most commonly for that wonderful effusion of those miraculous virtues that [were] poured out at Pentecost on the apostles; by which their spirits were not only exalted with extraordinary degrees of zeal and courage, of authority and utterance, but they were furnished with the gifts of tongues and miracles."[18]

In concluding his exploration of the work of the Holy Spirit, Burnet's prose took on the air of a doxology. "The Holy Ghost," he said, "is truly God—of the same substance with the Father and the Son." His ministry is that of "teaching all things, guiding into all truth, telling things to come, searching all things, even the deep things of God, his making intercession for us [and] his changing us into the same image with Christ." Last of all, Burnet wrote, the Holy Spirit is "one substance, majesty, and glory, with the Father and the Son."[19] Such teachings, and such an understanding of miracles, are an ornament to the Church of England. They were in Burnet's lifetime, and they are now.

17 ✦ Jonathan Edwards: Miracles and the Great Awakening

In [his book,] A History of the Work of Redemption, *Edwards had worked out what he was sure was the key to history. God worked through periodic awakenings. That seemed demonstrated through biblical history.*

—George Marsden[1]

The Great Awakening was not a religious dogma. . . . The sun shone on the West when its cultural leaders understood that the Holy Spirit had actually enabled [the apostle] Peter's original readers—the believers—to live the way that Christ lived.

—Vishal Mangalwadi[2]

In October 1703, four years after Gilbert Burnet published his *Exposition of the Thirty-Nine Articles of the Church of England*, a boy was born in colonial New England whose ministry would be marked by a time of renewal so famous that its name has become a byword for the outpouring of the Holy Spirit: the Great Awakening.

The boy's name was Jonathan Edwards. He became a pastor, theologian, philosopher, and, briefly, president of the institution we know today as Princeton University. By late August 1741, Edwards was a central figure in a spiritual awakening (and controversy) that was flowing through New England, bringing hope to many, and calling down the scorn of others hostile to this challenging of established notions of how God moved and worked.[3]

If Burnet in his historical moment had been "a reasonable man in an unreasonable time," Edwards was no less so in his own—nearly two generations later and across the ocean in the New World.

When Edwards arrived in New Haven, Connecticut, to deliver a commencement address at his alma mater, Yale, he arrived amid a storm of controversy. The flashpoint for conflict centered on James Davenport, "a radical and sensational itinerant preacher" who had taken to encouraging congregations to leave their pastors, leading "corporate fits of passion which sometimes involved the burning of theological books," and "claiming to hear the very voice of God."[4]

By the time Edwards had arrived in New Haven, Davenport had brazenly declared that the Reverend Joseph Noyes, pastor of New Haven's First Church, was a "wolf in sheep's clothing." Since the young men attending Yale were required to attend First Church, Davenport's call for Noyes' congregants to leave "their pharisaical pastor" and attend separatist "pure" meetings had generated a firestorm. Rector Thomas Clap, charged with the spiritual welfare of the young men attending Yale, issued a directive forbidding students to attend any itinerant services. But by the time this edict was handed down, many students were already becoming grossly insubordinate, imitating incendiary evangelists like Davenport, presuming to act as faultless judges of one another's spiritual condition, or that of the established clergy, or college officials themselves. It was particularly alarming that one of Yale's most gifted students, David Brainerd, was foremost among these students.

In such circumstances, Yale's trustees met during commencement week. At Rector Clap's insistence, a measure was voted through declaring that "if any student of this college shall directly or indirectly say, that the rector, either of the trustees or tutors are hypocrites, carnal or unconverted men, he shall for the first offence make public confession in the hall, and for the second offence be expelled."[5]

Edwards's distinguished biographer, George Marsden, wrote that "perhaps Rector Clap and his allies had hoped that Edwards, as a renowned friend of both true awakening and orthodox order, would warn the students [in his commencement address] that they must temper their enthusiasm with respect for constituted authority." Yet Edwards, of whom this was indeed a most accurate description, instead gave "a ringing endorsement" of the awakening now underway—one all the more potent because he freely admitted the facts that had prompted their stern complaints, namely, "that there were many strange and unusual phenomena and even excesses" associated with the awakening.[6]

And so, with this qualification established at the outset, Edwards proceeded to his task. "In the apostolic age," Edwards wrote, "there was the greatest outpouring of the Spirit of God that ever was; both as to His extraordinary influences and gifts, and His ordinary operations, in convincing, converting, enlightening, and sanctifying the souls of men."[7]

However, Edwards noted, where the influences of the true Spirit abounded, counterfeit manifestations were likely to crop up. Satan, Edwards firmly believed, delighted in sowing discord and confusion by mimicking the ordinary and extraordinary influences of the Spirit of God. And in support of this view, he pointed to "innumerable passages of the apostles' writings."[8]

In the face of such realities, Edwards thought it only prudent to say it was "very necessary that the church of Christ should be furnished with some certain rules, distinguishing and clear marks, by which she might proceed safely in judging of the true from the false."[9]

Continuing to set the parameters of his argument, Edwards next introduced an important principle concerning the operations of the Spirit of God. "The Holy Spirit," he stated, "is sovereign in His operation." Within the divine economy, God often works in a variety of ways. We cannot tell how great a variety He may use, Edwards said. Therefore, "we ought not to limit God where He has not limited Himself."[10]

This was a crucial point. For as Edwards observed, there is a great tendency in people to doubt things that may seem strange, especially among those who are older. They question things, Edwards said, that they have never been used to in their day, or "had not heard of in the days of their fathers."[11]

But such a tendency, Edwards argued, was misplaced. If it is a good argument to say that a work is not from the Spirit of God because it is very unusual, he said, it ought to be remembered that many unusual things took place in the time of the apostles.

Here, Edwards urged his readers to recall that the work of the Spirit in those ancient times was carried on in a manner that, in very many respects, was altogether new; such as never had been seen or heard of in the world. Sudden changes had taken place. But had that not been precisely what God had wished to do? The very intent of such "mighty and wonderful works" had been to produce a sudden alteration in towns, cities, and countries.[12]

This was the more important, Edwards said, because Scripture prophecies indicate that "in the latter ages of the world," the "last and greatest outpouring of the Spirit of God" will be such that "the manner of the work will be very extraordinary." Things will unfold that have never before taken place.[13]

A work ought not to be disparaged, Edwards continued, because it might prompt tears—or cause people to tremble, groan, cry aloud, or even faint. The influence persons are under, he said, is not to be judged, one way or other, by effects on the body. The reason was simple and straightforward: nowhere in Scripture is any rule given concerning such things.[14]

Edwards then introduced an example from common life to under-score what he meant. Our nature is such, he said, that when we are "in danger of some terrible calamity," say, in a time of war, many are "ready to tremble at the shaking of a leaf," expecting the enemy any minute. It is little wonder, then, Edwards concluded, that an awareness of "the wrath of God, when manifested but a little to the soul, overbears human strength."[15]

Given such reasoning from common experience, Edwards thought that it should come as no surprise that "a true sense of the glorious excellency of the Lord Jesus Christ," His wondrous love, or a deep sense of joy, should be such as might overcome the bodily strength of some. For if we admit, as so many would readily do, "that no man can see God and live," why should it be thought strange that if "God should some-times give his saints . . . foretastes of heaven . . . their bodily strength [is overcome]?"[16]

Still others, Edwards noticed, object to extraordinary events because there are instances of them recorded in the New Testament, as having been brought about by "extraordinary effusions of the Spirit."[17]

But Edwards could see no force in this type of objection. "I do not know," he said, "that we have any express mention in the New Testament of any person's weeping, or groaning, or sighing through fear of hell, or a sense of God's anger." But is there anybody so foolish as to say that in whoever these things might appear, their convictions are not from the Spirit of God?[18]

~

Few think of Jonathan Edwards employing humor in his writing, but a flash of humor might have been present when he addressed another type of objection to the work of God's Spirit. He insisted that it is no argu-ment that a work is not of the Spirit of God if some people experience at times a kind of ecstasy, are carried beyond themselves, or have had their minds transported into a train of strong and pleasing thoughts, visions, or have felt as though they had been caught up to heaven, and there saw glorious sights.[19]

Here Edwards could speak from personal experience of things he had witnessed during times of revival. "I have been acquainted with some such instances," he said, and here there may have been a twinkle in his eye as he said, "I see no need of bringing in the help of the devil [to] account [for] these things. . . . Human nature, under these intense exercises and affections, is all that need be brought into the account."[20]

To support this idea, Edwards invoked "the visions of the prophets" as recorded in Scripture, and also the biblical account of "St. Paul's rapture into paradise." He finished this line of thought by saying, "I have already shown . . . that persons under a true sense of a glorious and wonderful greatness and excellency of divine things, and soul-ravishing views of the beauty and love of Christ [are often] overpowered."[21] Therefore, he concluded, "I think it is not at all strange, that [many] are thus affected and overborne, [or that] there should be some persons of particular constitutions that should have their imaginations thus affected."[22]

∼

Edwards moved next to the positive side of the ledger. He had dealt with various misplaced objections to a work being brought about by the Spirit of God. Now he would speak of scriptural evidence demonstrating that a work *had* been brought about by the Holy Spirit.

First of all, Edwards stated, a work "is a sure sign from God" if it fosters "an increase of esteem for Jesus," confirming and establishing in a person's mind "the truth of what the gospel declares to us about His being the Son of God, and the Saviour of men."[23]

Further, a work is brought about by God if it fosters "in men a greater regard to the Holy Scriptures, and establishes them more in their truth and divinity." The devil, Edwards insisted, would never "attempt to beget in persons a regard [for] that divine word which God has given to be the great and standing rule for the direction of his church in all religious matters."[24]

The Spirit of God is also at work, Edwards believed, if love of God and others is on the increase. And here he referenced the writings of the apostle John to reinforce his point: "Beloved, let us love one another, for love is of God; and everyone who loves is born of God and knows God. He who does not love does not know God, for God is love" (1 John 4:7–8).[25]

As he drew to a close, Edwards offered both a summary and a potent conclusion. "I have spoken," he said, of several distinguishing characteristics "of a work of the true Spirit."[26] Then, very forcefully, he said, "These [are] things which the devil *would not do* if he could."

Satan, Edwards adamantly insisted, would not awaken the conscience and make men sensible of their sin. Nor would he make people "sensible of their great need of a Saviour." The enemy of our souls "would not confirm men in the belief that Jesus is the Son of God, and the Saviour of sinners, or raise men's value and esteem of Him." The evil one "would not beget in men's minds an opinion of the necessity, usefulness, and truth of the Holy Scriptures, or incline them to make much use of them." Last of all, Edwards declared, Satan would not "show men the truth, in things that concern their souls' interest; to undeceive them, and lead them out of darkness into light, and give them a view of things as they really are."[27]

∼

Edwards's gift to the church in setting out these "distinguishing marks of the Spirit of God" was, in the end, a gift of biblically based discernment. Many harbored a misplaced prejudice against extraordinary events, or miracles, simply because such events did not fit well with their preconceived notions. Others had gone too far the other way and given themselves over to habits of unhealthy excess. Filled with spiritual pride, they thought themselves specially gifted by God, when in reality they were deeply misguided.

What Edwards held up for people on both sides of this divide was the rule of Scripture. What did it say? What did it commend as praiseworthy and normative? What did it censure as being false and harmful? These were the considerations that were to outweigh all others.

In an age highly charged with religious controversy, Edwards's voice was a voice of reason. That miracles do occur, he stoutly defended. At the same time, discernment dictates that we not be too trusting and credulous. In such matters, Scripture is always the sure and unfailing guide.

18 + David Hume: The Case Against Miracles and the Reasons for Faith

There are some, I think, who would perhaps find it more possible to accept the New Testament story if the miracles did not stand in the way. But perhaps . . . it would be easier for them to accept both if they could once look into the true heart of these miracles. So long as they regard only the surface of them, they will, most likely, see in them only a violation of the laws of nature: when they behold the heart of them, they will recognize there at least a possible fulfilment of her deepest laws.

—George MacDonald[1]

I f any one man's name is associated with the rejection of miracles as a supernatural phenomenon, it is that of the Scottish philosopher David Hume. Eight years younger than Jonathan Edwards, he outlived the great American philosopher and theologian by nearly twenty years, dying in 1776.

Hume was brilliant, as Edwards was, making his mark in the fields of philosophy, history, and political economy. For vigor of intellect and logical flow in argument, Hume had few peers in his time.[2] His place in the pantheon of the great philosophers of history is secure, and his influence on schools of philosophy since the 1700s is far-reaching.

This has certainly been the case so far as Hume's reflections on the subject of miracles are concerned. Any discussion of miracles, learned or more popular in nature, takes his ideas into account. Seldom has one definition prompted greater and more sustained debate than Hume's definition of a miracle. In his view, "a miracle may accurately be defined as '*a transgression of a law of nature by a particular volition of the Deity, or by the interposition of some invisible agent.*'"[3]

This, it must be confessed, is rather heavy going so far as specialized language is concerned. And it may be helpful to cite a more concise definition Hume offered on another occasion. A miracle, he said at this time, is "a violation of the laws of nature."[4] This was a partial citation of a one-sentence quote that may be said to sum up his case for the rejection of miracles. "A miracle," he wrote, "is a violation of the laws of nature; and as a firm and unalterable experience has established these laws, the proof against a miracle, from the very nature of the fact, is as entire as any argument from experience can possibly be imagin'd."[5]

In stating this, Hume, after his fashion, had thrown down a philosophical gauntlet. There have been more than a few writers and thinkers in the 235 years since his death who have taken up that gauntlet and attempted to counter Hume's premise.

It should come as no surprise that many Christian thinkers have joined the conversation with Hume. After all, the whole of Christianity rests upon a belief in a miracle of divine revelation, namely the teachings of Scripture—and all that is said there of the creation of the world, God the Father, the Son, and Holy Spirit, and much else besides.

Space doesn't allow for a full consideration of the many Christian thinkers who have engaged Hume's definition and argument, but we may touch on several of the important replies that have appeared.

In 1911, the *Encyclopaedia Britannica* published a classic essay by the learned theologian Alfred Ernest Garvie (1861–1945). A winner of first-class honors at Mansfield College, Oxford University, Garvie possessed a searching intellect and was especially noted in later life for his "devotion in evangelical love and faith to the unity of the Church of Christ."[6] Few scholars were better suited than he to offer a critique of Hume at this time in history.

Taking up Hume's argument, as well as a complimentary reply from John Stuart Mill, Garvie stated,

Hume maintains that no evidence, such as is available, can make a miracle credible. Mill states the position with due care. "The question can be stated fairly as depending on a balance of evidence, a certain amount of positive evidence in favour of miracles, and a negative presumption from the general course of human experience against them."[7]

To this Garvie replied that

the existence of "a certain amount of positive evidence in favour of miracles" forbids the sweeping statement that miracles are "contrary to experience." The phrase itself is, as [William] Paley has pointed out, ambiguous. If it means all experience, it assumes the point to be proved; if it means only common experience then it simply asserts that the miracle is unusual—a truism. The probability of miracles depends on the conception we have of the free relation of God to nature, and of nature as the adequate organ for the fulfilment of God's purposes. If we believe in a divine revelation and redemption, transcending the course of nature, the miracles as signs of that divine purpose will not seem improbable.[8]

Garvie was surely right to point out that in answering Hume, everything depends on where you start. If one presupposes a "free relation of

God to nature," certain things follow. Since God created nature, He is free, if He so chooses, to perform any number of works beyond nature—miracles—since He Himself is beyond nature and all-powerful. For those who start with this basic assumption, the concept of a miracle is not a difficult concept to embrace.

But if one presupposes that God is bound by the laws of nature, miracles become problematic, as Hume rightly points out. A miracle, by definition, is supernatural—literally "beyond nature." And so it has to be said that if natural laws can never be broken or transcended, as Hume maintains, miracles can never occur.

Here, orthodox Christians part company with him. For from the first chapter of Genesis, "the free relation of God to nature" is enshrined. God spoke the heavens and earth into being, out of nothing. His almighty declaration was a miracle of the highest order, because nature itself sprang from His omnipotent word. God created nature and endowed it with the laws we have since come to recognize in studies of how nature functions.

Moving to a consideration of the New Testament, Garvie said that for the Christian Church, "the miracles of Jesus are of primary importance; and the evidence—external and internal—in their favour may be said to be sufficient to justify belief." The gospels, he continued, assumed their present form between AD 60 and 90. In their pages, the representation of the moral character, the religious consciousness, and the teaching of Jesus inspire confidence. Miracles are woven into the very texture of this representation. In them Jesus reveals Himself as Savior.

Delving more deeply into this line of thought, Garvie continued, "The Jesus Christ presented to us in the New Testament would become a very different person if the miracles were removed." Further, Jesus' sinless perfection and filial relation to God make Him unique. His works, of which miracles are a centerpiece, are consistent with His deity.

Last of all, there is more early evidence for the supreme miracle of

Christ's resurrection than of any other miracle spoken of in Scripture. Here Garvie referred his readers to 1 Corinthians 15:3–7, which was written before AD 58.[9] Christ's conquest of death, Garvie said, "is most frequently appealed to in the apostolic teaching. The Christian Church would never have come into existence without faith in the Risen Lord. The proof of the supernaturalness of His Person sets the seal to the credibility of His supernatural works."[10]

~

Beyond this, it is important to recall that a passage cited earlier in Garvie's essay spoke of the English clergyman and philosopher William Paley (1743–1805). Later in this chapter, current scholarship regarding Paley will be considered in contrast with Hume. But here, it is worth taking a few moments to give a sense of what Paley contributed to the field of apologetics when his two most important books were published.

These books were *The Evidences of Christianity* (published in 1794) and *Natural Theology* (published in 1802). The great merit of these books lies in their "strong reasoning power," and Paley's gift for "clear arrangement and forcible statement."[11] He also possessed a gift for distillation—isolating the most compelling arguments of philosophers who preceded him and presenting them to best advantage.

All of this made for an effective apologetic style, and for Paley, miracles were at the heart of the case to be made for Christianity. In the opening pages of *The Evidences of Christianity*, Paley set about laying the groundwork for his case. "Mankind," he wrote, "stood in need of a revelation"—that is, there was a great and persistent need for us to understand how we, and our world, came about.[12]

Paley then introduced a further premise. What if we suppose, he asked, that "the world we live in had a Creator? Is it improbable that a revelation should be made, [or] is it incredible that God should interpose for such a purpose?"[13] Paley thought it logical to assume that if there were a Creator, He would most certainly want His creatures to know about their origins.

Since such a revelation could only come from God, it was by definition supernatural, that is, outside of or beyond nature. And so Paley could deduce that this divine revelation to humanity was therefore, *by definition*, a miracle.

Those who profess faith in Christianity understand that God's revelation about Himself, His plans, His purposes, and our origins is but another name for Scripture, or the Holy Bible. They are one and the same. In Scripture, we learn that God spoke the world into being from nothing. He created the natural world and set its laws in motion.

For Paley, this was a vital distinction to bear in mind, and it had much to do with the ideas of David Hume. Arguing on the basis of experience, Hume had said that miracles cannot occur because "the course of nature is invariable," and that if variations to the course of nature did occur, they would "be frequent and general"—not rare.[14]

But, Paley asked, "has the necessity of this [view] been demonstrated?" What if "the course of nature [is] the agency of an intelligent Being?" Should we not therefore "expect that such a Being, on occasions of peculiar importance, may interrupt the order which He had appointed?" Further, what if such a Being, whom we call God, should confine such interruptions "to the experience of a few"? Is that not His prerogative?[15]

Paley believed all this to be true, and that it was "a matter neither of surprise nor objection" that God, who had set in motion "the course of nature," could interrupt that course as often or as little as He liked. As the sovereign of the universe, which Scripture teaches God to be, He can issue royal decrees as He wishes, and of any kind—whatever may suit His good will and pleasure.[16] It all depends on where one starts in terms of basic assumptions, Paley contended. Thus he did not find Hume's argument from experience to be conclusive.

As we shall see, recent and very compelling scholarship has revisited Paley's counter to Hume, placing renewed emphasis on it. But here, it bears repeating that A. E. Garvie was right to draw attention to Paley as a key figure in the history of debates about the nature of miracles, and Garvie's essay in the *Encyclopaedia Britannica* was an important contribution to a wide audience on this subject.

∼

Some eleven years before A. E. Garvie died, the writer G. K. Chesterton published an article that addressed David Hume's concerns regarding the credibility of miracles. Chesterton's article appeared in the October 27, 1934, edition of the *Illustrated London News*, and bore the title "On Believing in Miracles."

Chesterton's tone in this piece was conversational, and it bore the hallmarks of his prose—wit, colorful illustration, even a dash of his celebrated penchant for paradox—but he was in truth making a very cogent point.

The article began in a lighthearted vein, with a clever play on words. He then moved quickly to the heart of the matter. Chesterton stated,

> There is a point of fallacy or false logic raised by some correspondents in connection with . . . such articles as I wrote . . . about the Loch Ness Monster or the Arabian Nights. The point appears in connection with all sorts of things; traveller's tales, ghost-stories, faith-cures, table turning, psychic phenomena, miracles and marvels of all kinds. But my interest in it here is not psychological or anthropological or biological or theological or cosmological, but logical.

This was whimsical, but the humor Chesterton used here was that of a jester: commending a potent truth through the use of wit or satire. On one hand, he was skillfully juggling words like *psychology*, *anthropology*, *biology*, and *cosmology*. On the other, he held just one key word in place: *logic*. It was a word picture meant to say, "Don't be distracted by what you see over here. Keep your eye on the one word that matters. Logic is my purpose. Let's consider what it may have to teach us."

And so, Chesterton proceeded to his task. There is a statement, he began, which we've all heard hundreds of times, generally made by modern disputants in the following way. They say that a marvel, or magical event, in its nature demands much stronger evidence to support it than do ordinary events—and especially ordinary speeches.

Based upon this, Chesterton said, people proceed, apparently, to believe the whole of any record of speeches and events, but they leave out the magical events and dismiss them. To this Chesterton strenuously objected. This is a monstrous fallacy, he said. "There is no question of wanting stronger or weaker evidence for extraordinary or ordinary events in such a case." We have the same evidence for both, "and the only question is whether it is credible evidence; or, in other words, whether the witness is telling lies. But if he is *not* telling lies, then his evidence is much stronger for a startling event than it is for a commonplace event."[17]

Chesterton's thoughts here bear a striking resemblance to a famous scene from C. S. Lewis's *The Lion, the Witch and the Wardrobe*, first published in 1950, some sixteen years after Chesterton's article appeared in the *London Illustrated News*.

The setting for Lewis's scene was this: Lucy Pevensie had just returned from her first journey into the land of Narnia. Full of wonder, she told her brothers and sister about it. But they, Peter, Edmund, and Susan, refused to believe her. Going to Professor Kirke, the owner of the house where they were staying, they asked him about all that Lucy had told them. They got an answer, but nothing like what they expected.

"Logic," Professor Kirke said half aloud. "Don't they teach logic where you attend school?" Clearly, he insisted, there can only be three possibilities to consider. Either your sister is lying, she is under a delusion, or she is telling the truth. In your experience, she is not known to be a habitual liar, and she doesn't seem to be mad. There can therefore be only one conclusion. In the absence of any evidence to the contrary, she must be telling the truth."[18]

At this, Susan gave the professor a sharp look. But all the same, she felt certain, judging from the expression on his face, that he was not ridiculing them.

Peter, for his part, wondered aloud how such a thing could be true.

In reply, the professor asked why he would say that.

Peter thought for a moment, and then asked Kirke why it was that if Narnia was real, people didn't find their way there every time they went into the wardrobe. He hadn't seen anything when he looked in, he said, and not even Lucy had said she did when they all looked in.

Professor Kirke seemed not to be bothered by this. He told Peter that what he'd just described had little to do with the heart of the matter.

Peter wasn't so easily convinced, saying to Kirke that if things are real, they must be there all the time.[19]

Susan, hearing all this, was incredulous. There wasn't any time, she said, for Lucy to have done what she said she had—even if a place like the one she'd described really existed. And further, she said she'd been gone for hours, but only a moment had gone by when she'd come running to catch them.

But, the professor insisted, that was the very thing that lent the air of truth to her story. If there truly was a door somewhere in his home that led to another world—which he was perfectly willing to admit—since it was a *strange* house, and he knew little about it—well then, if Lucy had gone there, why shouldn't this other world have a time all its own? To this he added that *he* didn't think Lucy, being so young, could have made up such an idea as this for herself. Further, if she had been pretending, wouldn't she have remained hidden for a while before coming out to tell her story?

"But do you really mean, sir," said Peter, "that there could be other worlds—all over the place, just round the corner—like that?"

"Nothing is more probable," said the Professor, taking off his spectacles and beginning to polish them, while he muttered to himself, "I wonder what they do teach them at these schools."[20]

For the readers of the *Illustrated London News*, Chesterton had been playing the role of Professor Kirke. His article wasn't fiction, as Lewis's story was, but the ideas and principles of logic were very much the same.

Indeed, Chesterton introduced his own fanciful story to drive his point home. Its similarity to Lewis's imaginary construct in *The Lion, the Witch and the Wardrobe* is really rather astounding. "If my cousin George," Chesterton began, "tells me that he saw my Uncle Samuel jump from the top of St. Paul's Cathedral into Cheapside and walk cheerfully away, explaining that he could do this through being constantly upheld by angels—then I may disbelieve the incident, but it will necessarily mean that I disbelieve the witness. I know my Cousin George too well."

Tongue planted firmly in cheek, Chesterton continued by saying that he would not feel a kindly tolerance toward George as a notorious liar. But he would, however, "feel an acute and active annoyance with George as an infernal fool, if he expects me to believe that he can repeat every word of uncle's subsequent discourse on angels, when he does not know whether a man jumped off the dome of St. Paul's or not."

Chesterton followed this with an important distinction. "The fact," he said, "that the leap and survival would be called miraculous, while the sermon on angels would only be called mystical, makes no difference to the logic of the case." If a witness like his cousin George could be mistaken about seeing "a human figure, in a top-hat and whiskers, flying in the air above Cheapside, he could certainly be mistaken about the fine shades of doctrine in a discourse about the difference between the Cherubim and Seraphim." If, as was perhaps more than likely, George had simply "said anything that came into his head, in the way of tales and wonder, then he might equally say anything that came into his head in reporting the talk of the wonder-worker." What conclusion should we therefore draw? "Evidence about a miracle," Chesterton said, "is either obviously worthless or it is more worthy of credence than evidence of all the hundred fine shades of mind and mood which we all miss or misread every five minutes."[21]

~

Chesterton proceeded next to directly engage the thinking of David Hume. He had set the stage; now he was ready to lift the curtain on the crucial act of his play. "I have taken the point here," he said, "in connection with all sorts of fanciful or remote circumstances that have nothing to do with anything that I myself believe or disbelieve—because I am not now talking about belief, but about proof." He was, he insisted, talking about logic and the laws of evidence, as they ought to apply to any tale told by any person. In all such cases, he said, it will be found that the old rationalistic tag advanced by Hume—namely that "miracles in their nature need stronger evidence"—is decidedly the wrong way of putting things. Hume had said such things, and so, too, had T. H. Huxley— he didn't, he said, have the precise quote—which was a wry reference to Chesterton's self-confessed penchant for quoting from memory. However, he said, "if they did use this now very ordinary argument, they used a very bad argument."

Why so? It is not really true, Chesterton maintained, "that we demand absolute proof about abnormal things, and accept less than proof about lesser things." This would mean people only tell lies about large things, and never speak lies about little things. It is not really true that we want more than one proof for one thing or less than one proof for another. People desire adequate proof for anything; "or at least anything

for which we want it at all." If people gloss over problems in more pro-
saic or trivial narratives, it is not because people need less evidence to
show they are correct. It is only because they care much less whether
they are correct or not.

Here, Chesterton introduced another example. "If I am told that
a man turned a cat into a griffin and then took the 2:15 train for
Finsbury Park, I do not really believe that a man who believes in grif-
fins must be right about trains." As a matter of fact, he did not (on the
whole) think the first statement was true, but he did not care whether
the second statement was true or not. The crux of the matter was that
when such a fallacy was "applied to more important facts, and men
read a record full of miracles and monologues, deny all the miracles
and believe all the monologues, their ghastly lack of logic is likely to
have worse effects."[22]

In all this, Chesterton had adopted an inimitable and very creative
way of engaging a central tenet of Hume (and Huxley's) worldview. His
article for the *Illustrated London News* was, by turns, witty, whimsical,
and colorful. But as with Lewis's scene from *The Lion, the Witch and the
Wardrobe*, Chesterton was also making a very profound point.

In Lewis's story, there were two very important reasons why Lucy
Pevensie could be believed: she was neither known to be a liar, nor was
she mad. If people in real life, or from the pages of history, give no evidence of being either liars or mad, and they speak to us about miracles
they say they have witnessed, we might just want to believe them. We
might, in fact, discover something very important and life-changing if
we do.

∼

If in the 1930s, Chesterton framed a very creative reply to an argument raised by Hume, John C. Lennox, professor of mathematics at the

University of Oxford, has in recent years framed a more traditional set of apologetic counterarguments to the great Scottish skeptic.

In his book *God's Undertaker: Has Science Buried God?* Lennox explored the case for Christianity in terms of the apologetic writings of Hume's younger contemporary, William Paley, the archdeacon of Carlisle. Further, Lennox considered an oft-repeated claim of the modern era that "Hume's onslaught against design arguments" demolished ideas articulated by Paley.

To what was Lennox referring? In the early 1800s, Paley became famous for his reflections on the celebrated "watchmaker metaphor." This passage appears in the opening pages of Paley's book *Natural Theology*, originally published in 1802. He wrote,

> In crossing a heath suppose I pitched my foot against a stone, and were asked how the stone came to be there: I might possibly answer, that for any thing I knew to the contrary, it had lain there for ever. . . . But suppose I had found a *watch* upon the ground, and it should be inquired how the watch happened to be in that place; I should hardly think of the answer which I had before given, that for any thing I knew, the watch might have always been there. . . . The watch must have had a maker . . . an artificer . . . who formed it. [Similarly,] every indication of contrivance, every manifestation of design, which existed in the watch, exists in the works of nature; with the difference, on the side of nature, of being [of necessity] greater.[23]

Since it was first published in the early nineteenth century, many have found Paley's analogy a rich and fascinating one. Yet many modern champions of Hume's worldview contend, as Lennox noted, that arguments from analogies do not always hold.[24] To make this point, Hume had originally written of an imaginary discussion in his book *A Treatise of Human Nature*. And in that discussion, the key passage was this:

If we see a house, Cleanthes, we conclude, with the greatest certainty, that it had an architect or builder; because this is precisely that species of effect which we have experienced to proceed from that species of cause. But surely you will not affirm, that the universe bears such a resemblance to a house that we can with the same certainty infer a similar cause, or that the analogy is here entire and perfect. The dissimilitude is so striking, that the utmost you can here pretend to is a guess, a conjecture, a presumption concerning a similar cause; and how that pretension will be received in the world, I leave you to consider.[25]

By way of response, Lennox stated that "for many people, Hume's argument carries the day" against Paley.[26] Thus any notion of the miracles God performed in creating the world and humanity fall to ruins. These miracles have no basis in fact, and no intelligent designer brought them about.

Not so fast, Lennox countered, for bearing the Paley/Hume debate in mind, contemporary philosopher Elliott Sober raised a very pertinent point. Sober wrote,

Although Hume's criticism is devastating if the design argument is an argument from analogy, I see no reason why the design argument must be construed in this way. Paley's argument about organisms stands on its own, regardless of whether watches and organisms happen to be similar. The point of talking about watches is to help the reader see that the argument about organisms is compelling.[27]

To this, Lennox added that "certainly, Paley's argument about organisms stands on its own; but it is strengthened even more by the observation that Sober is scarcely justified in saying that the analogy fails."

Here, Lennox turned to advances in modern science. He notes,

Since Paley's time, developments in science have shown that there are many kinds of systems within living organisms for which the term "molecular machine" is entirely appropriate and among which are to be found biological clocks that are responsible for the vital molecular timekeeping function within the living cell and which are of vastly greater sophistication than Paley's illustrative watch. Indeed, "machine" language is ubiquitous in cutting-edge molecular biology.[28]

Such advances in the sum of our knowledge of molecular biology would have astonished Hume, Lennox wrote. One day, Lennox continues, in the not-too-distant future, scientists will be able to "design biochemical systems and construct proteins" that will, in turn, make it "possible to construct simple organisms from their molecular components."[29]

Our understanding of such matters is being revolutionized, and in ways that bodes well for the insights Paley propounded so many years ago. Lennox concluded that the design argument was in truth much more robust than Hume thought, though it was important to keep Hume's caution about analogies in mind. On the whole, however, it could be said that "much of the force of [Hume's] objection has been dissipated by more recent progress in biology."[30]

Hume's reasoning about the concept of intelligent design was flawed in another sense as well, Lennox noted. This weakness could be seen in a comparison of inductive reasoning—which Hume employed—to "the method of abduction," so often used by historians today.[31]

Lennox wrote,

Not all science is inductive since we do not always have the luxury of repeated observation or experimentation. We cannot repeat the Big Bang, or the origin of life, or the history of life, or the history of the universe. Indeed what about any historical event? It is not repeatable.

Does that mean we can say nothing about these things? It would, if we followed Hume.[32]

In support of abductive reasoning, Lennox began by stating its advantages. This kind of reasoning works by way of "inference to the best explanation." Hume's argument against miracle, he went on to say, "leaves abduction untouched. An argument that does explain a given effect is always better than one that does not."[33]

That said, Lennox conceded that it was important, though it might seem at times difficult, to separate the design argument from the many negative connotations affixed to it by modern scientific rhetoric. But something else ought also to be borne in mind. The very mention of the word *design* immediately makes some people think of "the powerful image of clockwork that figured so prominently in older design arguments." The upshot is that the word *design* is associated consciously or unconsciously, with the clockwork universe of Sir Isaac Newton.[34]

In Newton's time, Lennox wrote, analogies likening the universe "to the smooth running of a master-clock had enormous appeal." But since that era, what with an ever-increasing knowledge of the biological sciences, many scientists in this field came to believe that "the biological world did not look much like a clock." At the same time, many theologians rejected the "master-clock analogy" because they reckoned "it could easily be used to support a deistic view of God," which held "that God wound up the universe as [its] Creator and Sustainer," and that God "caused the universe to exist at every moment." These views many theologians could not accept.[35]

While granting all of this by way of the history of science since Newton's time, Lennox stated that a great deal of recent scientific research has yielded "the fact that the biosphere is now known to contain endless sophisticated clocks." The import of this is that design arguments that now invoke a clock analogy "cannot so easily be dismissed."[36]

Beyond this, Lennox offered another important distinction. It would be a mistake, he wrote,

> to use [design arguments] with a reductionist spin in order to give the impression that the universe was *nothing more than clockwork.* Consequently, in order to avoid potentially misleading associations of ideas, it might well be better to talk about arguments inferring intelligent origin, than about design arguments.[37]

And so, William Paley might not be as irrelevant as many think. Indeed, Lennox has a great respect for Paley's intellect and contributions to philosophical thought. Until recently, few would have predicted Paley might have the better of the argument in countering Hume with constructs relating to intelligent design. Many thought the watchmaker analogy Paley advanced had been well and truly consigned to the dustbin of history.

But Lennox cited the distinguished English theoretical physicist Sir John Polkinghorne to show that Paley's day in the philosophical sun is far from over. "So where is natural theology today," Polkinghorne wrote, "two centuries after William Paley? The short answer is, 'Alive and well, having learned from past experience to lay claim to its insight rather than to coercive logical necessity; and to be able to live in a friendly relationship with science, based on complementarity rather than rivalry.'"[38]

~

There is one final note to add before closing.

The intent here has not been to mount a far-ranging discussion. The purpose of this chapter has simply been to discuss some of the objections Hume raised about the veracity of miracles and explore how some very fine thinkers within the Christian tradition have engaged them. It would require a book, perhaps several, to adequately explore all the facets of this robust debate. The idea here has been to set out some of the more basic and interesting parameters of a longstanding discussion—one that shows no signs of diminishing in importance.

19 ✦ George Washington: Miracles in the Midst of Battle

I Expected Nothing but death for Every One of us, for they had us surround[ed] all but a little in the Rear, which they strove for with all their Force.

—The Journal of a Soldier from the Battle of the Monongahela[1]

I expected every moment to see [Washington] fall. His duty and his situation exposed him to every danger. Nothing but the superintending care of Providence could have saved him from the fate of all around him.

—James Craik[2]

The allwise disposer of events has hitherto watched over my steps."[3] These words were written in the 1790s by the Anglican vestryman known to history as George Washington—the first president of the United States and America's commander in chief during the War of Independence.[4]

There was more, far more, to Washington's recognition of God's providential care in his life than meets the eye. For he knew, and could remember, a time nearly forty years earlier when his life had been spared in extraordinary circumstances. And he knew as well, on the eve of deciding to seek a second term as America's first president, that had his life not been spared, he never would have served in that office—to say nothing of leading America's forces during the years of desperate struggle needed to secure independence.[5] Had his life not been spared in July 1755, it is not at all certain that America *would* have secured her independence. Indeed, she might not have. For as James Thomas Flexner has so memorably written, Washington was America's "indispensable man."[6]

In the fog of war, a miracle unfolded in the life of young George Washington. He always looked on it as such. Not a few historians and biographers have marveled at it in the two hundred years since his death.

Washington's miraculous escape took place during the conflict historians call the Battle of Monongahela, fought on July 9, 1755. He was then an aide to the British commanding general, Edward Braddock. The battle, fought on a wilderness road, was part of the French and Indian War, and during the fight, the slaughter was horrific. Decades later, the scenes of death and dying were things Washington could still vividly recall. The following account is taken from his manuscript recollections of the battle.

About ten o'clock on the ninth, the forward part of Braddock's command was attacked. Withering volleys of gunfire seemed to burst in upon them from every direction, unleashed by an enemy they could not see. The rear guard of Braddock's forces came forward to offer reinforcement, but even as they did, they came under murderous fire. "A general panic took place among the Troops," Washington recalled, "from which no exertions of the Officers could recover them."

In the early part of this action, some of the Colonial troops, or Irregulars, as they were called, advanced to the right at their own initiative, in loose order, to attack. They were only too familiar with the kind of guerilla warfare the French and Indians had loosed upon them when fighting from concealed locations, and they were doing what they could to combat it. However, the British officers were unused to such unorthodox defensive tactics, mistook the actions of the Irregulars for cowardice, and strove to halt them. Further confusion ensued, where-upon Washington himself, knowing the wisdom of what the Irregulars were trying to do, offered to "[lead] the Provincials and engage the enemy in their own way." But by the time he was able to convince his superior officers to let him try this tactic, it was too late to use it.

Instead, "[several] attempts were made to dislodge the enemy from an eminence on the Right, but they all proved ineffectual, and fatal to the Officers, who by great exertions and good examples endeavored to accomplish it." In one of these attempts, General Braddock "received the wound of which he died; but previous to it, had several horses killed and disabled under him." To make matters worse, two British captains, Orme and Morris, were disabled by their wounds and were therefore unable to help lead these assaults. Washington, the only aide who was unwounded, "remained the sole Aide through the day to the General; [but] he also had one horse killed and two wounded under him, a [mus-ket] ball through his hat, and several [more] through his clothes, but escaped unhurt."

Meanwhile, the other remaining officers were either killed or so severely wounded that they were unable to assume command once General Gage began to succumb to his wounds. Washington's summary of how this engagement ended makes for somber reading. He wrote,

Of about 12 or 13 hundred which were in this action, eight or 9 hun-dred were either killed or wounded, among whom a large proportion of brave and valuable officers were included. The folly and conse-quence of opposing compact bodies to the sparse manner of Indian fighting in woods, which had in a manner been predicted, was now so clearly verified that from henceforward another mode obtained in all future operations. . . . At an incampment near the Great Meadows the brave but unfortunate Genl. Braddock breathed his last. He was interred with the honors of war, and as it was left to [me] to see this performed, and to mark out the spot for the reception of his remains— to guard against [the desecration of his grave], if the place should be discovered—[So] they were deposited in the Road over which the army wagons . . . passed to hide every trace.[7]

Several days later, on July 18, 1755, Washington wrote to his brother, John Augustine Washington. The bare recital of all that had happened reflected deep gratitude that God had mercifully carried him through this horrible battle. Reports had begun to circulate that he had been killed, and he wrote as soon as he could to allay the fears of family and friends. "Dear Jack," the letter began,

As I have heard since my arrival at this place, a circumstantial account of my death and dying speech, I take this early opportunity of contradicting both, and of assuring you that I now exist and appear in the land of the living by the miraculous care of Providence, that protected me beyond all human expectation; I had 4 Bullets [pass] through my Coat, and two Horses shot under me, and yet escaped unhurt.

We have been most scandalously beaten by a trifling body of men; but fatigue and want of time prevents me from giving any of the details till I have the happiness of seeing you at home. . . . [I am in a] Weak and Feeble state of Health, [which] obliges me to halt here for 2 or 3 days, to recover a little strength. . . . You may expect to see me there on Saturday or Sunday Se'night, which is as soon as I can well be down. . . . Pray give my Compliments to all my Friends.

I am, Dear Jack, your most Affectionate Brother.[8]

~

Washington's deliverance unscathed from the Battle of the Monongahela was truly remarkable, but an event that happened far earlier in his life was no less important. For had it ended differently, the world would never have heard of George Washington, the hero of Monongahela, the man who would become America's first president.

The setting for this event was Washington's boyhood home, Ferry Farm, located close to Fredericksburg, Virginia. He moved there at the age of six and lived there until the age of nineteen.[9] This home, and Washington's years there, were chronicled in a recent National Geographic Channel documentary *George Washington Revealed*. Many, the film's trailer states, think they know the real George Washington, but there is far more to his life than they might realize—including a disaster from his boyhood years that could well have taken his life. "Washington's correspondence," said the film's narrator, "hints that a fire struck his childhood home on Christmas Eve, 1740, destroying much of the living quarters. He was only eight years old, and life has already dealt him a severe blow."[10] The documentary went on to state that recent archaeological research has indeed confirmed that this catastrophic event took place, that for the first time its full story can be recounted.

With historical hindsight, can we say that this, too, was a miracle? Stop to consider. If Washington had perished with his family in that horrific fire, there would have been no young man to acquit himself so bravely during the Battle of the Monongahela, no man of sterling character and leadership to be the "indispensable man" during the years when America fought to secure her independence. And there would have been no leader to guide the fortunes of a young nation as her first president once independence was secured. Had Washington not been saved from that fire as a boy, history as we know it would have been very different.

If we are reluctant to call this preservation from death a miracle, it ought to be considered in the light of what Washington believed about Providence. Scholar Jeffry Morrison wrote that "Washington's favorite word for describing both God and God's relation to the world was 'Providence.'"[11] Morrison went on to say that Washington's "favorite locution was 'divine Providence,'" a term he used nearly two dozen times in his writings. Most of all, a phrase from the letter he wrote in July 1755 bears repeating. "I now exist," Washington had then written, "and appear in the land of the living by the miraculous care of Providence, that protected me beyond all human expectation."[12] It is irrefutable evidence that Washington believed in miracles in connection with Providence.

But what of Providence itself? What does it mean? The word *providence* refers to "God's support, care, and supervision of all creation, from its beginning to all eternity. The term comes from the Latin word *providentia*, which in turn derives from the Latin verb 'provideo,' which means 'to foresee.'" But as we learn from the *Zondervan Illustrated Bible Dictionary*, far more is meant by the Latin verb *provideo* than mere foresight or foreknowledge. The heart of this word's meaning is the notion of "prearrangement." And historically speaking, the theological term *providence* has always meant "nothing short of the universal sovereign rule of God." As the Westminster Shorter Catechism expresses it, "God's works of providence are his most holy, wise and powerful preserving and governing all his creatures, and all their actions." Divine Providence, therefore, is the outworking of divine decrees, which are "the purpose of Him who works all things according to the counsel of His will" (Eph. 1:11).[13]

"General providence," the *Zondervan Illustrated Bible Dictionary* also states, "encompasses the government of the entire universe, but especially of human beings." Here the words of Deuteronomy 10:14 have special meaning: "Indeed heaven and the highest heavens belong to the LORD your God, also the earth with all that is in it." And as we read in Hebrews 1:3, God by His providence is revealed as "upholding all things by the word of His power."[14] Thus the word *providence* is a word of deep and multi-layered meaning. When Washington used it, as he did often, he was saying a very great deal. Steeped as he was in the Anglican tradition, this rich, multilayered context was one he knew well.[15]

And so it was that three months before he died, Washington drew from the language of the Book of Common Prayer to tell a kinsman where his hopes for eternity lay. "I was the *first*, and now I am the *last*, of my father's children by [his] second marriage who remain. When I shall be called upon to follow them, is known only to the Giver of life."[16] Here Washington was citing a passage he had often heard and said. It was one he ardently believed. On the pages of the 1769 edition of the Book of Common Prayer one can read, "O God, Who art the Giver of life, of health, and of safety; we bless thy name."

20 + Transforming Grace: Miracles in the Life of William Wilberforce*

We are amazed at the Riches of his Free Grace. . . . We see the Means of Grace by Miracle brought into a World of Reprobates and Rebells. We find the Best made of the very Worst.

—THOMAS TRAHERNE[1]

The miracle of salvation has to be the greatest miracle of all, for it meets the greatest need, brings the greatest results (and they last forever), and cost the greatest price.

—WARREN WIERSBE[2]

E arlier we learned that God intervened in an incredible way to bring about the conversion of Paul of Tarsus. He who had once persecuted the church and was complicit in the death

*Note: Many of the quotations in this chapter are taken from Robert and Samuel Wilberforce, *The Life of William Wilberforce*, 5 vols, (London: John Murray, 1838). Other quotes are taken from John Harford, *Recollections of William Wilberforce*, (London: Longman, Green, Longman, Roberts, & Green, 1865), and the author's books on William Wilberforce. *William Wilberforce: A Hero for Humanity* (Grand Rapids, MI: Zondervan, 2007), and *A Journey Through the Life of William Wilberforce* (Green Forest, AR: New Leaf, 2007).

of Stephen became instead a follower of Christ and a herald of God's grace. Though he was for a time stricken with blindness, his sight was restored through intercessory prayer. In time, he would be called "the apostle to the gentiles," and was the person God used in large measure to bring Christianity to that part of the world we know today as Europe. Taken in its entirety, what unfolded in his life was, without question, miraculous.

But have there been other believers and other occasions where God has intervened miraculously in drawing people to Himself?

Many saints have said as much of God's dealings with them. And while we might spend much time exploring the many stories that have come down to us of this nature, one story from more recent history is a powerful reminder of God's extraordinary dealings in the conversion process.

It is the story of William Wilberforce.

Many know of this statesman today because of the film *Amazing Grace*, and he is best remembered for having led the twenty-year fight in the British Parliament to abolish that country's slave trade.

Far less well-known is the spiritual transformation that resulted in Wilberforce's embrace of Christianity. He called it a "miracle of mercy," and it is by any measure a remarkable story.[3]

We are highly fortunate that Wilberforce left us with so many written recollections of this time in his life. Drawing upon them, it is possible to reconstruct the series of events that culminated in his embrace of faith.

In the spring of 1784, just after staging a stunning upset, Wilberforce became one of only two very powerful parliamentary representatives for the entire county of Yorkshire. So decisive was his victory that its momentum carried over into many other electoral contests throughout Britain, greatly strengthening the governing majority of his great friend, Prime Minister William Pitt.

Wilberforce was the toast of England, and a dazzling political future seemed assured. However, God would intervene in his life in ways that no one, least of all he, could have foreseen.

Flush with his great success, Wilberforce thought to embark on a continental tour of Europe. Such a grand tour was much the fashion in those days, and he had not been able to take one during his college years, as many people had done.

Now he could indulge himself, and he meant to savor his great electoral victory by using his wealth and newly found political prominence to make his tour something to remember.

But who to take with him? His mother and sister, he knew, would be joined by his cousin Bessy Smith. He desired the company of a friend who would be a welcome addition to his traveling party, a conversationalist who could enliven the miles of transit by coach.

Wilberforce thought he knew just the person. Dr. William Burgh was one of the leading citizens of the city of York. Intelligent and agreeable, Burgh had shown Wilberforce many marks of kindness. Learned, cheerful, and lively, Burgh was in every way ideally suited to be a companion for a grand tour. And how could he resist such an invitation, especially since all his expenses would be paid?

To Wilberforce's great surprise, and for reasons unknown, Burgh declined his generous offer. Now at a loose end, Wilberforce cast about him for a replacement. Unexpectedly, while in Scarborough, a town on the North Sea coast of Yorkshire, he fell in with his former tutor from his days at grammar school, Isaac Milner.

A Cambridge University don, Milner was a man Wilberforce fondly remembered as being cheerful, good-natured, and entertaining. And so, on impulse, he invited Milner to join him on the grand tour. Delighted by this unforeseen opportunity, Milner gratefully accepted.

Yet in one very important respect, Milner was now different from the man Wilberforce remembered as a schoolboy.

Wilberforce recalled,

When I engaged him as a companion in my tour, I knew not that he had any deeper [religious] principles. The first time I discovered it, was at the public table at Scarborough. The conversation turned on a Mr. [James] Stillingfleet [the Rector of Hotham]; and I spoke of him as a good man, but one who carried things too far.

"Not a bit too far," said Milner; and [he held] to this opinion . . . when we renewed the conversation in the evening on the sands. This declaration greatly surprised me; and it was agreed that at some future time we would talk the matter over.

Had I known at first what his [religious] opinions were, it would have decided me against making him the offer [to accompany me on my tour].

Why such a reaction from Wilberforce? Simply put, he'd become a religious skeptic. Attending the London Unitarian Chapel established by Theophilus Lindsey, Wilberforce had turned away from the boyhood faith he'd once professed. Ambition and the pursuit of political prominence now dominated his life. On those few occasions when he felt the need for something more, Lindsey's chapel was a place he could frequent without having too much asked of him in return. Religious skepticism was then something of a fashion. Visiting Lindsey's chapel, he could be seen to be thoughtful by others whose good opinion he sought. An occasional smattering of spiritual reflection—that was all he really cared for. In no way did he wish to be perceived as one who carried such things to excess.

James Stillingfleet was part of a burgeoning but largely despised wing of the Church of England: evangelical Anglicanism. The ministry of the Wesleys, John and Charles, along with George Whitefield, were both a scandal and a reproach to adherents of the spiritual minimalism that then dominated the Anglican Church. Many clergy within the Church of England differed little from Theophilus Lindsey in the extent of their religious skepticism. Many had actually abandoned their belief in the divinity of Christ. Apathy, corruption, and spiritual indifference were the norm. Ritual and ceremony were largely all that remained of a once vibrant and vital orthodox faith. James Stillingfleet, as with the Wesleys and Whitefield, longed to foster a return to the first things of the faith, and for this he was branded fanatical and excessive.

Now Wilberforce was saddled with a friend who approved of Stillingfleet. Wilberforce's pride kept him from withdrawing his invitation to Milner. Only time would reveal what Milner's presence might mean for their forthcoming journey.

There was yet another reason why Wilberforce reacted so strongly when Stillingfleet's name was mentioned—one of which Milner was unaware, and one that had formerly been a source of great pain to Wilberforce.

The story was this: Wilberforce's father, to whom he had been close, died when he was only eight years old. His mother soon after contracted a serious illness, and it was feared she might not survive. Little William, whose world had been shaken to its core, was sent to live with his childless aunt and uncle.

This aunt and uncle had been converted under the ministry of George Whitefield, and they were no less loving than they were devout. A boy grieving the loss of his father and fearing the loss of his mother could scarcely have failed to be touched by their kindness, love, and faith. Soon after coming to stay with them, he showed every indication that he too had placed his hope in God.

In this, young William was encouraged by one of his aunt and uncle's great friends, a former slave ship captain turned pastor named John Newton. Newton regaled the boy with stories of the sea and with vivid sermons that explored the world of *The Pilgrim's Progress*. The two grew close, so much so that Wilberforce later said he had "reverenced [Newton] as a parent when I was a child."

Wilberforce stayed with his aunt and uncle for about two years. Meanwhile, his mother had recovered from her dangerous illness and was gradually gaining strength. All the while, the bond deepened between her son and her in-laws, as it did with Newton.

Then, suddenly, it all came to an end. Young William's letters home had begun to reflect his ardent, newly born faith. His mother, whose religious views tended toward the very staid, high-church end of the spiritual scale, was horrified at the thought that her boy, and the sole male heir to the Wilberforce family fortune, might turn "methodist"— then a pejorative term that meant religious enthusiast or fanatic. As soon as she could, she went to London and removed her son from an influence she considered little less than poison.

Young William left his uncle's family with sorrow. "I deeply felt the parting," he remembered, "for I loved them as parents: indeed, I was almost heart-broken at the separation." Soon after, he wrote to his uncle, "I can never forget you, as long as I live."

Wilberforce's aunt expressed openly her grief that he should be removed from the benefits of a religious life. "You should not fear," replied his mother cuttingly, "if it be a work of [what *you* call] grace, you know it cannot fail."

His elderly grandfather was no less implacably opposed to any threat of Methodist leanings. "If Billy turns Methodist, he shall not have a sixpence of mine." Young Wilberforce now faced the very real threat of being disinherited.

How does a young man cope with so many sources of pain—the death of his father, the grave sickness of his mother, the cruel removal from care of relations who had become like parents to him as well as the fatherly kindness of a mentor like John Newton? Add to this that two of Wilberforce's three sisters died as children.

Gradually, he did what many in his place would do: push all the pain, or the perceived sources of pain, as far away as he could. That meant stepping away from so ardent a faith as he had professed and embracing the heedless, affluent life of a young man born to wealth. The family wished him to be ambitious and focus solely on advancing the family's standing in society, perhaps through elective office, as his grandfather had done—or his cousin, who had been elected to Parliament.

"At first," he remembered, "all this was very distasteful to me, but by degrees I acquired a relish for it, as so the good seed was gradually smothered, and I became as thoughtless as any amongst them."

And so Wilberforce lost himself in the life his family insisted on. He would later recall:

The theatre, balls, great suppers, and card-parties, were the delight of the [great] families in the town. The usual dinner hour was two o'clock, and at six they met at sumptuous suppers. As grandson to one of the principal inhabitants, I was everywhere invited and [indulged].

The religious impressions which I had gained at Wimbledon continued for a considerable time after my return to Hull, but . . . no pains [were spared] to stifle them. No pious parent ever laboured more to impress a beloved child with sentiments of [faith], than [was done] to give me a taste for the world and its diversions.

And so, one early biography noted, "with the self-indulgent habits formed by such a life, [Wilberforce] entered St. John's College, Cambridge, [in] October 1776, at the age of seventeen. [He had been] left, by the death of his grandfather and uncle, the master of an independent fortune."

Wealth, position, and the glittering prospect of advancing as far as his ambition would take him—these were the focal points of Wilberforce's life. Any concern for matters of faith had long since withered away.

~

Yet all the while, though he did not know it, someone had never ceased to think of him, nor to pray for him.

That someone was John Newton.

So it was that when Wilberforce set out on his grand tour, there was a backstory of which he then knew nothing, but would soon come to know a great deal.

And once they were on their way, any concerns he had about Isaac Milner proving a dull or sanctimonious traveling companion were completely unfounded.

"Milner and I," he recalled, "were fellow-travellers in one carriage, and the rest of our party in another. Milner was lively and dashing in his conversation—very much a man of the world in his manners [and conduct]." So the party crossed France to Lyons and set sail on the Rhone—"dropping down its stream to Avignon—a voyage of four days under a cloudless sky."

Still, as charming a companion as Milner was, there was something different about him. Wilberforce remembered,

> He was a sincere believer, and when I let loose, as I sometimes did, my sceptical opinions, or treated with ridicule the principles of vital religion, he [challenged] my objections, and would sometimes say, "Wilberforce, I don't pretend to be a match for you in this sort of running fire; but if you really wish to discuss these topics in a serious way, I shall be most happy to do so."

Wilberforce had a competitive nature and likely relished the idea of refuting any notions of faith Milner possessed. He took up the challenge.

The setting could not have been more advantageous for such

discussions as Milner wished to have with his friend. They were constantly together, particularly during the long carriage rides that were a necessity of travel.

Milner, in explaining the basis of his principles, justified them "by referring to the word of God." This led to their reading the Scriptures together.

Wilberforce soon discovered that he could not so easily dismiss what his friend said. Milner, who held the Lucasian Chair of Mathematics at Cambridge, was so brilliant a scholar that his graduate examiners had once described him with a single word: *incomparabilis*. Engaging Milner in serious discussions of faith was not unlike asking C. S. Lewis to make the case for Christianity.

So, at least, Wilberforce found Milner to be. "At length," he confessed, "I began to be impressed with a sense of the weighty truths which were more or less the continual subjects of our conversation."

And Wilberforce held nothing back. "I pressed on [Milner] my various doubts, objections, and difficulties. The final result of our discussions was a settled conviction in my mind of the truth of Christianity."

But then another impasse loomed before him. He had accepted Milner's arguments, but he had to admit that

> they long remained merely as opinions assented to by my understanding, but not influencing my heart.
>
> I began to think what folly it was, nay, what madness, to continue month after month, nay, day after day, in [such] a state. . . . I was firmly convinced [of] the great truths taught us in the New Testament, [and] that the offers of the gospel were universal and free, in short that happiness, eternal happiness, was at my option.

Returning to England in the autumn of 1785, he entered on a period of soul-searching marked by "deep and earnest prayer." Brought under

deep convictions of sin, he knew he needed to confide in a trusted counselor. But who to turn to?

It was then he remembered the friend of his youth.

Almost the first person to whom I unfolded my heart was [the poet
William] Cowper's friend—good old John Newton—whom I had
often heard preach when I lived with my uncle and aunt. I had no
other religious acquaintance. He entered most kindly and affection-
ately into my case, and told me he . . . had never ceased to pray for me.

Moreover, "he told me he always had entertained hopes and confidence that God would some time bring me [back] to Him."

Newton steadied his young friend in the midst of his spiritual crisis.
"When I came away [from this visit]," Wilberforce recalled, "I found
my mind in a calm, tranquil state, more humbled, and looking more
devoutly up to God."

Newton helped Wilberforce find solid ground spiritually, but he also
gave him unconventional advice that would mean much for the course
of history. Wilberforce confessed he was tempted to leave the world of
politics, perhaps for pastoral ministry. Much to his surprise, Newton
disagreed. As Wilberforce remembered, "Mr. Newton, in the [visits] I
had with him, advised me . . . to keep up my connection with Pitt, and
to continue in Parliament."

Newton's counsel could not have been more momentous. For within
two years, Wilberforce would take up the cause that would come to domi-
nate his political life: the abolition of the British slave trade. He could not
have done so had he left Parliament. Newton's advice had been crucial.

Nor did it stop there. Newton, the former slave ship captain, visited with Wilberforce on the very Sunday in late October 1787 when
Wilberforce wrote his diary, "God Almighty had placed before me two
great objects," the first of which was "the suppression of the slave trade."

The second was a resolve to do what he could to foster moral and cultural renewal.

On that day, the two friends had spoken of the slave trade and Newton's role in it. A man once complicit in the enslavement of hundreds now became a catalyst for his young protégé to become the leader of the parliamentary struggle to end the slave trade. Had it not been for Newton's counsel at these two pivotal moments, Wilberforce might well have left Parliament, and might never have taken up the fight to end the slave trade. Looking back on it all, Wilberforce could only marvel. "God," he wrote, "can effect whatever He will, by means the most circuitous, and the least looked for."[4]

21 ✦ The Lion of Northfield: Miracles and the Story of D. L. Moody

I can almost throw a stone from Tremont Temple to the spot where I found God over forty years ago. I wish I could do something to lead [others] to that same God. I wish I could make people understand what He has been to me. He has been a million times better to me than I have been to Him.

—D. L. Moody[1]

On November 23, 1892, a ship set sail from Southampton, England, for New York City. Aboard the North German ocean liner, the *Spree*, were D. L. Moody with his eldest son, Will. As the ship left the pier, neither man had any way of knowing they were about to face as close a brush with death as they would ever have. "My last day in London," Moody recalled, "was a pleasant one; a day of promise it might have been called, for the sun shone out brightly after some of those dark, foggy days so common in London."

A company of friends had gathered at the station to see him off, and he suggested they sing a song that had become a favorite for him, "Then

Shall My Heart Keep Singing." But their hearts weren't in it, they said. "I was the only one in the group," Moody said, "who seemed to feel like singing."[2]

The *Spree* was three days out from port when, in the early morning hours, as Moody remembered, "I was suddenly startled by a terrible crash and shock, as if the vessel had been driven on a rock." Will Moody jumped from his berth and rushed on deck. He returned a few moments later, saying, "The propeller shaft has broken and the vessel is sinking."[3]

Moody did not at first believe it could be as bad as that, but decided nonetheless to dress and go out on deck. Once there, he soon discovered that what his son had told him was true. Initially, the captain had told frightened passengers there was no danger. But, when some of the second-cabin passengers tried to return to their berths, they were driven out again by in-rushing water. They had no choice but to leave all their belongings behind.[4]

The captain and crew now began to do all they could to save the ship. But despite their best efforts, it seemed that the pumps were useless, for water poured into the ship too rapidly to be controlled. "There was nothing more in the power of man to do," Moody recalled. "We were utterly, absolutely helpless. We could only stand still on the poor, drifting, sinking ship and look into [what would become] our watery graves."[5]

Meanwhile, unbeknownst to the passengers, the captain and officers had begun making preparations for the last resort. The lifeboats were put in readiness, provisions prepared, and life preservers distributed. The officers were armed with revolvers to enforce their orders. All that remained was a final decision over whether to launch the boats at once or wait.

However, the seas were so heavy that the crew reckoned the lifeboats could hardly stay afloat. At the same time, Moody learned that two of the passengers "had loaded revolvers ready to blow out their brains if the vessel should go down, preferring death by bullet to death by drowning."[6]

At noon the following day, the captain told everyone he had the flow of water under control and was now in hopes of drifting in the way of some passing vessel. All the same, many were alarmed to see that the ship's bow was now high in the air, while the stern seemed to settle into the water more and more.

The seas continued to be very rough, and the ship rolled from side to side with fearful lurches. It seemed that if she were to pitch violently but once, the bulkheads would have burst and the end come. The captain did what he could to keep up hope by telling everyone they should probably drift in the way of a ship by three o'clock that afternoon. But as night closed in upon them, there had been no sign of a sail.[7]

Everyone aboard passed an awful night. There were seven hundred men, women, and children who did not know what awaited them. No one dared sleep. Everyone had gathered together in the saloon of the first cabin. "The agony and suspense," Moody recalled, "were too great for words. The passengers looked at one another, as if trying to read what no one dared to speak. Rockets flamed into the sky, but there was no answer. We were drifting out of the track of the great steamers. Every hour seemed to increase our danger."[8]

Sunday morning dawned with no sign of help or hope. Up to that time no suggestion of holding religious services had been made. It was thought that to have done so would almost certainly have produced a panic. But as the second night after the accident came on, Moody asked his friend and fellow passenger General Oliver Otis Howard to request the captain's permission to hold a service in the saloon.[9]

To this, the captain readily assented. Notice was quickly given of the meeting and, to Moody's surprise, nearly every passenger attended. "I think everybody prayed," he said, "skeptics and all."[10]

And so, standing with one arm clasping a pillar to steady himself on the reeling vessel, Moody tried to read the Ninety-First Psalm. Everyone then prayed that God would still the stormy sea and bring them safe to port.

As this happened, Moody experienced something extraordinary. The words of Psalm 91 took on a meaning they had never held for him before. "It was a new psalm to me from that hour," he remembered. "The eleventh verse touched me very deeply. It was like a voice of divine assurance, and it seemed a very real thing as I read: 'He shall give His angels charge over thee, to keep thee in all thy ways.'"[11]

Thinking that reading more Scripture would prove a help, Moody began to read aloud from Psalm 107. As he did, a German passenger translated each verse for the benefit of his countrymen.[12]

Even as he read, Moody was himself being transformed. "I was passing through a new experience," he would later say. "I had thought myself superior to the fear of death. I had often preached on the subject, and urged Christians to realize this victory of faith." During the Civil War he had been under fire without fear. He had also been in Chicago during the great cholera epidemic, and gone around with doctors visiting the sick and dying. He remembered a case of smallpox where the flesh had literally dropped away from the backbone, yet he had gone to the bedside of that poor sufferer again and again, to read his Bible and pray. "In all this," Moody said, "I had no fear of death."[13]

But on the sinking ship it had proved a far different experience. It wasn't that he had no sense of peace with God. "There was no cloud between my soul and my Savior," of that he felt assured. "I knew my sins had been put away, and that if I died there it would be only to wake up in heaven. That was all settled long ago."[14]

But as his thoughts turned to his loved ones at home—his wife and children, his friends on both sides of the sea, the schools he had established, and all the interests so dear to him—and as he realized that perhaps the next hour would separate him forever from all these, it nearly broke him down. "It was," he said, "the darkest hour of my life!"[15]

Moody felt he could not endure it. He had to have relief, and at last, relief came in prayer. "God heard my cry," he remembered, "and enabled me to say, from the depth of my soul: 'Thy will be done!' Sweet peace came to my heart."[16]

Returning to his room, Moody almost immediately fell asleep. In later years, he would say that he "never slept more soundly in all my life." The peace God gave him was indeed a peace that passed all understanding. "I cried unto the Lord," he said, "and He heard me and delivered me from all my fears. I can no more doubt that God gave answer to my prayer for relief than I can doubt my own existence."[17]

About three o'clock in the morning, Moody was aroused from a sound sleep by the voice of his son. "Come on deck, Father!" Moody got out of bed and followed his son out onto the deck. Once they were there, Will pointed to a far-off light, which was rising and sinking on the sea. It proved to be the light of the steamer *Lake Huron*, whose lookout had seen their distress signals and supposed it was a vessel in flames. "Oh, the joy of that moment," Moody recalled. "Seven hundred despairing passengers stood on deck and beheld the approaching ship! Who can ever forget it?"[18]

~

Moody's life and those of his fellow passengers had been spared. To what purpose, in Moody's case, became crystal clear for him in the year that followed. For had he perished in November 1892, he never would have been able to spearhead a Christian mission the like of which the world had never seen.

The setting was the Chicago World's Fair of 1893. The fair opened on May 1 of that year, but Moody had been thinking about it for far longer. As far back as his trip to Palestine one year earlier, he had been praying for this unique event. As his son Will recalled, "Among his other qualifications for the career of an evangelist, Father had a peculiar genius for recognizing opportunities."[19]

At no time during Moody's many years of public ministry was this gift better illustrated than in the campaign conducted in Chicago during the World's Fair in 1893. The idea of making such a venue the scene of a widespread evangelistic effort was as novel as it was daring. Planning for it took place over several months, and final arrangements were made while the Exposition buildings were still under construction. As early as 1892, while Moody was abroad conducting his mission in Great Britain, he alluded frequently to this project and sought to enlist the prayers of Christians everywhere for the effort.[20]

Though reared in rural New England, Moody had retained a love for cities ever since his early adulthood in Chicago. And that city, of all others, was especially dear to him. As he saw it, Chicago, during the World's Fair, represented "the opportunity of a century."

Into Chicago Moody knew that multitudes would be pouring from every state and territory and town in America, and from many nations abroad. Where would they turn when they reached their destination? The White City, their goal, would be visited, but so would many places of sin and sorrow. The contrast of closed church doors and open saloons, darkened houses of God and the brilliantly lighted devil's dens burdened his soul. For thirteen months prior to the start of the World's Fair, these were all Moody could think of.[21]

At the same time, Moody was deeply, profoundly aware of something that few others knew of. In 1892, just prior to taking ship aboard the *Spree* for New York City, Moody had visited a London physician.

The news was worrisome. The doctor told him his heart was weakening and that he must let up on his work. He was sternly admonished to take better care of himself. Chastened by this news, Moody had taken ship with the thought that he would not work quite so hard.

Then had followed all the events onboard the *Spree*—events during which his life and the lives of several hundred others might have been lost. There had been times during those crowded hours when Moody thought he would never again have the privilege of preaching the gospel. One night during that ordeal, the first night of the accident, he had made a vow that if God would spare his life and bring him back to America, he would go to Chicago, "and at the World's Fair preach the gospel with all the power that He would give me."[22]

~

God did indeed spare Moody's life, both in terms of heart trouble and being lost at sea. He knew he was living on time divinely given to him, and he was determined to make the most of it.

His plans were proceeding apace when opposition arose from another, and most unexpected, source. When it became known that the Fair's managers had decided to keep it open on Sundays, many Christians resolved to boycott the Fair. Others thought to initiate legal action and bring a lawsuit compelling them to close on Sundays.

This Moody strongly resisted. "Let us open so many preaching places," he said, "and present the Gospel so attractively that the people will want to come and hear it."[23]

And so, as a general would marshal his troops, Moody and his co-workers set to work in earnest. Their plan for the campaign was simple, though it would require incredible dedication and hard work.

Chicago was then naturally divided into three sections by the forking river: the north side, the west side, and the south side. In each section a church center was selected: the Chicago Avenue Church (Moody's home church) on the north, the First Congregational Church on the west, and Immanuel Baptist on the south. Later, many other churches were offered and occupied.

Moody, as his son Will recalled, "was not able to carry on the work alone, but worked with many prominent Christian workers from all parts of America and Europe." Accordingly, buildings and tents sufficient to hold large audiences were secured and funds raised to cover the expenses of speakers and singers, buildings and advertising.[24]

Raising funds proved a stupendous task in itself. At one point during the mission to the World's Fair, the daily expenditures involved in the renting of halls, costs of advertising, salaries, and entertainment of speakers, clerks, and others amounted to $800 (or more than $20,000 daily in today's money).[25]

This sum had to be met by Moody's personal efforts. A large force of secretaries wrote appeals under his direction. And his efforts to secure the cooperation of the religious press in giving full notice to the work aided greatly in securing the generous support of the Christian public.

But this was only a portion of the work to which Moody gave himself. Under his supervision meetings were extended in every direction. As there were great districts that it was desired to reach, where residents would not enter a church—even if one were accessible—he decided to hire theaters. Soon a footing was obtained in the Haymarket Theater, and here he preached every Sunday morning until the end of the World's Fair campaign, with the exception of two Sundays when he was absent from the city. As the movement grew, other theaters and halls were rented until eight or nine were under his control, some on Sundays only, but others throughout the week.

Added to this, five huge tents were in constant use, pitched at strategic points in the midst of non-churchgoing communities. Two "gospel wagons" were utilized from which tracts were distributed, addresses given, and gospel hymns sung to audiences that would gather wherever a halt was made in the thickly populated tenement district.

A shop in the heart of Chicago was also rented and fitted up as a mission hall. Meetings were held not only every afternoon and evening, but a special squad of volunteers came on at ten at night in order to reach the drunkards and harlots who were known to haunt the vicinity far into the morning hours.

Special efforts were made as well to influence the neighborhood of the fairgrounds. There, on the open prairie, hotels and other buildings had grown up like gourds, without any effort to keep corresponding pace in providing church accommodations. But Moody secured the use of half a dozen tents, tabernacles, and hotel parlors.

The most notable meetings of the campaign, judged from popular response, were probably those held in Tattersall's Hall and Forepaugh's circus tents. When Moody announced the meeting in Tattersall's, with its seating capacity of ten to fifteen thousand, he said memorably, "We have got something better than Buffalo Bill's Wild West Show, and we must get a bigger audience than he does."[26] The influx of vast audiences proved his hopes were not misplaced.

Forepaugh's circus had come to Chicago in June 1893 and established itself on the lakefront. Its manager rented the tent to Moody and his coworkers for Sunday morning, but reserved it for his own shows in the afternoon and evening. Many people long remembered that when the circus advertisement appeared, the manager had included Moody's Sunday morning meeting in his announcement as follows:

> *Ha! Ha! Ha!*
> *Three Big Shows!*
> *Moody in the Morning!*
> *Forepaugh in the Afternoon and Evening!*[27]

The great canvas ellipse of Forepaugh's circus covered an immense area. It had a seating capacity of ten thousand with standing room in the arena for ten thousand more. While it was being prepared for the Sunday meeting, a circus man chafingly asked Mr. Moody if he expected to get three thousand hearers. The man was astonished when on two successive Sundays the large area of the tent was crowded to overflowing with those who were eager to hear the "Old Gospel." In the center of the arena a rude platform was erected for the speakers and a few of the singers while the rest of the song corps were ranged around them.

One observer long remembered what could be seen during one of those Sunday meetings at Forepaugh's circus. All about the interior of the huge tent were ropes, trapezes, gaudy decorations, etc., while in an adjoining canvas building was a large menagerie, including eleven elephants. There were, this observer recalled, "clowns, grooms, circus-riders, men, women, and children, eighteen thousand of them, and on a Sunday morning too! Whether the Gospel was ever before preached under such circumstances I know not, but it was wonderful to ear and eye alike."

It was an amazing sight and sound to witness when tens of thousands began to sing the hymn "Nearer, My God, to Thee." And to many, a visible sense of awe fell upon the multitude. After an hour of singing and prayer, Moody typically rose to preach, his text being *"The Son of Man is come to seek and to save that which was lost"* (Luke 19:10 KJV, emphasis added).

At all times, the Spirit of God seemed to be present. "The hush of Heaven was over the meeting," one attendant recalled.

> Towards the close of the address there was a slight disturbance, and a "lost child" was passed up to the platform. Mr. Moody held her up so that her parents might see her; and when her anxious father reached the platform Mr. Moody placed the child in his arms and said: "That is what Jesus Christ came to do: to seek and to save lost sinners, and restore them to their Heavenly Father's embrace."[28]

Still others recalled that it was a revelation to the circus manager that so many people would come to listen to songs and sermons. The afternoon and evening shows staged by the manager himself were so thinly attended that he abandoned all thought of holding Sunday exhibitions and asked Moody to keep him supplied with an evangelist to hold gospel meetings in the tent on Sundays in other cities, promising to bear all the traveling and other expenses of such an arrangement.[29]

Aside from the meetings in Forepaugh's circus, every variety of gospel meeting was held in other venues: men's meetings, women's meetings, children's meetings; temperance meetings, soldiers' meetings, jail meetings; open-air and cottage meetings; meetings for Germans, Poles, Bohemians, French, Jews, and Arabs in the fairgrounds; meetings for praise and for prayer; all-day and all-night meetings.

Strangers from all parts of the world came in the thousands, and it was Moody's purpose, as far as possible, to reach all people, of all nationalities. To do this, he enlisted the aid of prominent European ministers and evangelists. Dr. J. W. Pindor of Silesia came to preach to the Poles; Joseph Rabinowitz of Russia to the Jews; Theodore Monod of Paris to the French; and Dr. Adolf Stoecker of Berlin to the Germans.

To mention Americans who ministered in German, Swedish, Bohemian, and other tongues, as well as in English, would be to name most of the prominent evangelical preachers, teachers, and singers in America at that time. In addition to them were John Paton of the New Hebrides and Thomas Spurgeon and Henry Varley of Australia. Still others from England, Scotland, and Ireland took part. The cooperation of many World's Fair visitors, like Count Bernstorff of Berlin, and Lord Kinnaird of London, was also secured during their stay in Chicago. As the last weeks of the fair approached, the work gathered momentum. A large hall in the center of the city was secured, where a two-hour midday service was held daily.

Moody urged Christians everywhere to pray and labor with unremitting diligence. He said,

> It seems as if we had only been playing during the past weeks; now we are going to work. We have just been fishing along the shore; now we are going to launch out into the deep. Friends, help fill up

the churches. Let us see whether we can't wake up this whole city. There is now before us the grandest opportunity for extending the Kingdom of God that this country has ever seen. Hundreds of thousands of people will come in during these last weeks of the World's Fair. It is possible to reach them with the gospel message.[30]

All this required a redoubling of effort. Still more buildings were needed for meetings near the World's Fair grounds. Moody sought to hire all the theatres he could get. Heretofore with expenditures as much as $800 a day, Moody now reckoned that he could spend $8,000 a day (or $200,000 a day in today's currency) if only sufficient funds could be obtained.[31]

In the end it was the concerts of prayer that Moody instituted which seemed to have made all the difference. Many came to look on them as a continuing miracle in which the spirit of God drew thousands of hearts and minds to Christ. As Will Moody later recalled,

> On several of those last Sundays Father coordinated as many as one hundred and twenty-five different meetings—assuming, when it was necessary, the expenses of rent and incidentals, furnishing speakers and singers, and working up the attendance, which would aggregate upwards of one hundred thousand each Sunday.[32]

On Chicago Day, October 8, Chicago determined to celebrate, on a colossal scale, the twenty-second anniversary of the great fire of 1871. Moody was also determined to make a special effort. The World's Fair had arranged extra attractions, and more than seven hundred thousand people would pass through the gates that day. Moody, for his part, arranged to hold continuous meetings in three large central halls, and in one notable instance, the attendance was so large that the speakers had difficulty pushing their way in.[33]

In the end, the work of hundreds of volunteers under Moody's leadership, and the blessing of God, produced an incredible result. Moody's own estimate of the results of the work, given in an interview at the close of the campaign, described the six months' effort. In replying to various questions, he said, "The principal result is that millions have heard the simple Gospel preached by some of the most gifted preachers in the world; thousands have been genuinely converted to Christ, and Christians all over this land have been brought to a deeper spiritual life."[34]

22 + Eastern Orthodoxy: Miracles of Majesty and Mystery

To be a Christian is to be a traveller. Our situation, say the Greek Fathers, is like that of the Israelite people in the desert of Sinai: we live in tents, not houses, for spiritually we are always on the move. We are on a journey through the inward space of the heart, a journey not measured by the hours of the watch or the days of the calendar, for it is a journey out of time into eternity.

—KALLISTOS WARE[1]

Byzantium. The majestic dome of the Hagia Sophia. The four ancient Patriarchates of Constantinople, Alexandria, Antioch, and Jerusalem. Monuments all to the mystery and inspiration of an ancient and much revered faith.

In recent years, many in the West have been drawn to the beauty and meaning of Orthodox liturgy, iconography, history, and literature. Miracles, too, are an integral part of its epic story. In worship, art, and teaching, Eastern Orthodoxy has imparted a great and enduring legacy.

The Orthodox Study Bible defines a miracle as "a sign whereby God supersedes the laws of nature in a mystery."[2] Elsewhere, within the pages of the book *In the Heart of the Desert: The Spirituality of the Desert Fathers and Mothers*, miracles are described as follows: "Miracles . . . are a part of creation and invoke our creativity. They are insights into another way of life, involving openness to mystery and welcoming the surprise of grace. We do not in fact make miracles happen; we merely witness them happening."[3]

Stories of the Desert Fathers and Mothers are greatly revered with the Orthodox Church. For it is understood that these saints chose to sojourn in the desert so that they might "overcome earthly discriminations and limitations." They were ardent in pursuit of holiness and gave their lives to this quest. What were they seeking? As one scholar of this period in church history noted, "What is real differed in the desert; or at least, reality acquired a different perspective. Somehow, *the order of this world was infiltrated and influenced by the order of another world*. It is no wonder, then, that the *Sayings* [*of the Desert Fathers and Mothers*] are literally filled with stories about miracles and visions."[4]

The accounts that have come down to us of these desert *Sayings* read much like the parables we find in the New Testament. These saints, in their own unique way, had chosen to seek first the kingdom of God. And so it is that their stories are intended to teach us about the reality of who God is. Miracles are often at the heart of these narratives, as in the case of one event from the life of Abba Bessarion. As it is told:

Abba Doulas, the disciple of Abba Bessarion, said: "One day, when we were walking by the sea, I was thirsty and said to Abba Bessarion: 'Father, I am very thirsty.' He said a prayer and told me: 'Drink some of the sea water.' The water proved sweet when I drank some. I even poured some into a leather bottle for fear of being thirsty later on. On seeing this, the old man asked me why I was taking some. I replied: 'Forgive me, it is for fear of being thirsty later on.' Then the old man said: 'God is here, God is everywhere.'"[5]

Author John Chryssavgis has written compellingly about why the Desert Fathers and Mothers speak to our historical moment—indeed all times—with such richness of meaning and depth of spiritual experience. Chryssavgis said,

For the desert elders, miracles are paradoxical responses resulting from God's paradoxical love. They confirm God's absolute love and celebrate God's absolute freedom in a world that means everything to God as its creator. For the Desert Fathers and Mothers, creation is a miracle. The world, too, is a miracle. In fact, it is not the desert dwellers that make miracles happen; they themselves comprise miracles of God. As vessels of another grace, they remind us of the miracle of human existence. They recall the cohabitation of all the glory of God in all the frailty of humanity.[6]

Closer to our own time, G. K. Chesterton captured the sense of wonder that ought to be the mark of the Christian. The idea that moved him to write is that we desperately need to remember who we are, who created us, and the miracle that the world itself exists. So Chesterton observed,

The sense of the miracle of humanity itself should be always more vivid to us than any marvels of power, intellect, art, or civilization. The mere man on two legs, as such, should be felt as something more heartbreaking than any music and more startling than any caricature.[7]

~

The miracle at Cana is of great significance within the Orthodox Church as it relates to the sanctification of marriage. *The Orthodox Study Bible* tells us that "the Bible and human history begin and end with marriages.

Adam and Eve come together in marital union in Paradise, before the Fall, revealing marriage as a part of God's eternal purpose for humanity in the midst of Creation."[8] Genesis 2:22–24 provides the scriptural basis for this teaching.

> Then the rib which the LORD God had taken from man He made into a woman, and He brought her to the man. And Adam said: "This is now bone of my bones and flesh of my flesh; she shall be called Woman, because she was taken out of Man." Therefore a man shall leave his father and mother and be joined to his wife, and they shall become one flesh.

Moving through to the end of Scripture, *The Orthodox Study Bible* teaches that "history closes with the marriage of the Bride to the Lamb, earthly marriage being fulfilled in the heavenly, showing the eternal nature of the sacrament."[9] The scriptural basis for that is found in the book of Revelation 19:7–9.

> "Let us be glad and rejoice and give [the Lord] glory, for the marriage of the Lamb has come, and His wife has made herself ready." And to her it was granted to be arrayed in fine linen, clean and bright, for the fine linen is the righteous acts of the saints.
>
> Then he said to me, "Write: 'Blessed are those who are called to the marriage supper of the Lamb!'" And he said to me, "These are the true sayings of God."

The Orthodox Church teaches that between Genesis and Revelation comes the centerpiece of Scripture so far as marriage is concerned. For in the gospel of John, chapter 2, verses 1 through 11, the Lord Jesus Christ blessed the wedding of Cana in Galilee. "In attending this wedding and performing His first miracle there," we read in *The Orthodox*

Study Bible, "Jesus Christ, the Son of God, forever sanctified marriage. As with all the Christian sacraments, marriage is sacramental because it is blessed by God."[10]

We can all be grateful to the Orthodox Church for presenting us with such a beautiful and compelling picture of marriage, one so richly rooted in Scripture and understood in the light of Holy Writ. These words of teaching conclude what *The Orthodox Study Bible* tells us of this ceremony:

> Marriage is a sacrament—holy, blessed, and everlasting in the sight of God and His Church. Within the bonds of marriage, husband and wife experience a union with one another in love. . . . And within the bonds of marriage there is both a fullness of equality between husband and wife and a clarity of order, with the husband as the icon [or likeness] of Christ and the wife as the icon [or likeness] of the Church.[11]

This last lovely phrase has its scriptural corollary in the apostle Paul's letter to the Ephesians, chapter 5, verses 25 to 29.

> Husbands, love your wives, just as Christ also loved the church and gave Himself for her, that He might sanctify and cleanse her with the washing of water by the word, that He might present her to Himself a glorious church, not having spot or wrinkle or any such thing, but that she should be holy and without blemish. So husbands ought to love their own wives as their own bodies; he who loves his wife loves himself. For no one ever hated his own flesh, but nourishes and cherishes it, just as the Lord does the church.

~

Notwithstanding all that has been said, the Orthodox Church seems a world apart for many Protestant Christians. Geography, tradition, the place of iconography, and much else seem to separate them from this ancient faith.

But the Nicene Creed, the most widely affirmed of all the creeds that have come down to us from ages past, serves as a place where unity abides. There may indeed be many things about the Orthodox Church that differ from Protestant churches, or, for that matter, the Catholic Church. The Nicene Creed is one that nearly all churches in Christendom affirm. The miracles it speaks of are miracles cherished across the denominational landscape. That is a very great thing. The Nicene Creed is mere Christianity at its finest and most enduring.

We read of this in the introduction to *I Believe: The Nicene Creed*, a book beautifully illustrated by Pauline Baynes, the illustrator of C. S. Lewis's *Chronicles of Narnia*. There it is stated:

> One of several early Christian creeds—among them the Apostles' and Athanasian Creeds—the Nicene Creed is regarded as the most ecumenical, representing the beliefs of more of the Christian world than any other creed. It is used by most Protestant Churches, as well as by the Roman Catholic Church, and Eastern Orthodox churches, and remains a rock of Christian belief to this day.[12]

The Nicene Creed has of course been published in many places, but the text that appears below is taken from *The Orthodox Study Bible*.

> I believe in one God, the Father Almighty, Maker of heaven and earth, and of all things visible and invisible;
>
> and in one LORD Jesus Christ, the Son of God, the Only-Begotten, begotten of the Father before all worlds,
>
> Light of Light, Very God of Very God, begotten, not made; of one essence with the Father; by Whom all things were made;

Who for us men and for our salvation came down from heaven and was incarnate of the Holy Spirit and the Virgin Mary, and was made man; and was crucified also for us under Pontius Pilate, and suffered and was buried; the third day He rose again according to the Scriptures; and ascended into heaven, and sits at the right hand of the Father; and He shall come again with glory to judge the living and the dead; Whose kingdom shall have no end.

And I believe in the Holy Spirit, the LORD and Giver of Life, Who proceeds from the Father, Who with the Father and the Son together is worshipped and glorified, Who spoke by the prophets.

And I believe in One Holy Catholic and Apostolic Church.

I acknowledge one Baptism for the remission of sins.

I look for the resurrection of the dead and the life of the world to come. Amen.[13]

Many miracles are described and affirmed in the text of the Nicene Creed. The first is that God made the heavens and the earth, which is taught in Genesis 1:1: "In the beginning God created the heavens and the earth."

The incarnation is the next miracle to be affirmed. Saint Athanasius, a saint revered by the Orthodox, Catholic, and Protestant traditions alike, wrote what many consider to be one of the finest introductions to the Nicene Creed's teaching on this miracle. It bears the title *On the Incarnation*, and was written prior to AD 319. Theologian A. E. Burn, writing in the early twentieth century, explained that we ought to feel a great and enduring debt to Athanasius for the strength of his conviction to this miracle, and for his courage in upholding that conviction during a time of great religious controversy. Further, to read Athanasius is to enter the world of fourth-century Christianity and discover a richness of belief that can deepen and strengthen our own faith. His teaching on the incarnation reads, in part:

The incorporeal and incorruptible and immaterial Word of God comes to our realm. . . . No part of creation is left void of Him: He has filled all things everywhere. . . . But He comes in condescension to show loving-kindness upon us, and to visit us. And seeing the race of rational creatures in the way to perish, and death reigning over them by corruption . . . He takes unto Himself a body, and that of no different sort from ours.

Thus taking from our bodies one of like nature, because all were under penalty of the corruption of death, He gave it over to death in the stead of all. . . . [Where] men had turned towards corruption, He [died that he] might turn them again towards incorruption, and quicken them from death by the appropriation of His body and by the grace of the Resurrection, banishing death from them like straw from fire.[14]

The resurrection is the third miracle affirmed in the Nicene Creed. Bishop Kallistos Ware, in his classic text *The Orthodox Way*, wrote very movingly about the resurrection, saying, "We do not merely say 'Christ rose' but 'Christ is risen'—he lives *now*, for me and in me."[15] Another stirring passage on the resurrection also appears in *The Orthodox Way*, where we read:

The deepest foundation of the hope and joy which characterize Orthodoxy and which penetrate all its worship is the Resurrection. Easter, the centre of Orthodox worship, is an explosion of joy, the same joy which the disciples felt when they saw the risen Saviour. It is the explosion of cosmic joy at the triumph of life, after the overwhelming sorrow over death—death which even the Lord of life had to suffer when He became man. "Let the heavens rejoice and the earth exult, and let all the world invisible and visible keep holiday, for Christ our eternal joy is risen." All things are now filled with the certainty of life, whereas before all had been moving steadily towards death. Orthodoxy emphasizes with special insistence the faith of Christianity in the triumph of life.[16]

The miracle of the coming of the Holy Spirit following Christ's ascension into heaven is also affirmed by the Nicene Creed. On the significance of Pentecost, Bishop Ware has written, "Hitherto it has been the Spirit who sends out Christ: now it is the risen Christ who sends out the Spirit. Pentecost forms the aim and completion of the incarnation: in the words of Vladimir Lossky, 'The Logos took flesh, that we might receive the Spirit.'"[17]

Moving next to a discussion of Matthew 18:20, where we read, "Where two or three are gathered together in My name, I am there in the midst of them," Bishop Ware asked a deeply important question: "How is Christ present in our midst?" It is, he answered, through the Holy Spirit. Further, one might look to Matthew 28:20, where we read, "Lo, I am with you always, even to the end of the age." How is Christ with us? Once again the answer came, "Through the Holy Spirit." Bishop Ware went on to say:

> Because of the Comforter's presence in our heart, we do not simply know Christ at fourth or fifth hand, as a distant figure from long ago, about whom we possess factual information through written records; but we know him directly, here and now, in the present, as our personal Saviour and our friend.[18]

~

This chapter commenced with an epigraph from the writings of Bishop Kallistos Ware, one of the most noteworthy and distinguished ambassadors of the Orthodox Church in the modern era. He has given many in the West gifts of rich and storied glimpses into the Orthodox Church. And so it seems fitting to close with one final reflection from him:

> To many in the twentieth-century West, the Orthodox Church seems chiefly remarkable for its air of antiquity and conservatism; the message of the Orthodox to their Western brethren seems to be, "We are your past." For the Orthodox themselves, however, loyalty to Tradition means not primarily the acceptance of formulae or customs from past generations, but rather the ever-new, personal and direct experience of the Holy Spirit *in the present*, here and now.[19]

23 ✦ Lady of the Radiant Smile: Miracles and the Life of Corrie Ten Boom

My times are in Your hand . . .

—Psalm 31:15

W hen I was a boy, my first real sense of the miraculous came from stories my mother read to me of Corrie Ten Boom, who had been imprisoned by the Nazis along with her entire family for their work in the Dutch underground hiding Jewish refugees who sought to escape internment in the death camps Germany had established. The title of her first memoir described the incredibly dangerous work she and her family had undertaken: *The Hiding Place.*

Corrie was arrested in late February 1944, at the age of fifty-one. Her elderly father, Casper, would die in prison, as would her beloved sister, Betsie. She herself escaped death through what can only be called a miracle. Just one week before all the women of her age group were put to death in a concentration camp called Ravensbrück, she was released due to what was later described as "a clerical error."

After World War II ended, Corrie began to travel the world, sharing the stories of her experiences—and her faith—with all who would listen.

English was not her first language. But the power of all that God did for her and through her shines resplendently in her simple, ungrammatical phrases. There is an immediacy to her words that takes one instantly to the scenes she was describing.

Among the things she left us, we have the audio transcript of one television appearance she made in America in the 1970s. Her words on that occasion are a treasure, a firsthand description of how God carried her when she needed Him most.

I was eleven months a prisoner. First, four months in solitary confinement, alone in a cell. And then in a concentration camp in Holland, a German concentration camp, and then, in Ravensbrück—a terrible place north of Berlin. And that's where my sister died.

Who kept me? I will tell you. There are circumstances [when] you cannot do anything. And it was only the Lord who carried me through. . . . I had always believed, now I know from experience that Jesus' light is stronger than the deepest darkness. And a child of God cannot go [into circumstances that are too] deep—always deeper are the everlasting arms to carry you.

The devil is strong, but his power is limited. And Jesus' power is unlimited. Indeed, [God's grace] was always sufficient, but sometimes I—I lost courage. And I remember that once I said—when I looked on the stars, I said, "O Lord, all the stars are in your guidance, but have you forgotten your child, Corrie Ten Boom?"[1]

One of the ways Corrie saw that God had not forgotten her was the utterly improbable way God provided a Bible for her while in the prison camp. When asked by her television host how a Bible had been permitted within the gates of a godless place where hope seemed lost, she smiled a great smile and said, "That was a miracle." She then continued, "When we entered [the camp] I had a little Bible. It was a small

Bible, but a whole Bible—Old and New Testaments—and I had it hidden under my clothes, and on my back.

"And I saw that they [were taking] away everything that we had hidden, eh. And I was so scared that I said, 'O Lord, send your angels. And they [can] surround me.' But then I thought, 'Yes, but angels are spirits and you can look through a spirit,' and I thought, 'O God, let your angels this time not be transparent.'

"God did it. The woman who stood before me was searched, and my sister was behind me, and they did not see me. And so I came in the prison with my Bible."

"Really," Corrie was asked, "God made his angels untransparent?!"

"Yes." She nodded. "We mustn't be too amazed when God does miracles."[2]

~

God's provision of this precious Bible was an incredible mercy. Yet wondrous as this answer to Corrie's unorthodox prayer was, she still knew the terrible pain of watching her sister, Betsie, waste away and die. Others, too, for whom she had come to care deeply, died amidst the oppressive cruelty of the hellish place they were forced to live in.

And so it is not surprising to learn that one of the greatest struggles Corrie had to face was one of forgiveness. She had come to hate her oppressors, and her struggle with that hatred threatened, by her own admission, to be her undoing. As she told her television host, "*We have to forgive.* I was not at peace with men. There was hatred in my heart." She then went on to explain:

> When guards were cruel [to] my friends, and [to] Betsie and me, there
> came such a hatred in my heart. [But it was] then I learned to take
> the promise of Romans 5:5—"The love of God is shed abroad into

our hearts by the Holy Spirit," and I learned this prayer: "Thank you, Jesus, that you have brought into my heart God's love, through the Holy Spirit [who has] given it to me, and thank you, Father, that your love in me is stronger than my hatred." And the hatred went, and I could love my enemies.[3]

As much as this story inspires, and as much as we can admire this Dutch saint for praying such a prayer, the struggle with forgiveness reared its head once more after her release from prison camp.

Some years later Corrie had an unexpected meeting with a man who had formerly been one of the cruelest guards during her time of imprisonment. Unlikely as it may have seemed, this man had become a Christian. And one evening, after Corrie concluded a talk about God's forgiveness, he approached her to ask a question, though he did not recognize her.

But she knew him at sight. In a flash, all her painful memories resurfaced.

Her heart froze. She could only stand still in shocked silence as fresh waves of grief threatened to overwhelm her. She then heard the man say, "Thank you for your message, fräulein! How good it is to know that, as you say, all our sins are at the bottom of the sea."

Corrie couldn't speak. Face-to-face with her captor, she didn't know what to do.

After a moment, the man continued speaking. He confessed that he had once been a prison guard at Ravensbrück, but had since become a Christian. "I know God has forgiven me for the cruel things I did there—but, fräulein, could *you* forgive me?" He then extended his hand.

In the silence of her mind, Corrie could only cry out to God. She couldn't move, couldn't say anything. "Jesus, help me!" she prayed to herself. "I can move my hand. I can do that much, but you must supply the feeling."

Woodenly, she extended her hand and took that of her former captor. It was then something incredible happened. As she recalled,

> [A] current started in my shoulder, raced down my arm, sprang into our joined hands. And then this healing warmth seemed to flood my whole being, bringing tears to my eyes.
>
> "I forgive you, brother!" I cried. "With all my heart!"
>
> For a long moment we grasped each other's hands, the former guard and the former prisoner. I had never known God's love so intensely as I did then. But even so, I realized it was not my love. I had tried, and did not have the power. It was the power of the Holy Spirit as recorded in Romans 5:5, "because the love of God is shed abroad in our hearts by the Holy Ghost which is given unto us."[4]

I was a boy when I first heard my mother read Corrie Ten Boom's words. Thirty-five years have passed. I have since read many moving books and heard many compelling stories.

But none have been more moving, or compelling, than the stories from a small paperback book that my mother read to me of the Dutch woman for whom God was deliverer, healer, and restorer.

As long as I live, I shall remember the cover of that book. It bore the picture of a lady eighty years old, carrying two light suitcases and bearing a radiant smile. With self-deprecating humor, Corrie Ten Boom was fond of calling herself "a tramp for the Lord." But for me, she will always be a herald of God's mercy, grace, and forgiveness. To look on her picture from that old book is to see the face of hope—and to remember that miracles still happen.

24 ✦ The King of Kings: Miracles in the Golden Age of Cinema

If ancient examples of faith and proofs of God's grace and deeds edifying to men have on that account been collected and written down, so that by the reading of them as though it made them once more present, both God is honoured and man is strengthened, why should not modern examples also be collected?

—TERTULLIAN[1]

Most people think of director Cecil B. DeMille in connection with the film *The Ten Commandments*, and rightly so. It is considered by many to be the greatest of all biblically based epic films. But there was another, earlier film for which he deserves to be remembered—perhaps even more so than for *The Ten Commandments*.

That film is *The King of Kings*, which was released in 1927. Though a silent film, few motion pictures have spoken so powerfully, for so long, to so many. Newly remastered as part of the distinguished cinematic series, the Criterion Collection, motion-picture historians have written that during the creation of this film, DeMille was allowed to work

> with one of the biggest budgets in Hollywood history, DeMille spun the life and Passion of Christ into a silent-era blockbuster. Featuring text drawn directly from the Bible, a cast of thousands . . . *The King of Kings* is at once spectacular and deeply reverent—part Gospel, part Technicolor epic.[2]

Blockbuster though it may have been upon its initial release, *The King of Kings* became a blockbuster of a wholly different order of magnitude in the years following. Writing in the *Wall Street Journal* in the spring of 2011, educator and author John Murray said that "because it was produced as a silent film, Protestant and Catholic missionaries alike were able to use [*The King of Kings*] for decades to share the Gospel with non-English-speaking peoples." This led to an absolutely astounding statistic. Given this set of circumstances, viewership of *The King of Kings* was "estimated at over 800 million people by 1959."[3]

Murray then went on to state that "the most powerful story related by DeMille in his autobiography about the influence of *The King of Kings* involved a Polish man named William E. Wallner." The story that Wallner had to tell was a harrowing one. And it involved the miracle of martyrdom.

Wallner began by saying that he first saw *The King of Kings* in 1928. Deeply touched, he resolved to devote his life to Christian ministry. Eleven years later, Wallner was the leader of a Lutheran parish in Prague. Shortly after Hitler invaded Czechoslovakia, a doctor in Wallner's parish was sent to a Nazi concentration camp. This man, a Jewish convert to Christianity, encouraged his fellow prisoners "to die bravely, with faith in their hearts." As a result of his sterling courage and vibrant witness, the doctor became a target of Gestapo officers.[4]

Suffering and torture were brutally inflicted on this steadfast believer. He was repeatedly struck with an iron rod until one of his arms had to be amputated. Still, he refused to be silent about his faith. Ultimately, as DeMille's autobiography reveals, "one Gestapo officer beat the doctor's head against a stone wall until blood was streaming down his face." The officer then brandished a mirror before the doctor's face. "Look at yourself now," he said with incredible cruelty. "Now you look like your Jewish Christ."[5]

Lifting the one hand he had left, the doctor said, "Lord [Jesus], never in my life have I received such honor—to resemble You." Those proved to be his last words.

These words seared the conscience of the sadistic Gestapo officer. Racked with guilt, the officer sought out Wallner, desperate to be free of the terrible burden of guilt that had come upon him like a death knell.

So it was that a pastor led an oppressor to faith. "Perhaps God let you kill that good man," Wallner said, "to bring you to the foot of the Cross, where you can help others." Deeply repentant, the officer returned to the concentration camp. In the years that followed, in concert with Wallner and the Czech underground, this man who had beaten a man to death risked his life to free many Jews.[6]

In 1957, Wallner met Cecil B. DeMille. He told the filmmaker about the impact *The King of Kings* had on his life, as it had influenced so many who had since come in contact with him. Deeply moved, he told DeMille that had it not been for this film, he never would have become a Lutheran pastor. "Three hundred and fifty Jewish children," he said, "would have died in the ditches."[7]

DeMille was greatly humbled by this. All he knew to say was,

If I felt that this film was *my work*, it would be intolerably vain and presumptuous to quote such stories from the hundreds like them that I could quote. But all we did in *The King of Kings*, all I have striven to do in any of my Biblical pictures, was to translate into another medium, the medium of sight and sound, the words of the Bible.[8]

So it was that a filmmaker had become caught up in something larger than himself, and he discovered with unmistakable clarity that "the word of God is living and powerful," even if conveyed in a silent film. Though it was not his intent, for how could he have known, he became part of a miracle—indeed a series of miracles. Through the story that Pastor Wallner shared with him, DeMille learned that God is able "to do exceedingly abundantly above all that we ask or think" (Eph. 3:20).

In concluding his article for the *Wall Street Journal*, John Murray reflected on the Easter holiday that had prompted him to write. He said,

Millions world-wide will celebrate Easter this weekend with the proclamation, "Jesus Christ is risen today, Alleluia!" Knowing this has inspired men and women throughout the ages to claim the words of Saint Paul, "that you may know what is the hope of His calling . . . the exceeding greatness of His power toward us who believe, according to the working of His mighty power which He worked in Christ when He raised Him from the dead." A resurrection hope found not only in film, but in the lives of those that follow.[9]

25 + Joy Lewis:
The Miracle of Healing

> *O Love that wilt not let me go,*
> *I rest my weary soul in thee;*
> *I give thee back the life I owe,*
> *That in thine ocean depths its flow*
> *May richer, fuller be.*
> *O Joy that seekest me through pain,*
> *I cannot close my heart to thee;*
> *I trace the rainbow through the rain,*
> *And feel the promise is not vain,*
> *That morn shall tearless be.*

> —GEORGE MATHESON[1]

H ere begins a story about miracles that involve C. S. Lewis, who wrote a classic text bearing the title *Miracles*. We will not speak here of his famous book, but rather of how one miracle was bestowed upon him and his wife, Joy.

Many know something of their story from the widely acclaimed film *Shadowlands*. C. S. Lewis, a longtime bachelor, world famous, and firmly established in his life and habits as an Oxford don, met Joy Davidman in 1952, after corresponding with her for two years.

She was a former atheist and member of the Communist Party in America. Highly talented in her own right and blessed with a brilliant mind, she had in her early thirties won the Yale Series of Younger Poets Competition for her collection of poems, *Letter to a Comrade*. In 1938, she was a cowinner, with Robert Frost, of the Russell Loines Memorial Prize.

No less a lion of the American literary scene than Pulitzer Prize–winner Stephen Vincent Benét had written the foreword for *Letter to a Comrade*, which was published by the prestigious Yale University Press in 1938. Praising Davidman's power of vivid conception, Benét stated that "[she] is able to say things so they stick in the mind." He quoted several times from her verse, as in this instance, saying, "Miss Davidman can see, with accuracy and freshness, the thing in front of her eyes."[2]

In drawing attention to Davidman's gifts, Benét offered this telling summary: "There are echoes here, as there are in almost any first book, and there are a few practice pieces. They occur, as they are bound to occur, because the poet learns his craft by exercising it. But there is also genuine power—and that's rather harder to come by."[3] Many critics singled out her poem "Snow in Madrid" for special praise. It speaks of a conflict, the Spanish Civil War, which touched the lives of many Americans, including Ernest Hemmingway. Of this desperate struggle, Davidman had written:

> *Softly, so casual,*
> *Lovely, so light, so light,*
> *The cruel sky lets fall*
> *Something one does not fight.*[4]

Beautiful lines from a great soul.

This C. S. Lewis discovered first through correspondence with Joy—a correspondence that began in 1950. For two years, they exchanged letters, a spirited and vibrant set of letters to judge from Joy's description of the first letter she received from Lewis. Writing to their mutual friend, Chad Walsh, on January 27, 1950, she said, "Just got a letter from Lewis in the mail. I think I told you I'd raised an argument or two on some point? Lord, he knocked my props out from under me unerringly; one shot to a pigeon. I haven't a scrap of my case left."[5]

In 1952, Joy visited Lewis in Oxford, during which time they and Lewis's brother, Warnie, "spent many happy times together . . . walking, talking and enjoying an occasional pub lunch, a pork pie or two and a pint of bitter."[6] When she had to leave, Warnie was not the only one to miss her or hope that they might meet again.

That meeting was to take place sooner than either Warnie or C. S. Lewis might have thought, for by 1953, Joy knew to her sorrow that her marriage to the American novelist William Gresham was in ruins. They would divorce one year later,[7] and it was Joy's fond wish to start her life over again in England with her two young sons, David and Douglas.[8]

Joy introduced her sons to C. S. Lewis during a visit to his home, The Kilns, on December 17, 1953. By January 1954, Joy's sons were enrolled at Dane Court School near Woking, Surrey. Later that year, in August, Joy and her family moved to Number 10 Old High Street, Oxford, so that they could see more of Lewis, who had become a cherished family friend. He showed them many marks of kindness, providing financial support in difficult times and fatherly affection to the boys.

Meanwhile, in June 1955, Joy had welcomed a visit from Chad and Eve Walsh and their two daughters. Still later, during their visit to the UK, the Walshes visited Lewis in Oxford. Recalling this visit in later years, Chad Walsh remembered that he and his wife "had a chance to observe Joy and Lewis together. She seemed to be at The Kilns a good deal. My wife firmly declared, 'I smell marriage in the air.'"[9]

In September 1955, Lewis departed for Ireland to enjoy a vacation there with his lifelong friend Arthur Greeves. He told Arthur that he was "thinking of marrying Joy in a private civil ceremony."[10] As it happened, there was a very pressing practical reason for Lewis to contemplate such a step. For reasons unknown, the British Home Office refused to grant Joy permission to live and work in England. However, "she wanted to stay and Lewis certainly wanted her to stay." In view of this, "the only solution he could think of was that they go through a civil marriage ceremony."[11]

And so, on Monday, April 23, 1956, Lewis and Joy were wed. He saw it as a practical, contractual matter wherein he and Joy would both live in separate residences. Lewis' brother, Warnie, thought that while this sounded well enough in theory, things are seldom so easy. As he wrote in his diary,

> [Jack] assured me that Joy would continue to occupy her own house as "Mrs. Gresham," and that the marriage was a pure formality designed to give Joy the right to go on living in England: and I saw the uselessness of disabusing him. Joy, whose intentions were obvious from the outset, soon began to press for her rights, pointing out with perfect truth that her reputation was suffering from [Jack's] being in her house every day, often stopping till eleven at night; and all the arrangement had been made for the installation of the family at The Kilns.[12]

It was clear enough that Lewis had come to have a deep affection for Joy, one that she fully returned. Sometimes love finds its true path in unexpected ways, and such was the case with them. They had every reason to look forward to future days at The Kilns.

But before the move took place, as Warnie Lewis remembered, "disaster overtook us."[13] It happened that for some time Joy, only just turned forty-two, had been feeling considerable pain in her left leg, back, and chest. She was diagnosed with "rheumatism and fibrositis, an inflammation of the tissues surrounding the muscles which causes pain and stiffness."[14]

On the evening of October 18, 1956, when Lewis was away at Cambridge University, God placed a holy prompting within the heart of a cherished family friend, Katherine Farrer. She could not explain it, but somehow she suddenly knew that something was wrong with Joy. "I *must* ring her!" she said to her husband. She began dialing Joy's number as quickly as she could. It had not as yet rung at Joy's apartment in Headington when Joy "tripped over the telephone wire, bringing the telephone down as she fell to the floor."[15] The femur of her left leg snapped like a twig. But even as she felt the searing pain and cried out, Joy heard Katherine Farrer's voice, asking if she could help.[16]

It was a miracle of divine intervention, for had Katherine not heeded God's holy prompting, Joy would never have received help so quickly. Rushed to the Wingfield-Morris Orthopedic Hospital, Joy's X-rays revealed that her left femur was almost eaten through with cancer— little wonder, then, that it had broken so easily when she fell. It was also learned that she had a malignant tumor in her left breast, and secondary sites in her right leg and shoulder.[17]

Joy's prognosis was dire indeed. As Lewis's biographer and friend George Sayer recalled, "In the following month, she underwent three operations: the cancerous part of the femur was cut out, and the bone was repaired. The tumour in her breast was cut out, but she was spared a mastectomy. Her ovaries were also removed."[18]

Some scholars have said that while C. S. Lewis felt deep compassion and "great pity" for Joy, he did not as yet love her in the romantic sense of the word.[19] Whatever the truth of this, he did a beautiful thing in stating his wish that a Christian marriage service be held for him and Joy, so that she could be taken to The Kilns to die with him as his wife.[20]

On March 21, 1957, they were married by the Reverend Peter Bide, happiness mingled with sorrow that the marriage might only endure for a brief season.

But their marriage was to be graced by something neither expected: a miracle. As Joy's son Douglas would later remember, "Come home mother did, but die she did not."[21] Very slowly at first, but then with increasing speed, her health began to improve. Her doctors, usually very circumspect professionally, began to guardedly use the word *miraculous*. Douglas Gresham's description of how it all unfolded is deeply moving. "There were no frills," he wrote, "no flashes of lightning, crashes of thunder or voices from the sky, no Steven Spielberg effects, just a simple, quiet, stunningly beautiful miracle. A dying woman being torn away from those who loved and needed her was gently restored to them."[22]

For a little less than two years Joy and "Jack" Lewis knew great and profound happiness. In July 1958, they had a honeymoon in Ireland. They were able to live at The Kilns as husband and wife, taking walks together, falling deeper in love, and finding that laughter was their portion as well. God had given them a gracious interval of great and unlooked-for blessing.

Sadly, it did not last forever. X-rays taken during a routine examination on October 13, 1959, revealed that cancerous spots were once again present on many of Joy's bones. Despite the increasing pain and worry, she and her beloved Jack were able to take a long-planned holiday in Greece with Roger Lancelyn-Green and his wife. They visited Athens, Mycenae, Rhodes, Herakleon, and Knossos—with a one-day stop in Pisa on the return leg of their trip.[23] Despite the pain that Joy felt, it was a golden time and fondly cherished.

Joy Lewis died on July 13, 1960, her devoted husband by her side. Their years together had been few. But they had been years when God came near in ways neither could ever forget. Following C. S. Lewis's death in 1963, the poignant story of their love and life together is one that millions have come to know. Jack Lewis had once written a famous book about miracles. But no account within its pages ever meant more to him than the story of the miracle he knew best: the miracle given to his beloved wife, Joy—something more, and something better, than either of them could have imagined.

26 ✦ Africa: Miracles in the Continent Beloved by God

Semper aliquid novi Africam afferre.
There is always something new out of Africa.

—Pliny the Elder[1]

A miracle of ever-expanding scope is unfolding in Africa, and has been for years. Not that it was expected. As early as the ecumenical conference held in Edinburgh in 1910, no less a person than Nobel Laureate J. R. Mott told his fellow conferees that he believed Africa would be taken over by Islam.[2]

Mott's prophecy proved decidedly false. By 2002, Christian expansion seemed to be constantly gathering momentum. Churches there "were bursting at the seams with an uninterrupted influx of new members."[3]

The history of the modern church in Africa is indeed wonderful. But it is important to note that this history extends into the past to the very advent of Christianity itself. In the New Testament book of Acts, we have the story of Philip and the Ethiopian eunuch, a story attended by miracles. Turning to Acts 8:26–40, we read,

Now an angel of the Lord spoke to Philip, saying, "Arise and go toward the south along the road which goes down from Jerusalem to Gaza." This is desert. So he arose and went. And behold, a man of Ethiopia, a eunuch of great authority under Candace the queen of the Ethiopians, who had charge of all her treasury, and had come to Jerusalem to worship, was returning. And sitting in his chariot, he was reading Isaiah the prophet. Then the Spirit said to Philip, "Go near and overtake this chariot."

So Philip ran to him, and heard him reading the prophet Isaiah, and said, "Do you understand what you are reading?"

And he said, "How can I, unless someone guides me?" And he asked Philip to come up and sit with him. The place in the Scripture which he read was this:

> *"He was led as a sheep to the slaughter;*
> *And as a lamb before its shearer is silent,*
> *So He opened not His mouth.*
> *In His humiliation His justice was taken away,*
> *And who will declare His generation?*
> *For His life is taken from the earth."*

So the eunuch answered Philip and said, "I ask you, of whom does the prophet say this, of himself or of some other man?" Then Philip opened his mouth, and beginning at this Scripture, preached Jesus to him. Now as they went down the road, they came to some water. And the eunuch said, "See, here is water. What hinders me from being baptized?"

Then Philip said, "If you believe with all your heart, you may."

And he answered and said, "I believe that Jesus Christ is the Son of God."

So he commanded the chariot to stand still. And both Philip

and the eunuch went down into the water, and he baptized him. Now when they came up out of the water, the Spirit of the Lord caught Philip away, so that the eunuch saw him no more; and he went on his way rejoicing. But Philip was found at Azotus. And passing through, he preached in all the cities till he came to Caesarea.

An angelic annunciation, the supernatural leading of the Holy Spirit, and an Elijah-like transport from Gaza to Azotus. Three mighty miracles, and all performed so that the gospel could go back with the Ethiopian eunuch to the court of Candace, the queen of the Ethiopians. Christianity was divinely sent to Africa. It found fertile ground and has flourished ever since.

Moving forward from the time of Philip, we come to the city of Hippo Regius, which, during the first three centuries of the Christian era, was one of the richest cities in Roman Africa. However, "the city's chief title to fame," as *Encyclopaedia Britannica* tells us, "was derived from its connexion with St. Augustine (354–430 A.D.), who lived here as priest and bishop for thirty-five years."[4]

As the noted church historian Gustav Krüger has written, Augustine's great work, "the most elaborate, and in some respects the most significant" that came from his pen is *The City of God (De civitate Dei)*. Krüger stated,

> It is designed as a great apologetic treatise in vindication of Christianity and the Christian Church,—the latter conceived as rising in the form of a new civic order on the crumbling ruins of the Roman empire,—but it is also, perhaps, the earliest contribution to the philosophy of history, as it is a repertory throughout of his cherished theological opinions.[5]

The City of God is generally regarded as "the highest expression" of Augustine's thought, while the other work that established his claim to literary immortality was his *Confessions*, considered by many "the best monument of his living piety and Christian experience." The *Confessions* were written shortly after he became a bishop, about 397, and "give a vivid sketch of his early career." As Krüger noted, "To the devout utterances and aspirations of a great soul they add the charm of personal disclosure, and have never ceased to excite admiration."[6] The earliest autobiography in Western literature, it is still considered one of the best, enshrined among such highly regarded collections as the Harvard Classics.

~

During medieval times in northeastern Africa, monastic Christianity, shaped largely by Monophysite or Coptic doctrine, exercised a wide influence. These believers used the canonical books of the Old and New Testaments, which had been translated from Greek into Ge'ez, the old Ethio-Semitic language of the northern highlands, thus transmitting to posterity what is still the liturgical language of the Ethiopian Orthodox Church.[7]

Ethiopian Christianity, which had its beginnings centuries before with the conversion of the Ethiopian eunuch under Philip's supernaturally guided ministry, imparted a great and lasting legacy to Africa. Its monastic nature "inspired large numbers of ordinary lay people to lead lives of great piety."[8]

Today, the Ethiopian Orthodox Church is the largest of the Oriental Orthodox or non-Chalcedonian Orthodox churches, with an estimated 33 million members. The majority of Ethiopian Orthodox live in Ethiopia, but there are also large expatriate communities in America, Canada, Australia, and part of Western Europe. Mention should also be made of the Orthodox Church in Eritrea, which had historically been part of the Ethiopian Orthodox Church, but formally separated from it in 1993. This Christian communion has about 2 million members, and in recent years has spread to the West Indies, where an estimated ninety thousand people have been converted.⁹

Thus it is that these expressions of African Christianity have shaped the growth of Christianity in nations of the West, each conversion a miracle that has resulted in transformed lives. They are part of the beautiful ripple effect of belief.

Further, it may surprise many to learn that the Ethiopian Orthodox Church is one of the oldest officially adopted and still flourishing national churches in the world. In the fourth century AD, Christianity was officially adopted as the religion of the Ethiopian royal court, during the patriarchate of Athanasius of Alexandria. The story of how Christianity was embraced in Ethiopia comes from the writings of Rufinus of Tyre (c. 345–410), who was told the story by Aedesius, an eyewitness to this watershed event.¹⁰

The story unfolds as follows. Two brothers, Frumentius and Aedesius, both native Christians from Tyre, were shipwrecked on the Red Sea coast. Taken as slaves to the Ethiopian royal court, Frumentius became the tutor for the king's son, while Aedesius became the king's cupbearer. Though suffering had brought them to this place, they were ideally suited to teach and commend the Christian faith. God wrought miracles of conversion through them, and a small community of believers soon developed. Rufinus also reported that "Roman merchants who were Christians" benefited as well from the teaching of Frumentius.¹¹

When the king's son succeeded to the throne, Aedesius returned to Tyre, but Frumentius went to Alexandria to seek a bishop for the growing Ethiopian Christian community. He was himself awarded this honor and returned to Ethiopia, becoming the first of a long succession of bishops appointed by the See of Alexandria.¹²

Moving south from the Ethiopian Orthodox Church—to the lower reaches of the African continent—and moving forward in time, there are stirring contemporary accounts of conversions taking place in South Africa and beyond. "Mission Africa," created in fellowship with the Third Lausanne Congress on Global Evangelization, commenced in Cape Town in October 2010. But the vision of Mission Africa has been truly continental in scope. Evangelists from around the world were paired with local ministry organizations at a total of twenty-one sites from Sudan to South Africa, from Liberia to Tanzania.[13]

Scott Lenning, who has led the Mission Africa initiative with colleagues Songe Chibambo and Eliot Winks, has been amazed by the response of people throughout the continent. "[God] has chosen Africa to carry the touch of the Gospel to the world," he said, and, indeed, if numbers are any measure of what has been taking place, God has been moving mightily. Early reports for Mission Africa estimate a total attendance of 488,394 at 890 meetings, with 58,245 responses from "individuals inquiring about a relationship with Christ."[14]

Mission Africa traces its spiritual inspiration to the precedent established by Billy Graham at the original Lausanne Congress in 1974, where a crusade was held in Lausanne in addition to the congress. And so, when it came to Mission Africa, local leaders "did not want to limit the potential evangelistic events to just Cape Town or even South Africa, but to take them to as much of Africa as possible."[15]

Lenning and Chibambo have both sensed the movement of God in all that has transpired to date with Mission Africa. As Lenning said: "Songe and I have adopted a saying to work by: 'Attempt something so big for God that it is doomed to failure unless God be in it.' We definitely feel God has been in Mission Africa to see this level of involvement and response."[16]

Lamin Sanneh, an eminent scholar of the history of missions and currently D. Willis James Professor of Missions and World Christianity at

Yale, has written widely about the spread of Christianity in Africa during the last forty years. Africa has been undergoing seismic political change, but amid the horrific violence of genocide and political conflict, Christianity has endured—indeed it has grown at an incredible rate. Sanneh reported,

> By 1985, it had become clear that a major expansion of Christianity had been under way in Africa in spite of prevailing pessimism about the imminent collapse of postindependent states, and of waning confidence in the church in Europe. Although they were little prepared for it, the churches found themselves as the only viable structures remaining after the breakdown of state institutions, and as such had to shoulder a disproportionate burden of the problems of their societies. Ironically, Christian Africans came predominantly from the poor and marginalized. By 1985 there were over 16,500 conversions a day, yielding an annual rate of over 6 million. In the same period, (i.e. between 1970 and 1985), some 4,300 people were leaving the church on a daily basis in Europe and North America.[17]

This is heartening news and, according to Sanneh, there seems to be no reason to think that more extraordinary trends won't continue. "The story of Christianity is still unfolding," he wrote, "[and] is still cutting for itself fresh channels in Africa. We do not yet know how that story will end. All we know is that many more are yet to join that story."[18]

~

What is taking place in Africa has touched a chord with many around the world who see Christianity as a great blessing and boon to a war-torn, disease-ravaged continent. On December 27, 2008, Matthew Parris, a prominent atheist, wrote an article for the Sunday *Times of London* that caught many readers' attention. It bore the title "As an Atheist, I Truly

Believe Africa Needs God." Parris's lengthy account is deeply moving and all the more powerful since it was written by someone who does not subscribe to a Christian worldview.[19]

Before Christmas 2008, after an absence of forty-five years, Parris returned to the country he'd known during his boyhood as Nyasaland. "Today it's Malawi," Parris wrote, "and *The Times* Christmas Appeal includes a small British charity working there. Pump Aid helps rural communities to install a simple pump, letting people keep their village wells sealed and clean. I went to see this work."[20]

Parris was inspired by what he saw, particularly as his faith in development charities, as such, had been diminished over the years. But there was something else that he could not account for. "Travelling in Malawi," he said, "refreshed another belief, too: one I've been trying to banish all my life, but an observation I've been unable to avoid since my African childhood. It confounds my ideological beliefs, stubbornly refuses to fit my world view, and has embarrassed my growing belief that there is no God."[21]

It was here that Parris, "a confirmed atheist," made an astounding statement. "I've become convinced of the enormous contribution that Christian evangelism makes in Africa: sharply distinct from the work of secular NGOs, government projects and international aid efforts. These alone will not do. Education and training alone will not do. In Africa Christianity changes people's hearts. It brings a spiritual transformation. The rebirth is real. The change is good."[22]

Parris's rare honesty made for a deeply compelling account. He wrote openly of how he used to engage in acts of avoidance when it came to the question of spiritual transformation—its very reality—let alone whether it did any good if it was real. He wrote,

> I used to avoid this truth by applauding—as you can—the practical work of mission churches in Africa. It's a pity, I would say, that salvation is part of the package, but Christians black and white, working in

Africa, do heal the sick, do teach people to read and write; and only
the severest kind of secularist could see a mission hospital or school
and say the world would be better without it. I would allow that if
faith was needed to motivate missionaries to help, then, fine: but what
counted was the help, not the faith.[23]

Wrestling with all that he'd witnessed, Parris had to change his way of
thinking. Valuing the "help" but not the "faith" component of things was
no longer tenable. As he reflected, "It doesn't fit the facts. Faith does more
than support the missionary; It is also transferred to his flock. This is the
effect that matters so immensely, and which I cannot help observing."[24]

Beyond this portion of Parris's article, his words took on the tone of
a testimony. What he'd seen of Christians in Africa, in the past and in
the present, touched him in ways that lingered in memory.

First, there were the missionaries Parris had known as a child. "As
a child I stayed often with them," he recalled. "I also stayed, alone with
my little brother, in a traditional rural African village. In the city we
had working for us Africans who had converted and were strong believers. The Christians were always different. Far from having cowed or
confined its converts, their faith appeared to have liberated and relaxed
them. There was a liveliness, a curiosity, an engagement with the world—
a directness in their dealings with others—that seemed to be missing in
traditional African life. They stood tall."[25]

Now, reflecting on his recent trip to Malawi, he had experiences
that were much the same.

I met no missionaries. You do not encounter missionaries in the lob-
bies of expensive hotels discussing development strategy documents,
as you do with the big NGOs. But instead I noticed that a handful of
the most impressive African members of the Pump Aid team (largely
from Zimbabwe) were, privately, strong Christians.

"Privately" because the charity is entirely secular and I never heard any of its team so much as mention religion while working in the villages. But I picked up the Christian references in our conversations. One, I saw, was studying a devotional textbook in the car. One, on Sunday, went off to church at dawn for a two-hour service.[26]

Little things that left a big impression, and ones not easy to dismiss. "It would suit me," Parris confessed, "to believe that their honesty, diligence and optimism in their work was unconnected with personal faith. Their work was secular, but surely affected by what they were. What they were was, in turn, influenced by a conception of man's place in the Universe that Christianity had taught."[27]

The close of Parris's article is startling in its implications for Africa and its future, and for Parris's perspective itself. "Christianity," he wrote, "post-Reformation and post-Luther, with its teaching of a direct, personal, two-way link between the individual and God, unmediated by the collective, and unsubordinate to any other human being, smashes straight through the philosophical/spiritual framework [of] crushing tribal groupthink."[28] A groupthink, Parris maintains, that has been the bane of Africa, leading to so many of the ills and atrocities that make for horrific news reports to the West.

"A whole belief system must first be supplanted," Parris concluded, "and I'm afraid it has to be supplanted by another. Removing Christian evangelism from the African equation may leave the continent at the mercy of a malign fusion of Nike, the witch doctor, the mobile phone and the machete."[29]

~

"God has chosen Africa to carry the touch of the Gospel to the world," Scott Lenning was quoted as saying earlier in this chapter. Just maybe, in view of all that has been said, Lenning is right. Maybe the faith of Africa can renew the faith of the West. If the way that that faith has touched Matthew Parris is any indication, such a renewal may be coming. If it does, would that not be a miracle of beautiful proportions, and devoutly to be wished?

27 ✦ Clyde Kilby: Joy and the Miracle of Being

The heavens declare the glory of God.

—Psalm 19:1

. . . like stars streaming splendour through the sky.

—James Montgomery[1]

The literary scholar Clyde Kilby bequeathed many gifts to posterity, not least his visionary commitment to establishing the Marion E. Wade Center at Wheaton College, a world-class research center for the books and papers of seven British authors: Owen Barfield, G. K. Chesterton, C. S. Lewis, George MacDonald, Dorothy L. Sayers, J. R. R. Tolkien, and Charles Williams.

Dr. Kilby, who died in 1986, also touched the lives of many students during the years that he taught literature at Wheaton. One of them was pastor John Piper, who earned his doctorate in theology from the University of Munich. Dr. Piper is a prolific and eloquent teacher and the author of many widely acclaimed books. They are, and have been, a source of blessing to many. But if one had to choose the blessing for which Dr. Piper himself is most grateful, near the top of the list might be a lecture he heard in October 1976 from Clyde Kilby. Piper wrote,

> It was an unforgettable lecture. I went to hear him that night because I loved him. He had been one of my professors in English Literature at Wheaton College. He opened my eyes to more of life than I knew could be seen. O, what eyes he had! He was like his hero, C. S. Lewis, in this regard. When he spoke of the tree he saw on the way to class . . . you wondered why you had been so blind all your life.[2]

To read Piper's recollection of this special event is to be reminded anew of the gifts great teachers can impart to their students, perhaps only one student, in ways that change their lives. "That night," Piper remembered, "Dr. Kilby had a pastoral heart and a poet's eye."

> He pled with us to stop seeking mental health in the mirror of self-analysis, but instead to drink in the remedies of God in nature. He was not naïve. He knew of sin. He knew of the necessity of redemption in Christ. But he would have said that Christ purchased new eyes for us as well as new hearts. His plea was that we stop being unamazed by the strange glory of ordinary things.[3]

Dr. Kilby concluded his lecture with a list of ten resolutions designed to remind us that, as the psalmist wrote, we are "fearfully and wonderfully made." So, too, is the world that we inhabit, the world that is "our Father's world."[4] As the poet and hymn writer Maltbie Babcock has written:

> *This is my Father's world, and to my listening ears*
> *All nature sings, and round me rings the music of the spheres.*
> *This is my Father's world: I rest me in the thought*

CLYDE KILBY · 257

Of rocks and trees, of skies and seas;
His hand the wonders wrought.

Babcock was a kindred spirit to Dr. Kilby. A gifted athlete, he had been a superb baseball pitcher and swimmer. To stay fit during the years of his pastorate at the First Presbyterian Church in Lockport, New York, he would hike in the early morning to the crest of a high hill two miles away and gaze into the distance at Lake Ontario. It was his habit before setting out on each day's sojourn to tell his church staff, "I am going out to see my Father's world."[5]

Dr. Kilby's resolutions strike a chord in unison with such thoughts. They celebrate the miracle God bestows on each of us in the gift of life and the world we inhabit. The gift of life was first given Adam and Eve, but before they had drawn their first breath, God had spoken the world into being from nothing through the almighty power of His word.

Here is mystery and wonder enough for a lifetime, something Dr. Kilby knew well. And so he wrote in resolution one: "At least once every day I shall look steadily up at the sky and remember that I, a consciousness with a conscience, am on a planet traveling in space with wonderfully mysterious things above and about me."[6]

For this thought, a scriptural counterpart could be found in the book of Job 9:8–10:

> *He alone spreads out the heavens,*
> *And treads on the waves of the sea;*
> *He made the Bear, Orion, and the Pleiades,*
> *And the chambers of the south;*
> *He does great things past finding out,*
> *Yes, wonders without number.*

In resolution number two, Kilby stated,

Instead of the accustomed idea of a mindless and endless evolutionary change to which we can neither add nor subtract, I shall suppose the universe guided by an Intelligence which, as Aristotle said of Greek drama, requires a beginning, a middle, and an end. I think this will save me from the cynicism expressed by Bertrand Russell before his death when he said: "There is darkness without, and when I die there will be darkness within. There is no splendor, no vastness anywhere, only triviality for a moment, and then nothing."[7]

Dr. Kilby's thinking here has a moving scriptural corollary in Revelation 21:5–6:

Then He who sat on the throne said, "Behold, I make all things new." And He said to me, "Write, for these words are true and faithful." And He said to me, "It is done! I am the Alpha and the Omega, the Beginning and the End. I will give of the fountain of the water of life freely to him who thirsts."

In his third resolution, Dr. Kilby described how each day is itself a gift from God, come what may. He stated,

I shall not fall into the falsehood that this day, or any day, is merely another ambiguous and plodding twenty-four hours, but rather a unique event, filled, if I so wish, with worthy potentialities. I shall not be fool enough to suppose that trouble and pain are wholly evil parentheses in my existence, but just as likely ladders to be climbed toward moral and spiritual manhood.[8]

Here, the words of the psalmist in Psalm 84:10 seem particularly appropriate: "For a day in Your courts is better than a thousand."

In resolution four, Dr. Kilby nailed his colors firmly to the mast, saying, "I shall not turn my life into a thin, straight line which prefers abstractions to reality. I shall know what I am doing when I abstract, which of course I shall often have to do."[9]

This is a line of thought that resonates deeply with the Amplified Bible's rendering of Job 11:13–15. "Set your heart aright," it begins, "and stretch out your hands to [God] . . . put sin out of your hand and far away from you and let not evil dwell in your tents; then can you lift up your face to Him without stain [of sin, and unashamed]; yes, you shall be steadfast and secure."

A determined resolve to see that we are, each of us, unique and made so by a gifting from God informs the fifth resolution Dr. Kilby crafted. There he wrote, "I shall not demean my own uniqueness by envy of others. I shall stop boring into myself to discover what psychological or social categories I might belong to. Mostly I shall simply forget about myself and do my work."[10] Here, 1 Thessalonians 5:5–6 is most fitting as a scriptural counterpart: "You are all sons of light and sons of the day. We are not of the night nor of darkness. Therefore let us not sleep, as others do, but let us watch and be sober."

"I shall open my eyes and ears," Dr. Kilby declared in resolution number six.

> Once every day I shall simply stare at a tree, a flower, a cloud, or a person. I shall not then be concerned at all to ask what they are but simply be glad that they are. I shall joyfully allow them the mystery of what Lewis calls their "divine, magical, terrifying and ecstatic" existence.[11]

Here, one cannot help but be drawn to the words of Isaiah 55:12: "For you shall go out with joy, and be led out with peace; the mountains and the hills shall break forth into singing before you, and all the trees of the field shall clap their hands."

"I shall sometimes look back," said Kilby in resolution seven, "at the freshness of vision I had in childhood and try, at least for a little while, to be, in the words of Lewis Carroll, the 'child of the pure unclouded brow, and dreaming eyes of wonder.'"[12] Here one seems to hear an echo, unmistakably, of the words of our Lord in Matthew 19:14: "But Jesus said, 'Let the little children come to Me, and do not forbid them; for of such is the kingdom of heaven.'"

In resolution eight, Kilby heeded wise counsel from an unlikely source, Charles Darwin. But it was good advice. So, Kilby declared, "I shall follow Darwin's advice and turn frequently to imaginative things such as good literature and good music, preferably, as Lewis suggests, an old book and timeless music." Here, the words of James 1:17 are a welcome companion: "Every good gift and every perfect gift is from above, and comes down from the Father of lights."

That God gives every moment of our lives and ought to be thanked for such was the overarching sentiment behind Kilby's ninth resolution. "I shall not," he wrote, "allow the devilish onrush of this century to usurp all my energies but will instead, as Charles Williams suggested, 'fulfill the moment as the moment.' I shall try to live well just now because the only time that exists is now." Here, the words of Ecclesiastes 3:1 seem most appropriate: "To everything there is a season, a time for every purpose under heaven."

A note of holy defiance shaped the last of Kilby's resolutions, the tenth. "Even if I turn out to be wrong," he stated emphatically, "I shall bet my life on the assumption that this world is not idiotic, neither run by an absentee landlord, but that today, this very day, some stroke is being added to the cosmic canvas that in due course I shall understand with joy as a stroke made by the architect who calls himself Alpha and Omega." And here we have a purposeful return to Psalm 19, cited in the epigraph for this chapter. There, in verses 4 to 6, we read, "He has set a tabernacle for the sun, which is like a bridegroom coming out of his chamber, and rejoices like a strong man to run its race. Its rising is from one end of heaven, and its circuit to the other end." To the cosmic canvas, indeed.

～

In September 2008, on what would have been Clyde Kilby's 106th birthday, John Piper once again paid tribute to his memory. Whereas many assayed to teach English literature, Piper remembered, Kilby seemed to *live* it. He seemed to possess an "extraordinarily awake, God-oriented palate for wonder in poetry and nature."[13]

To sit in Dr. Kilby's classroom, Piper continued, was to sit before a man who knew what it was to "exult in beauty and wonder." Never once did he say "this poem is amazing. He *was* amazed. He didn't just say the last chapters of the book of Job are mind-boggling glimpses of God's power and wisdom. His mind *was* boggled. It was irresistibly contagious."[14]

One might well wish to have been a student in Kilby's classroom, for as Piper recalled, "We sat there and for the first time we *saw* things. We *felt*. We were drawn into the bright day of wakefulness out of our self-preoccupied, adolescent slumbers."[15]

Kilby was a man who had drunk deep of literature, learning what it was to love God with one's mind. He had drunk deeply of laughter as well, as one day in class revealed. It was at that time, Piper stated, that Dr. Kilby came to the passage in Job that speaks of the ostrich. "This is the one I remember best. O how he laughed that God made the Ostrich 'stupid.' That's what his translation said. 'God has made her forget wisdom and given her no share in understanding.'"

In this seminal classic of ancient literature, God was confronting Job with breathtaking wonders. And God said, "I made the Ostrich stupid!

Match that, Job." This, Piper said, "was not a theological problem for Kilby. God was God. This was simply amazing. He gave us one of the greatest gifts—amazement at what we see."[16]

Kilby's closing words left an impression that has lingered for more than forty years. He said earnestly that "what America needs is a great poet. . . . A prophet-poet who could capture the heart of the nation and lift it out of itself to a transforming vision of the ultimately Beautiful."[17]

In the late 1960s, when Kilby spoke these words, it was a time of great ferment. Nineteen sixty-eight, in particular, was a time when many wondered if the nation was coming apart at the seams. So many were searching for ultimate answers, trying to find the true, the good, and the beautiful. John Piper's enduring debt to Clyde Kilby was that his teacher had reminded him and his fellow students where the true, the good, and the beautiful were to be found—miracles woven into the world around us and the cosmos beyond—to say nothing of the miracle of life. Dr. Kilby knew what it was to celebrate the miracle of our humanity. We are children of a mighty, matchless Creator. We ought to enjoy, even revel, in His good gifts.

28 ✦ The Grace of a Dream: Miracles in Academia

Now I beg all those that listen to this little treatise . . . or read it, that if there be anything in it that pleases them, they thank our Lord Jesus Christ for it, from whom proceeds all understanding and goodness.

—*The Canterbury Tales*[1]

I had built myself a fortress of atheism, secure against any attack by irrational faith. And I lived in it, alone." So runs the closing sentence from chapter 2 of *Not God's Type*, a moving modern conversion narrative written by Dr. Holly Ordway. Hers is the story of how a miracle unfolded within the halls of academia. Like so many in that setting, she was not looking for God. Quite the reverse. But she would discover, as Augustine had centuries before her, that God has formed us for Himself, and our hearts are restless until they find their rest in Him.

In ways she could not have imagined, Ordway was to discover the great truth given the world by the poet John Donne: no one is an island. God called to her in myriad ways: through poetry, the gift of a wise Christian friend, and last of all, the miracle of a dream that proved a final catalyst for her embrace of faith.

One of the most powerful aspects of Ordway's book is its unflinching honesty. She pulls no punches in describing her years as an atheist and the ways that she then regarded Christians. "At thirty-one years old," she wrote, "I was an atheist college professor—and I delighted in thinking of myself that way. I got a kick out of being an unbeliever; it was fun to consider myself superior to the unenlightened, superstitious masses, and to make snide comments about Christians."[2] She continued, "I knew next to nothing about Christianity, and cared less, I began to mock Christians and belittle their faith, their intelligence, their character."[3]

These comments all sound as though they were made by someone quite comfortable in her choice of worldview. And yet, as Ordway admitted, there was one shard of a stubborn truth she could not easily dismiss. So many atheists, she learned over time, felt the crushing weight of their conviction that life was ultimately meaningless. Given over to despair, several of them tragically took their own lives.

Ordway had no desire for a faith in any Christian sense, but she could not bring herself to believe that life had no meaning. "I felt that life had to be worth living,"[4] she wrote. Though she little knew at the time, or would have recognized it as such, this realization was to be the first of many intimations of immortality—an insight that began to foster a slow, even at times reluctant, pilgrimage that would eventually lead to faith's door.

Another gift that God had given her, though she didn't see it as such, was a self-described stubborn belief "that there was such a thing as truth." More than this, she "valued truth as an absolute good." This fostered within her a great desire "to know, and live by the truth—no matter what."[5]

From such a foundation of honesty within the human heart, God can do mighty things, and God began to do just that in Ordway's life. Poetry proved the road upon which she began to reconsider the truth claims of Christianity. In this, her journey to faith was to be not unlike that of C. S. Lewis, who once memorably said of his own path from atheism to belief: "A young man who wishes to remain a sound Atheist cannot be too careful of his reading. There are traps everywhere—'Bibles laid open, *millions of surprises*,' as [George] Herbert says, 'fine nets and stratagems.' God is, if I may say it, very unscrupulous."[6]

It was, in fact, poets like George Herbert who proved crucial to Ordway's embrace of faith. Herbert had written of the "heart in pilgrimage,"[7] and such was now the condition of her heart.

The path through poetry to faith began, she wrote, with John Keats, whose "Ode on a Grecian Urn" closed with the immortal lines: "Beauty is truth, truth beauty,—that is all ye know on earth, and all ye need to know."

Such lines are hard to dismiss with the kind of thought that says, "That's a nice sentiment," and let it go at that. Ordway found herself drawn to these lines in ways she never had been before. She wrote that she "could feel power thrumming" in the poetry she was now reading—verse that seemed to possess "an electricity of meaning."[8]

Another poem God placed on Ordway's path was John Donne's Holy Sonnet 14. It was a most potent "fine net and stratagem," to use C. S. Lewis's phrase. Four lines in particular from Donne's sonnet spoke to her heart with undisguised power:

> *Batter my heart, three-person'd God; for you*
> *As yet but knock; breathe, shine, and seek to mend;*
> *That I may rise, and stand, o'erthrow me, and bend*
> *Your force, to break, blow, burn, and make me new.*[9]

Upon reading these words, Ordway said she felt moved in a way she had never been moved before.[10] The close of the sonnet was utterly arresting. "I, except you enthrall me, never shall be free." Here, Ordway offered a forthright confession: "The words, once alien to me apart from my appreciation of their technical precision, now felt alive and powerful."[11]

At or about the same time, she began a careful reading of T. S. Eliot's classic poem "The Journey of the Magi." Ordway's recollection of that experience remains vivid and transformative. She wrote,

> That poem was, along with Donne's, one of the first to shake me out of my despair and wake me up to the possibility of something more. The narrator in Eliot's poem could easily have been myself on this journey—more than half convinced that the whole endeavor was foolishness, yet continuing on the journey anyway, drawn by something outside myself. And that critical realization at the end that this Birth was also Death—and that nothing, nothing, could ever be the same. When once I realized that Christ truly is who he claimed to be, I could not go back to the old country of atheism unchanged, clutching my old gods.[12]

The last of Ordway's poetic guiding spirits was in some ways the most welcome. She had been holding out for hope, longing for it, against a tide of despair that had attended the way of so many atheists. "Hadn't I been feasting on despair for years?"[13] she asked herself. She worried that it might overwhelm her. She was experiencing what she called "the winter of my soul."[14]

In such a setting Gerard Manley Hopkins spoke to her with a power no other poet possessed. For he, too, had once been driven to despair and was nearly shipwrecked there. Yet he had found the way home to hope. It was his poem "Carrion Comfort," a difficult and searingly honest poem, that charted a course for Ordway:

> *But ah, but O thou terrible, why wouldst thou rude on me*
> *Thy wring-world right foot rock? lay a lionlimb against me? scan*

With darksome devouring eyes my bruisèd bones? and fan,

O in turns of tempest, me heaped there; me frantic to avoid thee and flee?

It has been well said that when we try hardest to run from God, we in the end run to Him. All the while He has been waiting there, with arms open wide.

Ordway could not bring herself to admit she was looking for God, but she could admit, as Hopkins had written in another of his poems, "The Windhover": "My heart in hiding/Stirred." Something beyond her experience beckoned, and poetry had broken the hard ground of her heart. Once this was done, another guide to faith awaited her—a very unlikely guide indeed.

∼

Ordway's next guide on her journey to faith turned out to be her fencing coach. An avid fencer for many years, she now wished to become an elite competitor. Her coach would help her accomplish that goal, but he imparted a gift to her far beyond any mastery of technique he could have fostered during their years of training. He was, in point of fact, a committed Christian—a man who could winsomely and compellingly commend his faith. He came alongside her, and—displaying much wisdom, tact, and patience—urged her when he judged the time was right to carefully consider the intellectual case for Christianity.

The gift of two books proved crucial in their ongoing conversation about matters of faith. The first was the text *Does God Exist?* to which the noted scholar and apologist Peter Kreeft had contributed an introductory essay. The second was *Making Sense of the New Testament*, by Craig Blomberg. It says much for Ordway's integrity and honesty that though she felt highly wary of these gifts—rather like she'd just been handed a set of explosives—she agreed to read them, indeed talk about them with her coach when she'd finished. And so, taking notes as she read, Ordway began first with *Does God Exist?*

Straightaway, she encountered a rigorous and caring intellect in Peter Kreeft. In the opening pages of his introductory essay, Kreeft asked two important questions: "Why would someone want to prove God exists?" and, conversely, "Why would someone want to prove God does not exist?" Kreeft's main answer to both questions was one that resonated instantly with Ordway: "Simply for the sake of truth."[15]

Kreeft continued in his fascinating essay to describe two kinds of thinkers: those who are tender-minded and those who are tough-minded. Such a distinction appealed greatly to Ordway, who recalled, "I wanted to know the truth whether or not it helped me to be happy."[16] Clearly, she classed herself with those who would be considered tough-minded thinkers, for as Kreeft had written: "The 'tough-minded' put truth even above happiness."[17]

In the gift of this book, Ordway's coach had shown much wisdom. He knew that she, as an elite competitor, was already tough-minded. What she needed was a book that set out the case of Christianity in a rigorously reasoned, yet compassionate way. Since she had never read a book that made that case as Kreeft did, it was a particularly welcome gift.

But Ordway's coach was also well-schooled in matters of the heart. He had taken an overt step to commend his faith by giving her two books, but once this was done, he gave her time and space to consider what they had to say. "I tried to stay out of the way," he would later recall, "and just let God do the work."[18]

It proved just what was needed. Over time, Ordway reached a place of intellectual assent regarding the truth claims of Christianity. She was given time and space to let God speak to her heart. Such a mark of friendship and counsel is as fine and rare a thing as it is wise.

Following the publication of *Not God's Type*, Ordway herself wrote of how crucial this relational aspect of her coach's sharing his faith was, and also how the Holy Spirit, though she as yet knew little about Him, was guiding her steps in a way she knew not:

> If I were to add anything over and above what I wrote [in my book], at this point it would be to emphasize much more strongly the role that experiencing the Spirit in poetry and story played for me. At the time I wrote *Not God's Type*, I emphasized the apologetic arguments. . . . Now I see more clearly that the experience, of "tasting and seeing," moved me far closer to Christ than I realized before I started thinking about arguments. And I think the role of Christian fellowship and love was far more important than I realized as well.[19]

~

Having read the books her coach had given her, and after many discussions with him about matters of faith, Ordway had come a long way in her understanding of Christianity. She found much about it, and its history, that she felt drawn to. It was in this setting that the miracle of her dream unfolded, leading her at last to the threshold of faith.

One night, the evening before she was slated to fly out to Las Vegas to fence in a regional championship competition, she knew she needed rest. Turning in early, she almost instantly fell asleep.

It was then that she experienced a dream unlike any other she'd ever known. Walking alongside her coach, she saw to her amazement that they were walking the streets of Jerusalem. As they went along, he would point out famous places, holy places sacred to the Christian tradition. He was, as she recalled in the pages of her book, "a Virgil to my Dante, my guide and interpreter. Even in the dream itself I recognized that in some strange way I was acting out *The Divine Comedy*."[20]

At one point in the dream, Ordway and her coach sat down for a few moments on a bench across from a cluster of stone buildings. Pointing to them, her coach said, "That's Jesus' tomb." For several minutes, they watched as thronging crowds of tourists queued up, awaiting the few moments they would each be given to pay homage to the holy and sacred site.

Then, as sometimes is the case in dreams, came a moment of stark realization. Watching this scene unfold, Ordway understood and felt a profound awareness "that Jesus of Nazareth was the Son of the living God."[21] She found herself realizing as well that if Easter were all it was purported to be, if Christ had indeed risen from the dead, then His tomb was really nothing more than a hallowed place of curiosity. "What happened that day," she felt, "was so big, so shattering, that it overshadowed everything else. The tomb was important only because they laid the body of Jesus in it—and because on the third day it was *empty*."[22]

Even as she dreamed, her heart leapt. She awoke with a deep sense of joy in her heart, and one phrase in her mind: *He is risen.* "I lay there," she remembered, "in some small, quiet hour of the morning, abruptly and completely awake. The knowledge from my dream did not fade but stayed sharp and complete in my mind and in my heart."[23]

This gift of knowledge, imparted through a dream, helped Ordway overcome the last of the great barriers to her giving her heart fully to Christ. Heretofore, she had been unwilling to say, "Thy will be done, not mine." To do so meant losing control, the giving of her life to God.

But her dream had somehow instilled her with the strength to make what proved to be the final surrender. She felt released in her dream— free to believe, free to choose. Some fear still lingered, it was true. But she knew, and knew for certain, that she wanted to choose Christ.

∼

Are dreams, as one writer has clinically noted, "nothing but incoherent ideas, occasioned by partial or imperfect sleep"?[24]

Within the divine economy, they can be much more, far more, than incoherent ideas. They can be, if God so wills it, the stuff of which deliverance can come, as in the dream God gave to Joseph to flee from the wrath of Herod—or a means by which God bestows a gift to the human heart or mind, as He did in bestowing the gift of wisdom to young Solomon, the king of ancient Israel.

The book of Acts cites an Old Testament prophecy from the book of Joel to describe what will happen in the days following Christ's ascension into heaven: the age of the church. This prophecy has a direct bearing on the gift of dreams.

> And it shall come to pass, in the last days, says God, that I will pour out of My Spirit on all flesh; your sons and your daughters shall prophesy, your young men shall see visions, your old men shall dream dreams. And on My menservants and on My maidservants I will pour out My Spirit in those days. (2:17–18)

God gave Holly Ordway the gift of a dream as she learned about the Christian faith. Could there be a lovelier miracle? And here her story recalls one of the finest passages from G. K. Chesterton's writings. "The place," Chesterton wrote, "that the shepherds found, was not an academy or an abstract republic; it was not a place of myths . . . explained or explained away. It was a place of dreams come true."[25]

29 ✦ The God of All Hope: Miracles in the Place of Brokenness

For the sighing of the needy, now will I arise, saith the LORD; I
will set him in safety from him that puffeth at him.

—PSALM 12:5 KJV

Dwell upon the firstness of his love, dwell upon the freeness of his love,
the greatness of his love, the fulness of his love, the unchangeableness of
his love, the everlastingness of his love, and the activity of his love. . . .
Dwell upon what God hath undertaken for you. Dwell upon the choice
and worthy gifts that he has bestowed on you; and dwell upon that
glory and happiness that he has prepared for you.

—THOMAS BROOKS[1]

To speak with Pastor Mark Rivera is to speak with someone who knows firsthand that God is "mighty to save."[2] He's known many moments of hardship, but many moments as well of incredible blessing. Miracles have attended his way—gifts of a God who has graciously guided his steps. That thought is never far from his mind, and Mark would be the first to say, "Surely goodness and mercy shall follow me all the days of my life" (Ps. 23:6).

"I think that God's purpose is to constantly reveal the nature of His character, and his power in our lives," he said. "Miracles of God happen all around us."[3] Mark shared these words in a recent interview, and there could be no finer summary of what he has witnessed in his life—no finer summary of the hope he cherishes for all whom he meets. "Let me tell you what the Lord has done for me" is a phrase that comes easily to him. And it was in such a setting that a remarkable conversation took place—one in which Mark spoke of the extraordinary work of God in his life.

The first miracle that I ever experienced was when God came to me when I was fifteen years old. I was a very fractured and broken young man. I remember at nine years old walking away from my faith, wanting absolutely nothing to do with God.

I was a child evangelist. I would travel the country with my dad, preaching at some of the largest venues you could ever imagine. And for an eight-year-old kid to do that is unheard of.

But I remember that at eight years old, I could read and write both English and Spanish. I learned how to read and write English and Spanish from the Bible. I would remember reading passages of Scripture, and thoughts coming, and then my dad would say, "We're gonna go to Pennsylvania this week and you're gonna preach."

And I'd say, "Okay."

So I'd get before large groups, read a passage of Scripture, and the Holy Spirit would illuminate my little eight-year-old mind, and I'd get up and literally trance out, and just begin to speak before these audiences. And then, at the end, I would be so overwhelmed and overcome by the Holy Spirit that I would begin crying. And that's when my father knew that it was time for him to come up and close out the worship service. And we would see hundreds of people come to Jesus.

Now, that happened when I was just eight years old. And then, when I was nine years old, I found out that my father had an extramarital affair with one of the women from our church, and it literally just devastated and broke our family up. And I remember at nine years old going up to my mother and saying, "Mom, please don't force me to ever go to church again. I want nothing to do with God. 'Cause I don't understand why a good God would ever have allowed this to happen to our family."

And I don't know if this was the wisest move my mother ever made, or maybe it was a foolish move—but it was the decision obviously that God wanted her to make, and she said, "Son, I can't force you to accept my faith, so your faith has to be your own. But I need to tell you this: God will never leave you, nor forsake you."

And I said, "Well, okay, Mom, but please don't ever force me to go to church again." So for the next six years, I never set foot in a church.

During this time, my best friend—I was running in some really bad circles, doing a lot of horrible things over the course of my early teens—was murdered violently. He was shot sixteen times in the chest by another gang, and I remember calling my mother, saying, "Mom, the same death that my friend Larry experienced is probably gonna befall me. I need to get out of here. And as much as I hate my father, I need to probably go live with him."

And she said, "Well, I don't want to lose you. Just give me six months to move. I will move our family—wherever we need to move to."

I said, "Mom, I'm gonna give you six months. But in six months, if we're not out of here—I have to get out of here."

It was pretty audacious for a fourteen-year-old kid to draw that final line in the sand with my mom, but what a godly woman. She quit her job. We sold all of our belongings, and we moved down to Florida.

Well, in Florida, I wish I could say that my life had changed. But it didn't. I still was involved in many of the same patterns and behaviors, and I didn't have a very happy life.

I remember one morning—I was a pretty accomplished boxer, and I'd gotten into the habit of waking up pretty early in the morning, a lot of times before the sun was even up. And this one morning was no different. It was about 5 a.m., and in my bedroom I had a mattress on the floor under a large window. I didn't have a headboard or a footboard, it was just a mattress on the floor.

Well, like I said, it was five in the morning, and all I remember was this huge bright light coming into my room. The first thing I thought was, *Oh, maybe the Orange County Sherriff's Department has a helicopter or something close by, and they're chasing after someone.*

So I remember getting up and pulling the shades. But I couldn't see anything but light. And I knew that it wasn't a headlight from a car, or anything like that, because there was an eight-foot wall that ran around the perimeter of the property where we lived. And I remember lying back down and thinking to myself, *I can't explain it, but there's something holy about this moment*—because I wasn't afraid. I remember just lying there.

Then, all of a sudden, I heard an audible voice, saying, "I will never leave you, nor forsake you."

And I can't tell that story without breaking down in tears every time I tell it, because I'm awed—I'm so amazed at how God would use the same exact words that He put in my mother's mouth six years prior to that, when I wanted nothing to do with Him—that those same words and those same thoughts—that His words in Scripture would become alive to me that morning when He revealed Himself to me.

And that has been the only time that I ever heard God speak to me in an audible way.

But what ended up happening after that was that I remember this sense of awakening happening inside of me, and I remember all of a sudden hearing the Holy Spirit speak to me like He used to when I was eight years old.

And God gave me this little three-point plan for my life in that moment. He said, "I want you to be the best son you can be to your mother. I want you to reestablish your relationship with me, and I want you to dedicate yourself to your studies."

Just those three simple things He told this fifteen-year-old kid down in Orlando, Florida. And that was how He revealed Himself to me.

I became radically saved again that day. I got intimately involved in ministry at our local church, and I found a wonderful, God-believing church.

∼

Pastor Rivera had another incredible story to share. He said,

I have a half brother whose journey has been very troubled. He has never really committed his life to the Lord, and one morning, my wife and I were driving into work together, and I got a phone call saying, "Javier's been shot three times in the stomach. He was rushed to Boston, and he's not expected to make it."

And you know, my heart broke. Because of all the years that I'd had before that to spend with him, I felt this sense of urgency in wanting to share the gospel with him, and I was never successful in persuading him to make a decision for Christ.

I immediately thought, *Man, if he dies—I know what is waiting for him.*

I remember looking at my wife and saying, "We have to go down to Boston—now."

So I flew down to Boston. We parked the car, and we rushed upstairs. I grabbed my Bible, and I went into the hospital room. And as I did, the doctor came over to me, and he said, "Look, I need to prepare you for what's coming. I need to tell you right now that the next time I come into this room, be prepared to hear that you have lost your brother. There's uncontrolled bleeding, your brother is literally swollen to twice the size of his normal body because of all the bacteria and all of the adverse effects of the gunshot wound. Every vital organ in his chest has been ripped apart, and we cannot stop the bleeding. And I am so sorry to have to report this to you."

And then he said, "We can't even close him up because of all the swelling that's going on."

So he painted the grimmest picture I could ever imagine. And I looked at my wife. "This can't be how God ends this story."

I remember saying, "Guys, I want to pray—I want to pray. Because I don't believe that Javier's gonna die." I said, "They're telling us to prepare for death, and I pray today—I want to prepare for life."

We got together, and we prayed like you wouldn't believe. And the minute we joined hands, and we started praying—and I remember that prayer so vividly—I said, "Lord, where the modern medicine and wisdom of man ends, I want your glory to begin. They're saying, 'It's over' and I say it's just the start for you to do your greatest work in his life right now." I said, "Stop that bleeding, in Jesus' name."

The nurse came into the room as we were still praying, and I remember her saying, "Whoa, there's a power in here I can't explain," and she walked out.

We finished our prayer. Two minutes later the doctor walked in and said, "Folks, I can't explain what just happened in that operating room, but the bleeding has stopped. The swelling has gone down, and

Javier is stable now." Then he paused, and said, "But he probably will never walk again."

Well, I get to tell you that not only did Javier live, and has suffered zero ramifications of that shooting, but he can walk too. Even though he has broken fragments of his spine still inside him and modern medicine can't explain why he's walking.

And I just wanted to say that after it was all over that awful night, and the doctors and nurses had made sure Javier was stable, the nurse came in and said, "You guys prayed for the bleeding to stop, and when I walked into the operating room, the doctors all looked at themselves and said, 'Hey, guys, the bleeding has stopped.' And they started just giving each other high fives *as if they had done something*, but they couldn't explain *how* the bleeding had stopped."

~

Sometimes mercy runs to meet us at our point of greatest need. And sometimes mercy comes in the form of a miracle, like the father who runs to meet his prodigal son and embraces him, saying, "This was my son who was lost, and now is found."

It was Jesus who told that story in Luke's gospel, and it is Jesus whose mercy runs to meet all the prodigal sons and daughters lost to Him, and to themselves. It has been well said that gospel means finding the way home, finding one's way to Christ. Miracles are meant to point the way to Him. Mark Rivera has found that to be true, and in ways he will never forget.

Afterword + His names of goodness, wisdom, power, and love

God moves in a mysterious way,
His wonders to perform;
He plants His footsteps in the sea,
And rides upon the storm.

Deep in unfathomable mines
Of never failing skill;
He treasures up His bright designs,
And works His sovereign will.

—William Cowper[1]

There have been so many miracles over the years—I call them "God-incidences."

—Lady Davson, the third great-granddaughter
of William Wilberforce[2]

I see it every time I walk up the stairs of our home into the third-floor room we call "The Little Library." There, on a dry wooden beam near the gable end of our house, is the black scorch mark that constantly reminds us our home was miraculously saved from burning down.

My wife and I weren't home when the bolt of lightning struck, shattering part of a sixty-foot-high tree near our house, then ricocheting down from the tree to our roof. Where the bolt hit the roof, several shingles were blown away and scattered on the ground below. But what was most extraordinary was the scorch mark left on the gable end rafter. Our taciturn insurance adjuster said it best: "I don't use the word *miracle* often," he said, "but I can't understand why your house didn't burn down."

Nor was this the only time that we and our home were spared from serious injury or catastrophic damage. One night in late summer, after two weeks of steady, worrisome rain, a windstorm came through the seaside village where we live. It was about nine o'clock in the evening, when, all of a sudden, we heard a great crash and felt our house shudder.

A massive maple tree had come up by the roots in our backyard and fallen across our house. As it fell, it narrowly missed the in-law apartment where my parents reside over our carriage house. Nor did it strike the main part of our home, where my wife and I live. Instead, the tree fell onto the roof of our breezeway and screen porch.

Opening the front door of our home, I saw leafy branches hanging over the roof. Going back to the screen porch, which had taken the brunt of the fall, I fully expected to see the broken edges of branches that had come through the roof. All I could think was, *I'm so grateful everyone's okay, but boy, we're going to have some serious cleaning up and repairs to do.*

But I was wrong. There weren't any branches that had pierced through the roof of the screen porch or the breezeway. Going outside, I could see the great maple tree—looking for all the world as though it had merely decided to lean up against our house for a bit to rest.

When the tree removal company came the next day to remove the fallen maple, it proved quite a job. The tree was large and had to be carefully taken apart, one section at a time. Once the topmost portion of the tree had been cleared from our roof, what remained of the trunk of the tree sat back down, as it were, in its accustomed place on our lawn. From that point on, it was a simple matter of finishing the job of cutting the tree down.

However, once the tree had been cut away from the roof, our tree remover called down from the roof to say: "Hey, you won't believe this, but there isn't one shingle up here that needs to be replaced. Not one."

Among our collection of old snapshots, we have a picture of that large maple fallen across our roof. Should I ever need reminding that miracles do happen, or that they're closer than I think, I can pull that picture out, or simply walk upstairs to the Little Library. There, as it always will be, is the scorch mark from a lightning strike that never burst into a flame.

~

There are times when miracles find us in ways we cannot forget. I believe this book has explored something of that truth. I hope it has, and I hope those who've read it might better understand that we live in the midst of miracles. They are part of our history. They grace the present and are the hope of the future. We cannot know precisely how they will find us next, but we can know when we seek God they cannot be far away. It is certain that He is never far from our point of greatest need.

For myself, God came near in a way that is unmistakable.

For years, my wife and I tried to have children, but we could not. The shared pain of miscarriage caused us searing grief. For a long time, I found it very hard to speak of the children we had lost. I still do. Sometimes the wound is too tender to touch.

I found solace in remembering that God knows what it's like to lose a child. He understands.

Beyond this, however, I cannot know why He gathered our little ones to Himself. A wise elderly cousin, now departed, once told me that some things have to be left with God. I believe he was right.

But it helped me a great deal when I read one reflection from the writings of D. L. Moody, a saint to whom I owe many debts of gratitude. He loved God deeply and vibrantly, and I have learned many things from him.

One of the most enduring of my debts was incurred the first time I read the following story.

A bereaved father asked me the other day if I thought the little one he had lost had gone to be with Jesus. I could only tell him what David said when he lost his son, "I shall go to him, but he shall not return to me."

It is a very sweet thought to me, and it must be to you also who have lost little ones, that the King can take better care of them than we can. If we could look into the eternal city we should see the Shepherd leading them by the green pastures and the still waters.

"What will make heaven our home?" Moody asked on another occasion.

It is not so much the white robes, the golden crown, or the harps of gold; but it is the society we shall meet there that will make heaven our home. Who, then, are there? What company shall we have when we get there? Jesus is there, the Holy Father is there, the Spirit is there—our Father, our elder Brother, our Comforter. Who else is there? The angels are there; dear departed friends are there. And the little ones;—ah! they are there too.[3]

What a blessed hope.

But then, when I thought any chance of our having children had passed, God stepped into our lives. My wife gave birth to a son. We called him Samuel, that beautiful old Hebrew name that means "God hears." So He had—and He blessed us with the greatest gift I have ever known.

We laugh and tell ourselves that we won't put too much pressure on Sam by telling him that he's a living miracle. But beneath the laughter, we know it's true.

Sam isn't perfect; far from it. Now five years old, there are times when he tries our patience, and times when even living miracles don't want to go to bed yet. He gets scraped knees and talks back once in a while. But then he also shares sunsets with us, thinks ocean waves play tag, and holds my hand when I walk with him. He scores goals on me when we play soccer, and he's getting good with a baseball bat.

I tell him I smile inside when I see him. For a moment, he seems wiser than his years, and seems to know that I mean.

Others with whom we've shared Sam's story have found him a source of blessing too. I am really rather staggered by that thought. But I suppose miracles are like that. Something of their sacredness comes from being shared.

A friend told us once that seeing Sam's picture made God's goodness real to her. For that, Kelly and I can only feel gratitude beyond words. What can we say? Sam is a living, daily reminder to us that miracles happen.

Someday, when he is older, we will tell him why we look on him as our miracle child. I'm not quite sure how we'll do it, but in God's good time, I know He'll show us how.

ACKNOWLEDGMENTS

I could never have written this book were it not for the vision and commitment of Joel Miller, Vice President of Editorial and Acquisitions at Thomas Nelson Publishers. His was the original inspiration for this project, and his the guiding hand through every facet of the publishing process. I am deeply indebted to him for this, and for the gift of his friendship. The same holds true for my literary agent, Bucky Rosenbaum, whose wise counsel, unfailing kindness, and professionalism have been indispensable.

To all on the Thomas Nelson team who have had a hand in the creation of this book, particularly my editor, Kristen Parrish, my sincere and continuing thanks. The concert of your talents has made all the difference.

I should here like to pay tribute to the memory of Dr. John R. W. Stott, whose books have been an abiding source of inspiration and enrichment throughout my life. I fondly remember meeting him as an undergraduate, and shall never forget the warmth of his smile, nor his kind words of greeting and encouragement. As with so many the world over, my debt to his scholarship and vibrant witness is very great.

I wish to thank Os and Jenny Guinness for so many fine memories, and such a wonderful series of visits this past summer at Oxford. Bless you both.

Lady Davson, a treasured friend of many years, bestowed the gift of her description of what miracles are—and told me with a twinkle in her eye, "You may use that!" I am honored to do so, and honored by the gift of her friendship. Until we meet again in Rye, Kate.

Ranald Macaulay and Jonathan Aitken showed me much kindness likewise during Oxbridge 2011, as did Joseph Pearce, Malcolm Guite, Randy Alcorn, Vishal Mangalwadi, Colin Duriez, and Mary Poplin. To be one of "the three musketeers" along with Steve Bell and Holly Ordway was a most welcome gift, as was the time I spent in company with Andrew Lazo and DeAnn Barta—Oxbridge alums one and all. I should say as well that meeting Walter Hooper and Michael Ward during my time at Oxbridge was a privilege.

Among my UK friends, I am especially grateful to David Isherwood, Brian Edwards, Bill and Gill Aldred, and Marylynn Rouse. Your kind hospitality has been a hallmark of my visits across the pond.

To Charlie and Suzanne Olcott, and Eric and Margie Donaldson, I can never thank you enough for the wonderful visits I've had while staying in D. L. Moody's Northfield. And to Dave Powell (Mr. Moody's great-grandson), and his lovely wife, Lucia—the gift of your friendship is greatly treasured, especially time spent with you at Round Top, Northfield Mount Hermon, and visits to Rustic Ridge. Alex and Hilda Stewart have also shown me and my family much kindness, and for that I thank them very much indeed. To all other Northfield friends—space doesn't allow for me to thank you as fulsomely as I might wish, but every moment with you is fondly remembered.

Holly Ordway and Mark Rivera have graciously allowed me to share something of how miracles have unfolded in their lives. For that honor, I thank them most sincerely.

A quote from Keith Green appears as the epigraph for a chapter in this book, and I wish to acknowledge here how deep and abiding an influence his music has had upon me, ever since my teens. Just after his passing, I received a card from Last Days Ministries, asking me if I would be willing to serve as a counselor for a concert Keith was slated to give at Dartmouth College in October 1982. That concert was never to be, and I never did get the chance to meet him. But each time I listen to his music, I remember all over again the desire he fostered in me to want to live for God. It's never left me, and for that I bless his memory.

In a similar vein, and in view of kind correspondence, I wish to thank Michael Nachtigal, the manager of Classic Petra. The release of CP's album *Back to the Rock* has been a glad reunion with songs that are good friends. Many thanks to the guys in the band—for all the blessings, music, and memories. My son, Sam, is now a fan too—five years young—but old enough to know, "These guys rock!" We sing with every song—"Second Wind," "Godpleaser," "Adonai," and all the rest.

And, so far as Sam is concerned, he and my wife, Kelly, have, as ever, been models of patience and encouragement. They have given me time to write, and the gift of their love. These things, and their never-failing support, have helped me stay the course. Sam has made his father's heart glad by being a sports-bud, cheering on the Red Sox and the New England Patriots, and treating me to many good games of soccer, football, and baseball. Never has a man had a finer wife and son. I know how blessed I am, and thank God for it.

ABOUT THE AUTHOR

An award-winning author and historian, Kevin Belmonte served for six years as the lead historical and script consultant for the major motion picture *Amazing Grace*. His biography of William Wilberforce has also been taught as part of a course on leadership and character formation at Harvard's Kennedy School of Government, and he is the author of *Defiant Joy*, a critically acclaimed literary biography of G. K. Chesterton. On several occasions he has served as a script consultant for the BBC, and also for PBS. He resides in New England with his wife, Kelly, and their five-year-old son, Sam.

NOTES

1. Gerard Manley Hopkins, *Poems of Gerard Manley Hopkins*, ed. Robert Bridges (London: Humphrey Milford, 1918), 14.
2. Jeremy Taylor, *The Rule and Exercises of Holy Living* (New York: E.P. Dutton and Company, 1876), 414.
3. William Shakespeare, *All's Well That Ends Well*, act 2, scene 1, words spoken by Helena.

PREFACE

1. G. K. Chesterton, *The Innocence of Father Brown* (London: Cassell & Company, 1911), 6.
2. Walter A. Elwell, ed., *Evangelical Dictionary of Theology* (Grand Rapids, MI: Baker Academic, 2001), 420. Dr. Elwell (PhD, University of Edinburgh) is emeritus professor of biblical and theological studies at Wheaton College. He attended the University of Chicago and University of Tübingen before earning his PhD, and has edited numerous biblical reference works, including *The Baker Theological Dictionary of the Bible*.
3. Billy Graham, *The Holy Spirit* (Nashville: Thomas Nelson, 2000), 215.
4. Henry H. Halley, *Halley's Bible Handbook with the New International Version* (Grand Rapids, MI: Zondervan, 2007), 164.
5. Donald K. McKim, *The Westminster Dictionary of Theological Terms* (Louisville: Westminster/John Knox Press, 1996), 175. Here, McKim describes the miracles of Jesus as follows: "The various supernatural actions of Jesus as recorded in the Gospels. Theologically they are regarded as signs of his divinity and power over natural and cosmic forces and are revelatory of God's nature and purposes (see Matt. 8–9)."
6. Here, I have combined two separate statements from Martin Luther cited in Sidney Greidanus, *Preaching Christ from the Old Testament: A Contemporary Hermeneutical Method* (Grand Rapids, MI: William B. Eerdmans, 1999), 120.

7. Erwin Lutzer, *Seven Reasons Why You Can Trust the Bible* (Chicago: Moody Publishers, 2008), 42.
8. Greidanus, *Preaching Christ from the Old Testament*, 120.

PART I: MIRACLES OF THE ANCIENT WORD

CHAPTER 1: IN THE BEGINNING: THE MIRACLE OF OUR WORLD

1. St. John Chrysostom, as quoted in Kallistos Ware, *The Orthodox Way* (Crestwood, NY: St. Vladimir's Seminary Press, 1995), 44.
2. William Cowper, "The Winter Morning Walk," in H. S. Milford, ed., *The Complete Poetical Works of William Cowper*, Oxford Edition (London: Henry Frowde, 1905), bk. 5, lns. 686 – 87. Emphasis added.
3. Walter A. Elwell, ed., *Evangelical Dictionary of Theology* (Grand Rapids, MI: Baker Academic, 2001), 420.
4. William Cowper, "The Winter Morning Walk," in *The Poetical Works of William Cowper*, Book 5, *The Task* (London: Oxford University Press, 1926), lns. 810–12. For the sake of clarity, I have slightly paraphrased Cowper's lines.
5. Kallistos Ware, *The Orthodox Way* (Crestwood, NY: St. Vladimir's Seminary Press, 1979), 44.
6. The information presented in this paragraph and the quote therein are from Howard Clark Kee, "Miracles," in Bruce M. Metzger and Michael David Coogan, eds., *The Oxford Companion to the Bible* (New York: Oxford University Press, 1993), 519.
7. Ibid.
8. Ibid.
9. Ibid.
10. Ibid.

CHAPTER 2: CREATION: THE MIRACLE OF HUMANITY

1. Samuel Taylor Coleridge, *On the Constitution of the Church and State*, vol. 6 of *The Complete Works of Samuel Taylor Coleridge*, ed. W. G. T. Shedd (New York: Harper & Brothers, 1884), 54.
2. John Milton, *Paradise Lost*, in *Cowper's Milton, in Four Volumes*, vol. 2 (Chichester: W. Mason, 1810), bk. 4, lns. 362–63.
3. Matthew Henry, *An Exposition on the Old and New Testament* (London: Joseph Robinson, 1828), 1:6.
4. Ibid.
5. Ibid. Emphasis added.
6. Ibid, 13. Emphasis added.
7. Billy Graham, *The Secret of Happiness* (Nashville: Thomas Nelson, 2002), 18.
8. Ibid.
9. D. L. Moody, *Eleven Sermons Never Before Published* (New York: Christian Herald, 1911), 138.
10. Graham, *The Secret of Happiness*, 18.

11. John C. Lennox, *Seven Days That Divide the World* (Grand Rapids, MI: Zondervan, 2011), 72.

12. Ibid.

13. Ibid.

CHAPTER 3: GOD'S DECLARATION: THE MIRACLE OF OUR PROMISED REDEMPTION

1. C. S. Lewis, quoted in Clyde Kilby, ed., *A Mind Awake: An Anthology of C. S. Lewis* (New York: Macmillan, 1968), 21.

2. John Stott, *The Radical Disciple* (Downers Grove, IL: IVP, 2010), 49–50.

3. J. Edwin Hartill, *Principles of Biblical Hermeneutics* (Grand Rapids, MI: Zondervan, 1960), 111.

4. Stott, *The Radical Disciple*, 49–50. The author has added the words in brackets.

5. Matthew Henry, *An Exposition on the Old and New Testament* (London: Joseph Robinson, 1828), 1:15.

6. Ibid., 16.

7. Ibid.

8. J. D. Douglas, Merrill C. Tenney, and Moises Silva, *The Zondervan Illustrated Bible Dictionary* (Grand Rapids, MI: Zondervan, 2011), 1195.

9. Matthew Henry, *An Exposition of the Old and New Testament* (Philadelphia: Haswell, Barrington & Haswell, 1838) 1:43–44.

10. John Newton, *The Works of the Rev. John Newton: Complete in One Volume* (London: T. Nelson and Sons, 1853), 525.

CHAPTER 4: NOAH AND THE FLOOD: MIRACLES OF DELIVERANCE

1. C. H. Spurgeon, *Evening by Evening* (New York: Sheldon and Company, 1869), 346.

2. Matthew Henry, quoted in *The Christian Treasury* (Edinburgh: Johnstone, Hunter & Co., 1883), 287.

3. Matthew Henry, *An Exposition on the Old and New Testament* (London: Joseph Robinson, 1828), 1:40.

4. Ibid., 1:65.

5. All quotes are from Walter Kaiser, *Toward an Old Testament Theology* (Grand Rapids, MI: Zondervan, 1991), 80.

6. Ibid., 81.

7. Ibid., 80–81.

8. The information presented in this paragraph, and the quote therein, is from Howard Clark Kee, "Miracles," in Bruce M. Metzger and Michael David Coogan, eds., *The Oxford Companion to the Bible* (New York: Oxford University Press, 1993), 519.

9. Ibid.

10. Ibid.

11. Ibid.

12. Ibid.

13. John Newton, *The Works of John Newton* (Philadelphia: Uriah Hunt, 1839), 2:175.

CHAPTER 5: ABRAHAM: MIRACLES AND THE FRIEND OF GOD

1. Billy Graham, *Angels* (Nashville: Thomas Nelson, 1995), 98.
2. Douglas K. Stuart, *The New American Commentary* (Nashville: B&H Publishing Group, 2006), 2:113–14. I would here like to acknowledge the many kindnesses shown to me by Dr. Stuart during my graduate studies at Gordon-Conwell Seminary. Dr. Stuart was my student advisor and a source of much wit and wisdom. I have fond memories of time spent in his company.
3. Graham, *Angels*, 99.
4. Ibid.
5. Ibid.
6. Ibid., 98–100.
7. Warren W. Wiersbe, *The Bible Exposition Commentary: New Testament* (Colorado Springs, CO: Victor/Cook Communications, 2001), 2:300.
8. Ibid.
9. Ibid.
10. Bruce D. Barton, David R. Veerman, and Linda K. Taylor, *Hebrews*, eds. James Galvin, Ronald Beers, and Philip Comfort (Carol Stream, IL: Tyndale Publishers, 1997), 92.
11. Ibid.
12. Warren W. Wiersbe, *The Wiersbe Bible Commentary: The Complete Old Testament* (Colorado Springs, CO: David C. Cook, 2007), 77.
13. Ibid.
14. Ibid.
15. Ibid., 77–78.

CHAPTER 6: MOSES: MIRACLES OF THE EXODUS

1. Samuel Wilberforce, *Heroes of Hebrew History* (London: W. H. Allen and Co., 1890), 92–130.
2. M. D. Dunnam, *The Preacher's Commentary* (Nashville: Thomas Nelson, 2002), 2:23.
3. Douglas K. Stuart, *The New American Commentary* (Nashville: B&H Publishing Group, 2006), 2:109.
4. Dunnam, *The Preacher's Commentary*, 2:59.
5. Ibid.
6. Ibid., 64.
7. Ibid., 59.
8. Stuart, *The New American Commentary*, 2:113–14.
9. Wilberforce, *Heroes of Hebrew History*, 110–11.
10. Ibid.
11. Howard Clark Kee, "Miracles," in Bruce M. Metzger and Michael David Coogan, eds., *The Oxford Companion to The Bible* (New York: Oxford University Press, 1993), 519.
12. Ibid.

13. Ibid.
14. Wilberforce, *Heroes of Hebrew History*, 118.
15. John Piper, *The Pleasures of God: Meditations on God's Delight in Being God* (Sisters, OR: Multnomah Publishers, Inc., 2000), 103.
16. Ibid.
17. Ibid.
18. Peter Enns, *Exodus: The NIV Application Commentary* (Grand Rapids, MI: Zondervan/HarperCollins, 2000), 131. Peter Enns, a most distinguished scholar, holds a PhD in Near Eastern Languages and Civilizations from Harvard University.
19. W. G. Scroggie, *The Unfolding Drama of Redemption* (Grand Rapids, MI: Kregel Publications, 1995), 153.
20. Ibid., 154.
21. Ibid.
22. Ibid., 156.

CHAPTER 7: ELISHA: MIRACLES IN THE TIME OF THE PROPHETS

1. A letter from John Newton to Hannah More, September 7, 1791, see page 375 of *Memoirs of the Life and Correspondence of Hannah More*, vol. 1, edited by William Roberts, (New York: Harper & Brothers, 1834).
2. Herbert Lockyer, *All the Miracles of the Bible* (Grand Rapids, MI: Zondervan, 1988), 116.
3. Ibid.
4. Ibid.
5. Ibid.
6. Ibid.
7. Charles Simeon, *Horae Homileticae* (London: Richard Watts, 1819), 3:108.
8. Ibid., 108–109.
9. Ibid., 109.
10. Ibid.
11. Ibid.
12. Ibid.
13. Lockyer, *All the Miracles of the Bible*, 116.
14. Ibid.
15. Ibid., 119.
16. Matthew Henry, *An Exposition of the Old and New Testament* (London: Joseph Robinson, 1828), 1:936.
17. Ibid.
18. Simeon, *Horae Homileticae*, 5:49.
19. Ibid.
20. Ibid.
21. Ibid.
22. Lockyer, *All the Miracles of the Bible*, 126.
23. Ibid.

CHAPTER 8: THE PROMISE OF HIS COMING: THE
MIRACLE OF THE INCARNATION

1. Hannah More, *The Complete Works of Hannah More* (New York: Harper & Brothers, 1835), 1:376.
2. C. S. Lewis, *Miracles* (New York: HarperCollins, 2001), 173.
3. G. K. Chesterton, *Poems* (New York: Dodd, Mead and Company, 1922), 64.
4. The closing words of Rev. 22:16 (KJV).
5. For an excellent discussion of the incarnation, see the articles posted online by David Mathis at desiringgod.org, the ministry website for John Piper. The phrase used here is taken from David Mathis, "Advent and the Incarnation," *Desiring God* (blog), December 7, 2007, http://www.desiringgod.org/blog/posts/advent-and-the-incarnation. Accessed March 15, 2012.
6. Timothy George, "The Blessed Evangelical Mary," *Christianity Today*, December 1, 2003, http://www.christianitytoday.com/ct/2003/december/1.34.html?start=2. Accessed March 15, 2012.
7. Ibid.
8. Josh MacDowell, *Josh MacDowell's Handbook on Counseling Youth* (Nashville: Thomas Nelson, 1996), 221.
9. Warren W. Wiersbe, *The Wiersbe Bible Commentary: The Complete New Testament* (Colorado Springs, CO: David C. Cook, 2007), 140.
10. This and the quotes and information in the following paragraphs are taken from George, "The Blessed Evangelical Mary."
11. Ibid.
12. Ibid.
13. Ibid.
14. Ibid.
15. Ibid.
16. Ibid.
17. G. K. Chesterton, "The God in the Cave," in *The Everlasting Man* (New York: Dodd, Mead and Company, 1925), 209.
18. Packer's discussion of what the incarnation is appears in J. I. Packer, "Good Question: Incarnate Forever," *Christianity Today*, March 1, 2004, http://www.christianitytoday.com/ct/2004/march/25.72.html. Accessed March 15, 2012.
19. David Mathis, "Jesus Is Fully Human," *Desiring God* (blog), December 13, 2007, http://www.desiringgod.org/blog/posts/jesus-is-fully-human. Accessed March 15, 2012.
20. Packer, "Good Question: Incarnate Forever."
21. Jeremy Taylor, *The Great Exemplar of Sanctity and Holy Life According to the Christian Institution; Described in the History of the Life and Death of the Ever-Blessed Jesus Christ, the Saviour of the World* (London: Longman, Brown, Green, and Longmans, 1850), 55.
22. Ibid., 51.
23. Ibid., 52.

24. Thomas Aquinas, in Joseph Rickaby, ed., *Of God and His Creatures: An Annotated Translation (with Some Abridgement) of the Summa Contra Gentiles of Saint Thos Aquinas* (London: Burns & Oates, 1905), 359.

25. John Stott, *The Cross of Christ* (Downers Grove, IL: InterVarsity Press, 2006), 159.

26. Ibid., 176.

27. Ibid., 260–61.

28. Ibid., 284.

29. G. K. Chesterton, *Poems* (New York: Dodd, Mead and Company, 1922), 64.

CHAPTER 9: SIGNS AND WONDERS: THE MIRACLES OF JESUS

1. Jeremy Taylor, *The Whole Works of Jeremy Taylor* (London: Ogle, Duncan and Co., 1822), 15:21–22. Here, I have slightly altered the wording and punctuation of Taylor's prose.

2. T. S. Eliot, *Four Quartets* (New York: Mariner Books, 1968), 18.

3. Herbert Lockyer, *All the Miracles of the Bible* (Grand Rapids, MI: Zondervan, 1988), 152.

4. Ibid., 152.

5. Luke 4:17–19, where the story of Jesus reading out from the scroll of Isaiah in the synagogue is told.

6. John Stott, *Basic Christianity* (Grand Rapids, MI: Eerdmans, 2008), 42.

7. Ibid.

8. Ibid.

9. Ibid.

10. The two quotes in this paragraph are Ibid., 42–43.

11. Randy Alcorn, ed., *We Shall See God: Charles Spurgeon's Classic Devotional Thoughts on Heaven,* (Carol Stream, IL: Tyndale House Publishers, Inc., 2011), 119–20.

12. Albert Wolters, as quoted in Randy Alcorn, *Heaven* (Carol Stream, IL: Tyndale House Publishers, Inc., 2004), 89.

13. Charles H. Spurgeon, *Sermons Preached and Revised* (London: Passmore & Alabaster, 1877), 22:637.

14. Ibid.

15. These Greek words for *miracle* are fully explored in Lockyer, *All the Miracles of the Bible*, 15–16.

16. Ibid., 15.

17. Ibid.

18. Ibid.

19. Frédéric Louis Godet, *Commentary on the Gospel of St. John* (Edinburgh: T. & T. Clark, 1881), 13.

20. Lockyer, *All the Miracles of the Bible*, 16.

21. Ibid.

22. Herbert Lockyear, *All the Miracles of the Bible* (Grand Rapids, MI: Zondervan, 1988), 16.

23. John Laidlaw, *The Miracles of Our Lord: Expository and Homiletic* (New York: Funk & Wagnalls, 1892), 11–12. John Laidlaw, DD, was professor of theology at New College, the University of Edinburgh.
24. Ibid.
25. Ibid.
26. Ibid.
27. Ibid.

CHAPTER 10: THE CRUCIFIXION AND RESURRECTION: THE MIRACLES OF OUR REDEMPTION

1. John Bunyan, *The Pilgrim's Progress* (Hartford: Silas Andrus, 1827), 56.
2. G. K. Chesterton, *The Ball and the Cross* (New York: John Lane Company, 1909), 206–207.
3. John Stott, *What Christ Thinks of the Church* (Grand Rapids, MI: Eerdmans, 1972), 47.
4. Kenneth W. Osbeck, *Hallelujah, What a Savior: 25 Hymn Stories Celebrating Christ Our Redeemer* (Grand Rapids, MI: Kregel Publications, 2000), 25. Here it is stated that this public domain hymn was composed by Robert Lowry in 1874.
5. I have here combined a series of statements from Hannah More, *The Works of Hannah More: Including Several Pieces Never Before Published* (Philadelphia: Edward Earle, 1818), 8:258, 260.
6. "The risen Christ, our hope" is a phrase used as a heading by the NKJV for 1 Cor. 15:12–19.
7. The Episcopal Church, *The Book of Common Prayer* (Oxford: W. Baxter, 1825), 180.
8. Hannah More, *An Essay on the Character . . . of Saint Paul* (London: T. Cadell, 1815), 2:216–217.
9. Billy Graham and C. S. Lewis, as quoted in Nancy Gibbs et al., "The Message of Miracles," *Time*, June 24, 2001. The *Time* magazine article is posted online at http://www.time.com/time/magazine/article/0,9171,133993,00.html. Accessed March 15, 2012.
10. A. R. Fausset, *The Critical and Expository Bible Cyclopaedia* (London: Hodder and Stoughton, 1893), 478.
11. Alister McGrath, *What Was God Doing on the Cross?* (Eugene, OR: Wipf & Stock Publishers, 2002), 14.
12. The quote and information in this paragraph is taken from John Stott, *Basic Christianity* (Grand Rapids, MI: William B. Eerdmans, 1971), 46.
13. Ibid.
14. George MacDonald, *The Miracles of Our Lord*, (London: Strahan & Co., Publishers, 1870), 226. Emphasis added.
15. Ibid., 268.
16. C. H. Spurgeon, *The Metropolitan Tabernacle Pulpit* (London: Passmore & Alabaster, 1860), 36:452.

CHAPTER 11: A LIGHT FROM HEAVEN: THE MIRACLE OF PAUL'S CONVERSION

1. From the spoken prelude to Keith Green, vocal performance of "Altar Call," recorded 1983, on *I Only Want To See You There*, Sparrow Records.
2. John Stott, *Why I Am A Christian* (Downers Grove, IL: InterVarsity Press, 2003), 18–23.
3. Ibid., 19.
4. Ibid.
5. Ibid., 20.
6. Ibid., 21.
7. Ibid.
8. C. S. Lewis, *Surprised by Joy* (New York: Harcourt, Brace, 1955), 226. As quoted in Stott.
9. Stott.
10. Ibid., 23.
11. Ibid.
12. Robert Wilberforce and Samuel Wilberforce, *The Life of William Wilberforce* (London: John Murray, 1838), 1:381.
13. See 2 Peter 3:15–16, where Peter states, "Our beloved brother Paul, according to the wisdom given to him, has written to you, as also in all his epistles, speaking in them of these things, in which are some things hard to understand."

PART II: MIRACLES IN THE LIVES OF GOD'S PEOPLE

1. The Psalms, Hymns and Spiritual Songs of the Rev. Isaac Watts (Boston: Crocker & Brewster, 1858), 186.

CHAPTER 12: PERPETUA: MIRACLES IN THE LIFE AND DEATH OF A MARTYR

1. From an endorsement by Leighton Ford appearing in Gerald L. Sittser, *Water from a Deep Well: Christian Spirituality from Early Martyrs to Modern Missionaries* (Downers Grove, IL: Inter-Varsity Press, 2010), preface.
2. Tertullian, quoted in Samuel Eliot, *The History of Liberty: The Early Christians* (Boston: Little, Brown and Company, 1853), 1:246.
3. Ibid.
4. Ibid., 246–47.
5. Ibid., 247.
6. T. Herbert Bindley, trans., *The Epistle of the Gallican Churches* (London: The Society for Promoting Christian Knowledge, 1900), 62–63.
7. The text appearing above of Perpetua's prison biography is taken from Bindley, *The Epistle of the Gallican Churches* 62–76.

CHAPTER 13: AUGUSTINE: MIRACLES IN THE LIFE OF A PHILOSOPHER

1. Saint Augustine, *Confessions* trans. Garry Wills (New York: Penguin Classics, 2008), introduction.
2. Charles W. Eliot, "Introduction," in Saint Augustine, *The Confessions of St.*

Augustine, Harvard Classics (New York: P. F. Collier & Son, Company, 1909), 4.

3. *The Catholic Encyclopedia*, s.v. "St. Augstine of Hippo," http://www.newadvent .org/cathen/02084a.htm.

4. Saint Augustine, *The Confessions of St. Augustine*, trans. E. B. Pusey (New York: P. F. Collier & Son Company, 1909), 7:141–143. For the sake of clarity, I have here paraphrased from Pusey's translation.

5. Peter Brown, *Augustine of Hippo: A Biography* (Berkeley: University of California Press, 2000), 421.

6. Ibid.

7. Saint Augustine, *Essential Sermons*, trans. Edmund Hill (Hyde Park, NY: New City Press, 2007), 338.

8. Ibid., 256.

9. Ibid., 148.

10. Saint Augustine, *Sermons* (Hyde Park, NY: New City Press, 1992), 3:44.

11. Augustine, *Supra*.

12. Saint Augustine, *The City of God*, trans. and ed. Marcus Dods (Edinburgh: T & T Clark, 1888), 1:401.

13. Ibid.

14. Ibid.

15. Ibid., 408.

16. Ibid., 409.

17. Ibid.

18. Ibid. Emphasis added.

19. Saint Augustine, *The City of God* (Edinburgh: T & T Clark, 1888), 1:392.

20. Ibid., 393.

21. Ibid., 392–94.

22. Ibid., 394.

23. Ibid.

CHAPTER 14: JULIAN OF NORWICH: MIRACLES IN THE VISIONARY REALM

1. *An Essay Towards a Topographical History of the County of Norfolk*, (London: William Miller, 1806), 81.

2. Hugh Pearson, *Memorials of the Church and Parish of Sonning* (Reading: Edward J. Blackwell, 1890), xli.

3. Julian of Norwich, *Revelations of Divine Love*, ed. Warrack, xviii–xix. See also the brief biographical sketch of Julian that appears in Julian of Norwich, *Revelations of Divine Love*, trans. Elizabeth Spearing (London: Penguin Classics, 1999).

4. Julian of Norwich, *Revelations of Divine Love*, trans. Spearing.

5. T. S. Eliot's indebtedness to Julian's *Revelations* is acknowledged in the brief biographical sketch of Julian that appears in Julian of Norwich, *Revelations of Divine Love*, trans. Spearing.

6. T. S. Eliot, *The Four Quartets* (New York: Mariner Books, 1968), 45.

7. Julian of Norwich, *Revelations of Divine Love*, ed. Warrack, 62, 84.

8. John Bunyan, *The Pilgrim's Progress* (London: Nathaniel Ponder, 1678), 1.

9. Julian of Norwich, *Revelations of Divine Love,* ed. Warrack, 5.

10. Ibid., 8.

11. Ibid., 10.

12. Ibid., 11.

13. Ibid.

14. Saint Augustine, *The Confessions,* trans. J. G. Pilkington (Edinburgh: T & T Clark: 1876), 1.

15. Julian of Norwich, *Revelations of Divine Love,* trans. Spearing, biographical sketch.

16. Julian of Norwich, *Revelations of Divine Love,* ed. Warrack.

17. Ibid.

18. Ibid., 22.

19. Ibid., 23.

20. Ibid., 54.

21. Ibid., 54–55.

22. Ibid., 63.

23. Ibid., 69–70.

24. Ibid., 71.

25. Ibid., 72.

26. Ibid.

27. Ibid., 74. Emphasis added.

CHAPTER 15: MARTIN LUTHER: MIRACLES AND
THE DAWN OF THE REFORMATION

1. Rev. E. Mueller, trans. and Rev. P. Anstadt, ed., *Luther's Explanatory Notes on the Gospels* (York, PA: P. Anstadt & Sons, 1899), 93.

2. *The Encyclopaedia Britannica,* vol. 17, 11th ed., s.v. "Martin Luther" (New York: The Encyclopaedia Britannica Company, 1911), 17:133–140. This essay was written by the renowned church historian Thomas Martin Lindsey, LLD, DD, principal of the United Free Church College, Glasgow, and at one time assistant to the professor of Logic and Metaphysics in the University of Edinburgh, later professor of Church History, F.C. College, Glasgow. Among his works, Lindsey was the author of two highly regarded scholarly texts: *A History of the Reformation,* (New York: Charles Scribner's Sons, 1906) and *Luther and the German Reformation* (Edinburgh: T & T Clark, 1900).

3. Ibid.

4. Ibid.

5. Ibid.

6. Ibid.

7. Ibid.

8. Heiko Oberman, *Luther: Between God and the Devil* (New Haven: Yale University Press, 2006), 180.

9. Ibid., 182.

10. *The Encyclopaedia Britannica,* s.v. "Martin Luther."

11. "Bernard of Clairvaux: Medieval Reformer and Mystic," *Christian History*, http://www.christianitytoday.com/ch/131christians/moversandshakers/bernardclairvaux.html. Accessed March 15, 2012. See also Brian Patrick McGuire, ed., *Jean Gerson: Early Works* (Mahwah, New Jersey: Paulist Press, 1998), ix, xiv.
12. *The Encyclopaedia Britannica*, s.v. "Martin Luther."
13. Ibid.
14. Ibid.
15. Roland Bainton, *Here I Stand: A Life of Martin Luther* (New York: Penguin Books/Meridian, 1995), 63.
16. Ibid., 60.
17. Mueller, trans., Mueller, ed., *Luther's Explanatory Notes on the Gospels*, 49–50.
18. Ibid., 47.
19. Ibid.
20. Ibid., 48.
21. Ibid. Emphasis added.
22. Ibid. Emphasis added.
23. Ibid., 93–94.
24. Ibid.
25. Ibid.
26. Ibid., 65.
27. Ibid.
28. Ibid.
29. Ibid., 347.
30. Ibid.
31. Ibid.
32. Ibid.

CHAPTER 16: GILBERT BURNET: MIRACLES AND THE CHURCH OF ENGLAND

1. Gilbert Burnet, *An Exposition of the Thirty-Nine Articles of the Church of England* (Oxford: Oxford University Press, 1845), 24.
2. A description offered by the African American scholar and writer David Bradley in the PBS documentary created about U. S. Grant for the series, *The American Experience*. The transcript of this documentary containing Bradley's description of Grant is posted online at: http://www.pbs.org/wgbh/americanexperience/features/transcript/usgrant-transcript/.
3. Hugh Chisolm, ed., *The Encyclopaedia Britannica*, 11th ed. (New York: The Encyclopaedia Britannica Company, 1910), 4:851.
4. Ibid., 852.
5. T. E. S. Clarke and H. C. Foxcroft, *A Life of Gilbert Burnet: Bishop of Salisbury* (Cambridge: At the University Press, 1907), 328.
6. Burnet, *An Exposition of the Thirty-Nine Articles of the Church of England*, 28.
7. Ibid., 23.
8. Ibid., 46.

9. Ibid.
10. Lennox's summary of Lewis's argument, vis-à-vis David Hume's rejection of miracles, appears in Andrew Lazo and Mary Anne Phemister, *Mere Christians: Inspiring Stories of Encounters with C.S. Lewis* (Grand Rapids, MI: Baker Books, 2009), 163.
11. Burnet, *An Exposition of the Thirty-Nine Articles of the Church of England,* 46.
12. G. K. Chesterton, as quoted in Hugh Kenner, *Paradox in Chesterton* (London: Sheed & Ward, 1947), 104.
13. Burnet, *An Exposition of the Thirty-Nine Articles of the Church of England,* 65. Emphasis added.
14. Ibid., 66. Emphasis added.
15. Ibid.
16. Ibid.
17. Ibid., 76.
18. Ibid., 75.
19. Ibid., 77–78.

CHAPTER 17: JONATHAN EDWARDS: MIRACLES AND THE GREAT AWAKENING

1. George Marsden, *Jonathan Edwards: A Life* (New Haven: Yale University Press, 2004), 236.
2. Vishal Mangalwadi, *The Book That Made Your World: How the Bible Created the Soul of Western Civilization* (Nashville: Thomas Nelson, 2011), 378.
3. Marsden, *Jonathan Edwards: A Life,* 227.
4. I am here indebted to Jeff Lacine's excellent summary of Davenport's divisive actions, which is part of the article, "The Pastoral Touch of Jonathan Edwards: Three Examples," *Desiring God* (blog), September 11, 2010, http://www.desiringgod.org/blog/posts/the-pastoral-touch-of-jonathan-edwards-three-examples. Accessed March 15, 2012.
5. The information and summary used in this paragraph is from Marsden, *Jonathan Edwards: A Life,* 233.
6. Ibid.
7. Jonathan Edwards, *The Works of President Edwards* (New York: Leavitt & Allen, 1858), 1:525.
8. Ibid.
9. Ibid.
10. Ibid., 526.
11. Ibid., 527.
12. Ibid.
13. Ibid.
14. Ibid.
15. Ibid., 528.
16. Ibid.
17. Ibid., 528–529.
18. Ibid.

19. Ibid., 531.
20. Ibid.
21. Ibid. I have altered the word order slightly in this citation for clarity's sake.
22. Ibid.
23. Ibid., 539.
24. Ibid., 541.
25. Ibid., 543.
26. Ibid., 544.
27. Ibid.

CHAPTER 18: DAVID HUME: THE CASE AGAINST
MIRACLES AND THE REASONS FOR FAITH

1. George MacDonald, *The Miracles of Our Lord* (London: Strahan & Co. Publishers, 1870), 5.
2. A description of Hume's gifts as a controversialist is given in *The Encyclopaedia Britannica*, 11th ed. (New York: The Encyclopaedia Britannica Company, 1910), 13:883.
3. John Locke and Charles W. Eliot, *English Philosophers of the Seventeenth and Eighteenth Centuries: Locke, Berkeley and Hume* (New York: P.F. Collier & Son, 1910), 401.
4. David Hume, *Essays and Treatises on Several Subjects,* 3rd ed. (London: A. Millar, 1756), 2:175. Emphasis added.
5. Ibid.
6. *The Dictionary of National Biography,* s.v. "Garvie" (London: Oxford University Press, 1959).
7. *The Encyclopaedia Britannica,* 18:572.
8. Ibid. Emphasis in original.
9. The distinguished theologian Dr. Gordon Fee has written that 1 Corinthians may be safely said to have been written in the spring, between the years AD 53 to 55. See Gordon Fee, *The First Epistle to the Corinthians: New International Commentary on the New Testament* (Grand Rapids, MI: Eerdmans, 1987), 15.
10. *The Encyclopaedia Britannica,* 18:572.
11. Ibid., 20:629.
12. William Paley, *Archdeacon Paley's View of the Evidences of Christianity* (Philadelphia: James Kay, 1843), 15.
13. Ibid.
14. Ibid., 18.
15. Ibid.
16. Ibid.
17. G. K. Chesterton, ed. Lawrence J. Clipper, *The Collected Works of G. K. Chesterton: The Illustrated London News, 1932–1934* (San Francisco: Ignatius, 2011) 36:561.
18. C. S. Lewis, *The Chronicles of Narnia* (New York: HarperCollins Publishers, 2001), 131–32.
19. Ibid.
20. Ibid.

21. Chesterton, *The Collected Works of G. K. Chesterton* 36:561–62.
22. G. K. Chesterton, "On Believing in Miracles," *Illustrated London News*; cf. Chesterton 36:563–64.
23. William Paley, *The Works of William Paley, Complete in One Volume* (Philadelphia: J.J. Woodward, 1831), 387–91.
24. John C. Lennox, *God's Undertaker* (Oxford: Lion Books, 2007), 82.
25. David Hume, *A Treatise of Human Nature . . .* (London: Longmans, Green, and Co., 1909), 2:393.
26. Lennox, *God's Undertaker*, 82.
27. Elliott Sober, *Philosophy of Biology* (Boulder CO: Westview Press, 1993), 34.
28. Lennox, *God's Undertaker*, 83.
29. Ibid.
30. Ibid.
31. Ibid.
32. Ibid.
33. Ibid.
34. Ibid., 83–84.
35. Ibid., 84.
36. Ibid.
37. Ibid. Emphasis added.
38. Sir John Polkinghorne, as quoted in Lennox, *God's Undertaker*, 84.

CHAPTER 19: GEORGE WASHINGTON: MIRACLES IN THE MIDST OF BATTLE

1. Charles Hamilton, ed., *Braddock's Defeat: The Journal of Captain Robert Cholmley's Batman, The Journal of a British Officer, Halkett's Orderly Book, with an Introduction and Notes by Charles Hamilton*, (Norman: University of Oklahoma Press, 1959), 30.
2. James Craik, in Paul E. Kopperman, ed., *Braddock at the Monongahela* (Pittsburgh: U. of Pittsburgh Press, 1992), 302.
3. George Washington, as quoted in Jeffry H. Morrison, *The Political Philosophy of George Washington* (Baltimore: Johns Hopkins University Press, 2009), 144.
4. Jeffry H. Morrison, *The Political Philosophy of George Washington* (Baltimore: Johns Hopkins University Press, 2009), 137. Here, Morrison has written that Washington "was an Anglican from cradle to grave." Further, as Morrison noted, Washington "signed the oath of conformity to the established church in 1756 and was a parish vestryman and warden of Pohick Church and Christ Church in Alexandria [Virginia], within Truro Parish."
5. Ibid., 143. Here, Morrison noted that Washington made his statement about "the allwise disposer of events" in a letter to the attorney general of the U.S. during the period when "he was deliberating whether to stand for a second term as president."
6. A phrase from the title of James Thomas Flexner's classic study, *Washington: The Indispensable Man* (Boston: Little, Brown and Company, 1969).
7. George Washington, "The Braddock Campaign," *Scribner's Magazine* (New York: Charles Scribner's Sons, 1893), 13:530–37. For accuracy of punctuation and spelling, I have checked the Scribner's text against the more authoritative text presented in *The Library of America* edition of Washington's *Writings*.

8. I have updated the spelling in Washington's letter, which has been posted online by the Library of Congress at http://memory.loc.gov/cgi-bin/query/r?ammem/mgw:@field(DOCID+@lit(gw010115)).
9. "George Washington's Boyhood Home," Stafford Virginia Web site, http://www.tourstaffordva.com/George-Washingtons-Boyhood-Home.cfm.
10. Spoken text from the trailer for the National Geographic Channel documentary *George Washington Revealed*, http://video.nationalgeographic.com/video/national-geographic-channel/specials-1/history-events/ngc-george-washington-revealed/.
11. Morrison, *The Political Philosophy of George Washington*, 140.
12. This phrase, and the text of the letter containing it, have can be found at "George Washington Papers at the Library of Congress, 1741–1799," Library of Congress website, http://www.loc.gov/teachers/classroommaterials/connections/george-washington/history.html.
13. J. D. Douglas and Merrill C. Tenney, *The Zondervan Illustrated Bible Dictionary*, rev. Moises Silva (Grand Rapids, MI: Zondervan, 2011), 1185.
14. Ibid.
15. As Dr. Jeffry Morrison has written: "During the course of his life, Washington maintained active membership in the Anglican communion." In Morrison, *The Political Philosophy of George Washington*, 137.
16. Ibid.

CHAPTER 20: TRANSFORMING GRACE: MIRACLES IN THE LIFE OF WILLIAM WILBERFORCE

1. Thomas Traherne, *The Works of Thomas Traherne*, ed. Bertram Dobell (Cambridge: D. S. Brewer, 2005), 1:76.
2. Warren W. Wiersbe, *The Wiersbe Bible Commentary: The Complete New Testament* (Colorado Springs, CO: David C. Cook, 2007), 339.
3. Robert Wilberforce and Samuel Wilberforce, *The Life of William Wilberforce* (London: John Murray, 1838), 3:341. See also 4:344.
4. Ibid., 3:489.

CHAPTER 21: THE LION OF NORTHFIELD: MIRACLES AND THE STORY OF D. L. MOODY

1. A. P. Fitt and Paul Dwight Moody, *The Shorter Life of D. L. Moody* (Chicago: The Bible Institute Colportage Association, 1900), 1:20.
2. Ibid., 99–100.
3. Ibid., 100.
4. Ibid.
5. Ibid.
6. Ibid., 100–1.
7. Ibid., 101.
8. Ibid.

9. Ibid.
10. Ibid., 101–2.
11. Ibid., 102.
12. Ibid.
13. Ibid.
14. Ibid.
15. Ibid.
16. Ibid., 102–3.
17. Ibid.
18. Ibid., 103.
19. This story has been adapted from Will Moody's account of the Chicago World's Fair of 1893 as given in William R. Moody, *The Life of Dwight L. Moody* (Chicago: Fleming H. Revell, 1900), 409–18.
20. Ibid.
21. Ibid.
22. Ibid.
23. Moody, *The Life of Dwight L. Moody*, 413.
24. Ibid., 413–18.
25. This amount was determined using Consumer Price Index data via the website http://www.measuringworth.com/uscompare/result.php?use%5B%5D=DOLLAR&use%5B%5D=GDPDEFLATION&use%5B%5D=VCB&use%5B%5D=UNSKILLED&use%5B%5D=MANCOMP&use%5B%5D=NOMGDPCP&use%5B%5D=NOMINALGDP&year_source=1893&amount=800&year_result=2009. Accessed March 16, 2012.
26. John Pollock, *Moody* (Grand Rapids, MI: Zondervan, 1967), 284.
27. The information and quote in and around this paragraph is taken from Kevin Belmonte, *D. L. Moody* (Nashville: Thomas Nelson, 2010), 153. See also Moody, *The Life of Dwight L. Moody*, 415.
28. Moody, *The Life of Dwight L. Moody*, 415.
29. Ibid., 416.
30. Ibid.
31. The foregoing paragraphs draw on information and text found in Moody, *The Life of Dwight L. Moody*, 416–17.
32. Ibid., 417.
33. Ibid., 417–18.
34. This story has been adapted from Will Moody's account of the Chicago World's Fair of 1893 as given in Moody, *The Life of Dwight L. Moody*, 409–18.

CHAPTER 22: EASTERN ORTHODOXY: MIRACLES OF MAJESTY AND MYSTERY

1. Kallistos Ware, *The Orthodox Way* (Crestwood, NY: St. Vladimir's Seminary Press, 1979), 7.
2. Eugen Pentuic, Michael Najim, et al., *The Orthodox Study Bible* (Nashville: Thomas Nelson, 2008), 1783.

3. John Chryssavgis, *In the Heart of the Desert: The Spirituality of the Desert Fathers and Mothers* (Bloomington, IN: World Wisdom, Inc., 2008), 95.

4. Ibid., 93. Emphasis added.

5. Ibid.

6. Ibid., 94.

7. G. K. Chesterton, *Orthodoxy* (New York: John Lane Company, 1909), 82–83.

8. Eugen Pentuic, Michael Najim, et al., "Marriage," *The Orthodox Study Bible* (Nashville: Thomas Nelson, 2008), 1607.

9. Ibid.

10. Ibid.

11. Ibid.

12. Pauline Baynes, "About the Nicene Creed," in *I Believe: The Nicene Creed* (Grand Rapids, MI: William B. Eerdmans Publishing Co., 2003), front pages.

13. Eugen Pentuic, Michael Najim, et al., *The Orthodox Study Bible* (Nashville: Thomas Nelson, 2008), 1791.

14. Andrew Ewbank Burn, *The Nicene Creed* (New York: Edwin S. Gorham, 1909), 62–63.

15. Ware, *The Orthodox Way*, 94.

16. Ibid.

17. Ibid., 93.

18. Ibid., 93–94.

19. Ibid., 8.

CHAPTER 23: LADY OF THE RADIANT SMILE: MIRACLES AND THE LIFE OF CORRIE TEN BOOM

1. A transcription of recollections shared by Corrie Ten Boom during a CBN television interview recorded in 1974 and posted online via YouTube at: http://www.youtube.com/watch?v=038cuYe3Nis.

2. Ibid.

3. Ibid. Emphasis added.

4. This block quote, and the paragraphs immediate preceding, have been summarized from Corrie Ten Boom, "I'm Still Learning to Forgive," *Guideposts*, http://www.pbs.org/wgbh/questionofgod/voices/boom.html. Accessed March 16, 2012.

CHAPTER 24: THE KING OF KINGS: MIRACLES IN THE GOLDEN AGE OF CINEMA

1. Tertullian, *The Epistle of the Gallican Churches, Lugdunum and Vienna*, trans. T. Herbert Bindley (London: The Society for Promoting Christian Knowledge, 1900), 61.

2. From promotional copy written for the Criterion Collection's release of *The King of Kings*, http://www.criterion.com/films/949-the-king-of-kings.

3. John A. Murray, "The Gospel According to Hollywood," *Wall Street Journal*,

http://online.wsj.com/article/SB1000142405274870391600457627045268201 68
60.html. Accessed March 16, 2011.

4. Ibid.

5. Donald Hayne, ed., *The Autobiography of Cecil B. DeMille* (Englewood Cliffs, CA: Prentice-Hall, 1959), 283.

6. Murray, "The Gospel According to Hollywood."

7. Hayne, ed., *The Autobiography of Cecil B. DeMille*, 283–84.

8. Ibid., 284. Emphasis in original.

9. Murray, "The Gospel According to Hollywood."

CHAPTER 25: JOY LEWIS: THE MIRACLE OF HEALING

1. George Matheson, *The Christian Work and the Evangelist* (New York: Bible House, 1910), 88:562.

2. Stephen Vincent Benét, "Foreword" in Joy Davidman, *Letter to a Comrade* (New Haven: Yale University Press, 1938).

3. Ibid.

4. Ibid., 40.

5. Joy Davidman Gresham, as quoted in Walter Hooper, *C. S. Lewis: A Complete Guide to His Life & Works* (New York: HarperCollins Publishers, 1996), 59.

6. Douglas Gresham, *Lenten Lands* (New York: Macmillan, 1988), 45.

7. The divorce became final on August 5, 1954. Walter Hooper, ed., *The Collected Letters of C. S. Lewis: Narnia, Cambridge and Joy, 1950–1963* (New York: HarperCollins, 2007), 1675.

8. Douglas Gresham, *Jack's Life* (Nashville: Broadman & Holman Publishers, 2005), 146.

9. Hooper, *C. S. Lewis: A Companion and Guide*, 77–78.

10. Ibid., 78.

11. Ibid.

12. Ibid., 79.

13. Ibid.

14. Ibid.

15. Ibid.

16. Ibid.

17. Ibid., 79–80.

18. George Sayer, *Jack: C. S. Lewis and His Times* (San Francisco: Harper & Row, 1988), 222.

19. Hooper, *C. S. Lewis: A Companion and Guide*, 80. See also Sayer, *Jack: C. S. Lewis and His Times*, 222. Lyle W. Dorsett is among those scholars who have said that Lewis did have romantic feelings for Joy Davidman Gresham at this time.

20. Hooper, *C. S. Lewis: A Companion and Guide*, 80.

21. Gresham, *Lenten Lands*, 76.

22. Ibid.

23. Hooper, *C. S. Lewis: A Companion and Guide*, 697.

CHAPTER 26: AFRICA: MIRACLES IN THE CONTINENT BELOVED BY GOD

1. Thomas Benfield Harbottle, *A Dictionary of Classical Quotations* (New York: Macmillan, 1906), 262.
2. Lamin Sanneh, *Whose Religion Is Christianity? The Gospel Beyond the West* (Grand Rapids, MI: William B. Eerdmans Company, 2003), 14.
3. Ibid.
4. William Wade Fowler, "Bona Dea," *The Encyclopaedia Britannica*, 11th ed. (New York: The Encyclopaedia Britannica Company, 1910), 4:191.
5. Ibid., 2:909.
6. Ibid.
7. R. A. Oliver and Anthony Atmore, *Medieval Africa: 1250–1800* (Cambridge: Cambridge University Press, 2001), 14.
8. Ibid.
9. Ken Perry, ed., *The Blackwell Companion to Eastern Christianity* (Oxford: Blackwell Publishing, Ltd., 2010), 117.
10. Ibid, 118.
11. Ibid.
12. Ibid.
13. Trevor Persaud, "This Time for Africa," *Christianity Today*, http://www .christianitytoday.com/ct/2010/octoberweb-only/51-11.0.html.
14. Ibid.
15. Ibid.
16. Ibid.
17. Lamin Sanneh, *Whose Religion Is Christianity? The Gospel Beyond the West*, 15.
18. Ibid., 39.
19. Matthew Parris, "As an Atheist, I Truly Believe Africa Needs God," *Times of London*, December 27, 2008, http://www.timesonline.co.uk/tol/comment/ columnists/matthew_parris/article5400568.ece.
20. Ibid.
21. Ibid.
22. Ibid.
23. Ibid.
24. Ibid.
25. Ibid.
26. Ibid.
27. Ibid.
28. Ibid.
29. Ibid.

CHAPTER 27: CLYDE KILBY: JOY AND THE MIRACLE OF BEING

1. James Montgomery, *The Poetical Works of James Montgomery* (London: Longman, Rees, Orme, Brown, Green & Longman, 1836), 1:234.
2. John Piper, "10 Resolutions for Mental Health," *Desiring God*

(blog), December 31, 2007, http://www.desiringgod.org/blog/
posts/10-resolutions-for-mental-health.
3. Ibid.
4. See Ps. 139:14, and the words to the hymn "This Is My Father's World," by
Maltbie Babcock.
5. William Petersen and Ardythe Petersen, *The Complete Book of Hymns* (Carol
Stream, IL: Tyndale, 2006), 84.
6. Piper, "10 Resolutions for Mental Health."
7. Ibid.
8. Ibid.
9. Ibid.
10. Ibid.
11. Clyde Kilby, as quoted in John Piper, "Clyde Kilby's Resolutions for Mental
Health and for Staying Alive to God in Nature," *Desiring God* (blog), http://www.
desiringgod.org/resource-library/taste-see-articles/clyde-kilbys-resolutions-for-
mental-health-and-for-staying-alive-to-god-in-nature. Accessed March 15, 2012.
12. Lewis Carroll, *Through the Looking Glass and What Alice Found There*
(Philadelphia: Henry Altemus Company, 1897), 11.
13. John Piper, "Happy Birthday, Clyde Kilby," *Desiring God* (blog), September 25,
2008, http://www.desiringgod.org/blog/posts/happy-birthday-clyde-kilby/print.
14. Ibid.
15. Ibid.
16. Ibid.
17. Ibid.

CHAPTER 28: THE GRACE OF A DREAM: MIRACLES IN ACADEMIA

1. Geoffrey Chaucer, *The Canterbury Tales*, trans. Neville Coghill (London: Penguin
Books, 2003), 489.
2. Holly Ordway, *Not God's Type* (Chicago: Moody Publishers, 2010), 15–16.
3. Ibid.
4. Ibid., 25.
5. Ibid., 28.
6. C. S. Lewis, *Surprised by Joy* (New York: Harcourt, Brace Jovanovich, 1955), 191.
Emphasis in original.
7. George Herbert, *The Complete Works in Verse and Prose of George Herbert*, ed. Rev.
Alexander B. Grosart (Printed for Private Circulation, 1874), 2:lxxxi. This phrase
occurs in line 3 of Herbert's poem, "Prayer."
8. Ordway, *Not God's Type*, 31.
9. Herbert J. C. Grierson, ed., *Metaphysical Lyrics & Poems of the Seventeenth
Century, Donne to Butler* (Oxford: At the Clarendon Press, 1921), 88.
10. Ordway, *Not God's Type*, 31.
11. Ibid.
12. E-mail correspondence from Holly Ordway to Kevin Belmonte, September 9,
2011.

13. Ordway, *Not God's Type*, 32.
14. Ibid.
15. J. P. Moreland and Kai Nielsen, eds., *Does God Exist?* (Amherst, NY: Prometheus Books, 1993), 16. Cf. Ordway, *Not God's Type*, 58.
16. Ordway, *Not God's Type*, 58.
17. Moreland and Nielsen, eds., *Does God Exist?*, 18.
18. Ordway, *Not God's Type*, 60.
19. E-mail correspondence from Holly Ordway to Kevin Belmonte, September 5, 2011.
20. Ordway, *Not God's Type*, 133.
21. Ibid.
22. Ibid.
23. Ibid.
24. Benjamin Rush, *An Oration, Delivered Before the American Philosophical Society: An Enquiry into the Influence of Physical Causes Upon the Moral Faculty* (Philadelphia: Charles Cist, 1786), 10.
25. G. K. Chesterton, "The God in the Cave," in *The Everlasting Man* (New York: Dodd, Mead and Company, 1925), 209.

CHAPTER 29: THE GOD OF ALL HOPE: MIRACLES
IN THE PLACE OF BROKENNESS

1. Thomas Brooks, *The Complete Works of Thomas Brooks* (Edinburgh: James Nichol, 1866), 3:37.
2. Zeph. 3:17: "The LORD your God in your midst, The Mighty One, will save."
3. This quote, and all that follow, are from the transcription of an interview conducted by Kevin Belmonte with Pastor Mark Rivera at Bethany Church, Greenland, New Hampshire, on Thursday, September 15, 2011.

AFTERWORD

1. William Cowper, "Light Shining Out of Darkness," in *The Olney Hymns, The Complete Poetical Works of William Cowper*, ed. H. S. Milford (London: Henry Frowde, 1905), 455, lns. 1–8.
2. A quote from Lady Davson, President of International Ecumenical Fellowship, and third-great-granddaughter of William Wilberforce—spoken in phone conversation with the author on September 23, 2011.
3. D. L. Moody, *Life Words* (London: John Snow & Co., 1875), 92.

BIBLIOGRAPHY

Alcorn, Randy. *Heaven.* Carol Stream, IL: Tyndale House Publishers, Inc., 2004.

Aquinas, Thomas. *Of God and His Creatures: An Annotated Translation (with Some Abridgement) of the Summa Contra Gentiles of Saint Thomas Aquinas.* Edited by Joseph Rickaby. London: Burns & Oates, 1905.

———. *The Summa Contra Gentiles.* Translated by the English Dominican Fathers. London: Burns, Oates & Washbourne, Ltd., 1924.

———. *The Summa Theologica, Part I.* Literally translated by the Fathers of the English Dominican Province. London: R & T. Washbourne, Ltd., 1912.

Augustine. *Confessions.* Translated by Garry Wills. New York: Penguin Classics, 2008.

———. *Essential Sermons.* Translated by Edmund Hill. Hyde Park, NY: New City Press, 2007.

———. *The City of God,* vol. 1. Edited by the Rev. Marcus Dods. Edinburgh: T & T Clark, 1888.

———. *The Confessions.* Translated by J. G. Pilkington. Edinburgh: T & T Clark: 1876.

———. *The Confessions of St. Augustine, with an Introduction by Charles W. Eliot.* New York: P. F. Collier & Son, Company, 1909.

Bainton, Roland. *Here I Stand: A Life of Martin Luther.* New York: Penguin Books/ Meridian, 1995.

Barton, Bruce D., Veerman, David R., and Taylor, Linda K. *Hebrews.* Edited by James Galvin, Ronald Beers, and Philip Comfort. Carol Stream, IL: Tyndale Publishers, 1997.

Baynes, Pauline. *I Believe: The Nicene Creed.* Grand Rapids, MI: William B. Eerdmans Publishing Co., 2003.

Brown, Peter. *Augustine of Hippo: A Biography.* Berkeley: University of California Press, 2000.

Bruce, F. F. *The New Testament Documents: Are They Reliable?* Grand Rapids, MI: William B. Eerdmans Publishing Company, 1981.

Bunyan, John. *The Pilgrim's Progress.* London: Nathaniel Ponder, 1678.

Burn, A. E. *The Nicene Creed.* New York: Edwin S. Gorham, 1909.

Burnet, Gilbert. *An Exposition of the Thirty-Nine Articles of the Church of England*. Oxford: Oxford University Press, 1845.

Card, Michael. *The Name of the Promise Is Jesus*. Nashville: Thomas Nelson, 1993.

Charbonnier, Jean-Pierre. *Christians in China: A.D. 600 to 2000*. San Francisco: Ignatius Press, 2007.

Chesterton, G. K. *Collected Works of G. K. Chesterton: The Illustrated London News, 1932–1934*, vol. 36. San Francisco: Ignatius: 2011.

———. *Gloria in Profundis*. London: Faber and Gwyer, 1927.

———. *Orthodoxy*. New York: John Lane, 1909.

———. *Poems*. New York: Dodd, Mead and Company, 1922.

———. *St. Thomas Aquinas: The Dumb Ox*. New York: Random House, 1974.

———. *The Ball and the Cross*. New York: John Lane Company, 1909.

———. *The Everlasting Man*. New York: Dodd, Mead and Company, 1925.

———. *The Innocence of Father Brown*. London: Cassell & Company, Ltd., 1911.

Chryssavgis, John. *In the Heart of the Desert: The Spirituality of the Desert Fathers and Mothers*. Bloomington, IN: World Wisdom, Inc., 2008.

Clarke, T. E. S. and H. C. Foxcroft. *A Life of Gilbert Burnet: Bishop of Salisbury*. Cambridge: Cambridge University Press, 1907.

Daniels, William Haven. *D. L. Moody and His Work*. London: Hodder & Stoughton, 1875.

Davidman, Joy. *Letter to a Comrade*. New Haven: Yale University Press, 1938.

Dostoevsky, Fyodor. *The Brothers Karamazov*. Translated from Russian by Constance Garnett. New York: The Macmillan Company, 1922.

Dunnam, Maxie D. *Exodus*. Vol. 2 of *The Preacher's Commentary*. Nashville: Thomas Nelson, 2002.

Edwards, Jonathan. *The Works of President Edwards*, vol. 1. New York: Leavitt & Allen, 1858.

Eliot, T. S. *The Four Quartets*. New York: Mariner Books, 1968.

Elwell, Walter A., ed. *The Evangelical Dictionary of Theology*. Grand Rapids, MI: Baker Academic, 2001.

Enns, Peter. *Exodus: The NIV Application Commentary*. Grand Rapids, MI: Zondervan/HarperCollins, 2000.

Farrant, Jean. *Mashonaland Martyr: Bernard Mizeki and the Pioneer Church*. Cape Town: Oxford University Press, 1966.

Fausset, A. R. *The Critical and Expository Bible Cyclopaedia*. London: Hodder and Stoughton, 1893.

Fitt, A. P. and Paul Dwight Moody. *The Shorter Life of D. L. Moody*, vol. 1. Chicago: The Bible Institute Colportage Association, 1900.

Flexner, Thomas. *Washington: The Indispensable Man*. Boston: Little, Brown and Company, 1969.

Godet, Frédéric Louis. *Commentary on the Gospel of St. John*. Edinburgh: T & T Clark, 1881.

Graham, Billy. *Angels*. Nashville: Thomas Nelson, 1995.

———. *The Holy Spirit*. Nashville: Thomas Nelson, 2000.

——. *The Secret of Happiness*. Nashville: Thomas Nelson, 2002.

Grant, Michael. *Myths of the Greeks and Romans*. New York: Penguin Books USA Inc., 1962.

Greene, William Chase. *Moira: Fate, Good and Evil in Greek Thought*. Cambridge: Harvard University Press, 1948.

Greidanus, Sidney. *Preaching Christ from the Old Testament: A Contemporary Hermeneutical Method*. Grand Rapids, MI: William B. Eerdmans, 1999.

Gresham, Douglas. *Jack's Life*. Nashville: Broadman & Holman Publishers, 2005.

——. *Lenten Lands*. New York: Macmillan, 1988.

Halley, Henry H. *Halley's Bible Handbook with the New International Version*. Grand Rapids, MI: Zondervan, 2007.

Hamilton, Charles, ed. *Braddock's Defeat: The Journal of Captain Robert Cholmley's Batman, The Journal of a British Officer, Halkett's Orderly Book*. Norman: University of Oklahoma Press, 1959.

Hartill, Edwin J. *Principles of Biblical Hermeneutics*. Grand Rapids, MI: Zondervan, 1960.

Hayne, Donald, ed. *The Autobiography of Cecil B. DeMille*. Englewood Cliffs, CA: Prentice-Hall, 1959.

Henry, Matthew. *An Exposition on the Old and New Testament*, vol. 1. London: Joseph Robinson, 1828.

Hooper, Walter. *C. S. Lewis: A Complete Guide to His Life & Works*. New York: HarperCollins Publishers, 1996.

Hopkins, Gerard Manley. *The Poems of Gerard Manley Hopkins*. Edited by Robert Bridges. London: Humphrey Milford, 1918.

Hume, David. *Essays and Treatises on Several Subjects*, vol. 2, 3rd ed. London: A. Millar, 1756.

Julian of Norwich. *Revelations of Divine Love: A Version from the MS in the British Museum*. Edited by Grace Warrack. London: Methuen, 1901.

——. *Revelations of Divine Love*. Translated by Elizabeth Spearing and introduced by A. C. Spearing. London: Penguin Classics, 1999.

Kaiser, Walter. *Toward an Old Testament Theology*. Grand Rapids, MI: Zondervan, 1991.

Keble, John, ed. *The Works of that Learned and Judicious Divine, Mr. Richard Hooker*, vol. 3, part 2. Oxford: At the University Press, 1836.

Kilby, Clyde S., ed. *A Mind Awake: An Anthology of C. S. Lewis*. New York: Macmillan, 1968.

King, Don W. *Out of My Bone: The Letters of Joy Davidman*. Grand Rapids, MI: William B. Eerdmans Publishing Co., 2009.

Kopperman, Paul E. *Braddock at the Monongahela*. Pittsburgh: University of Pittsburgh Press, 1992.

Laidlaw, John. *The Miracles of Our Lord: Expository and Homiletic*. New York: Funk & Wagnalls Company, 1892.

Lazo, Andrew, and Phemister, Mary Ann, eds. *Mere Christians: Inspiring Stories of Encounters with C. S. Lewis*. Grand Rapids, MI: Baker Books, 2009.

Lennox, John C. *God's Undertaker*. Oxford: Lion Books, 2007.

——. *Seven Days That Divide the World: The Beginning According to Genesis and Science.* Grand Rapids, MI: Zondervan, 2011.

Lewis, C. S. *Miracles.* New York: HarperCollins, 2001.

——. *Surprised by Joy.* New York: Harcourt, Brace, 1955.

Lockyer, Herbert. *All the Miracles of the Bible.* Grand Rapids, MI: Zondervan, 1988.

Luther, Martin. *Luther's Explanatory Notes on the Gospels.* Compiled by the Rev. E. Mueller and translated by Rev. P. Anstadt. York, PA: P. Anstadt & Sons, 1899.

Lutzer, Erwin W. *Seven Reasons Why You Can Trust the Bible.* Chicago: Moody Publishers, 2008.

MacDonald, George. *The Miracles of Our Lord.* London: Strahan & Co. Publishers, 1870.

——. *The Miracles of Our Lord.* Edited by Rolland Hein. Wheaton, IL: Harold Shaw Publishers, 1980.

MacDowell, Josh. *Handbook on Counseling Youth: A Comprehensive Guide.* Nashville: Thomas Nelson, 1996.

Mangalwadi, Vishal. *The Book That Made Your World: How the Bible created the Soul of Western Civilization.* Nashville: Thomas Nelson, 2011.

Marsden, George. *Jonathan Edwards: A Life.* New Haven: Yale University Press, 2004.

McBrien, Richard P. *Catholicism: A New Study Edition.* New York: HarperOne, 1994.

McClure, J. B., ed. *D. L. Moody's Child Stories.* Chicago: Rhodes & McClure, 1877.

McGrath, Alister. *What Was God Doing on the Cross?* Eugene, OR: Wipf & Stock Publishers, 2002.

McGuire, Brian Patrick, ed. *Jean Gerson: Early Works.* Mahwah, NJ: Paulist Press, 1998.

McKim, Donald K. *The Westminster Dictionary of Theological Terms.* Louisville: Westminster/John Knox Press, 1996.

Metzger, Bruce, M. and Coogan, Michael David, eds. *The Oxford Companion to the Bible.* New York: Oxford University Press, 1993.

Milford, H.S. *The Complete Poetical Works of William Cowper.* Oxford Edition. London: Henry Frowde, 1905.

Montgomery, James. *The Poetical Works of James Montgomery*, vol. 1. London: Longman, Rees, Orme, Brown, Green & Longman, 1836.

Moody, D. L. *Eleven Sermons Never Before Published.* New York: Christian Herald, 1911.

——. *Twelve Select Sermons.* Chicago: Fleming H. Revell, 1884.

Moody, W. R. *The Life of D. L. Moody.* Chicago: Fleming H. Revell, 1900.

More, Hannah. *The Complete Works of Hannah More*, vol. 1. New York: Harper & Brothers, 1835.

Morrison, Jeffry H. *The Political Philosophy of George Washington.* Baltimore: Johns Hopkins University Press, 2009.

Newton, John. *The Works of the Rev. John Newton: Complete in One Volume.* London: T. Nelson and Sons, 1853.

Noll, Mark A., and Carolyn Nystrom. *Clouds of Witnesses: Christian Voices from Africa and Asia.* Downers Grove, IL: InterVarsity Press, 2011.

Oberman, Heiko. *Luther: Between God and the Devil.* New Haven: Yale University Press, 2006.

Oliver, R. A., and Anthony Atmore. *Medieval Africa: 1250–1800.* Cambridge: Cambridge University Press, 2001.

Osbeck, Kenneth W. *Hallelujah, What a Savior: 25 Hymn Stories Celebrating Christ Our Redeemer.* Grand Rapids, MI: Kregel Publications, 2000.

Paley, William. *Archdeacon Paley's View of the Evidences of Christianity.* Philadelphia: James Kay, 1843.

———. *The Works of William Paley.* Philadelphia: J.J. Woodward, 1831.

Pearson, Hugh. *Memorials of the Church and Parish of Sonning.* Reading: Edward J. Blackwell, 1890.

Perry, Ken, ed. *The Blackwell Companion to Eastern Christianity.* Oxford: Blackwell Publishing, Ltd., 2010.

Piper, John. *The Pleasures of God: Meditations on God's Delight in Being God.* Sisters, OR: Multnomah Publishers, Inc., 2000.

Reimann, Jim, ed. *Look Unto Me: The Devotions of Charles Spurgeon.* Grand Rapids: MI: Zondervan, 2008.

Rickaby, Joseph, ed. *Of God and His Creatures: An Annotated Translation (with Some Abridgement) of the Summa Contra Gentiles of Saint Thos Aquinas.* London: Burns & Oates, 1905.

Nadejda Gorodetzky. *St. Tikhon of Zadonsk.* Crestwood, NY: St. Vladimir's Seminary Press, 1976.

Sanneh, Lamin. *Whose Religion Is Christianity? The Gospel Beyond the West.* Grand Rapids, MI: William B. Eerdmans Company, 2003.

Sayer, George. *Jack: C. S. Lewis and His Times.* San Francisco: Harper & Row, 1988.

Scroggie, W. Graham. *The Unfolding Drama of Redemption.* Grand Rapids, MI: Kregel Publications, 1995.

Shedd, W. G. T. *The Complete Works of Samuel Taylor Coleridge*, vol. 6. New York: Harper & Brothers, 1884.

Simeon, Charles. *Horae Homileticae: Discourses Upon the Whole Scriptures*, vol. 3. London: Richard Watts, 1819.

Sittser, Gerald L. *Water from a Deep Well: Christian Spirituality from Early Martyrs to Modern Missionaries.* Downers Grove, IL: Inter-Varsity Press, 2010.

———. *Horae Homileticae: Discourses Upon the Whole Scriptures*, vol. 5. London: Henry G. Bohn, 1855.

Sober, Elliott. *Philosophy of Biology.* Boulder, CO: Westview Press, 1993.

Spurgeon, C. H. *Evening by Evening.* New York: Sheldon and Company, 1869.

———. *Sermons Preached and Revised*, vol. 22. London: Passmore & Alabaster, 1877.

———. *The Metropolitan Tabernacle Pulpit*, vol. 36. London: Passmore & Alabaster, 1860.

Stott, John. *Basic Christianity.* Grand Rapids, MI: Wm. B. Eerdmans Publishing Co., 2008).

———. *The Cross of Christ.* Downers Grove, IL: InterVarsity Press, 2006.

———. *The Radical Disciple.* Downers Grove, IL: Inter-Varsity Press, 2010.

———. *Understanding the Bible*. Grand Rapids, MI: Zondervan, 1999.

———. *Why I Am a Christian*. Downers Grove, IL: InterVarsity Press, 2003.

———. *What Christ Thinks of the Church*. Grand Rapids, MI: Eerdmans, 1972.

Stuart, Douglas K. *Exodus*. Volume 2 of *The New American Commentary*. Nashville: B&H Publishing Group, 2006.

Taylor, Jeremy. *The Rule and Exercises of Holy Living*. New York: E. P. Dutton and Company, 1876.

Ten Boom, Corrie. *Messages of God's Abundance*. Grand Rapids, MI: Zondervan, 2002.

Tenney, Merrill C. *The Zondervan Illustrated Bible Dictionary*. Revised by Moises Silva. Grand Rapids, MI: Zondervan, 2011.

Terras, Victor. *A Karamazov Companion: Commentary on the Genesis, Language and Style of Dostoevsky's Novel*. Madison, WI: The University of Wisconsin Press, 2002.

Tertullian. *The Epistle of the Gallican Churches, Lugdunum and Vienna*. Translated by T. Herbert Bindley, Merton College, Oxford. London: The Society for Promoting Christian Knowledge, 1900.

Eugen Pentiuc, Michael Najim, etat,. *The Orthodox Study Bible*. Nashville: Thomas Nelson, 2008.

Traherne, Thomas. *The Poetical Works of Thomas Traherne*. London: Bertram Dobell, 1903.

———. *The Works of Thomas Traherne*, vol. 1. Cambridge: D. S. Brewer, 2005.

Ware, Kallistos. *The Inner Kingdom*. Crestwood, NY: St. Vladimir's Seminary Press, 2000.

———. *The Orthodox Way*. Crestwood, NY: St. Vladimir's Seminary Press, 1979.

Wiersbe, Warren W. *The Bible Exposition Commentary: New Testament*, vol. 2. Colorado Springs, CO: Victor/Cook Communications, 2001.

———. *The Wiersbe Bible Commentary: The Complete Old Testament*. Colorado Springs, CO: David C. Cook, 2007.

Wilberforce, Robert, and Samuel Wilberforce. *The Life of William Wilberforce*, vol. 1. London: John Murray, 1838.

Wilberforce, Samuel. *Heroes of Hebrew History*. London: W. H. Allen and Co., 1890.

INDEX

SCRIPTURE INDEX

NOTE: Bold numbers are scripture chapters.

ALSO AVAILABLE FROM KEVIN BELMONTE

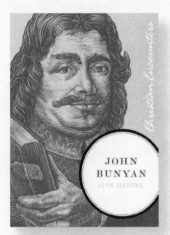

9781595553041
eBook: 9781418555221

The author of *The Pilgrim's Progress*, one of the most influential books in English literature, had little formal education. Born the son of a tinker, John Bunyan was expected to follow in his father's footsteps. He was allowed to go to school for a few years and purchase a few books, but his apprenticeship in the family business took precedence. Bunyan experienced his first sorrow in adolescence, when both his mother and sister died. It wasn't his last. Revolutions and wars were all around him, and he was jailed twice for preaching the Gospel. Yet amidst repeated imprisonments, civil war, and violent persecution, Bunyan crafted *The Pilgrim's Progress*, a testament unlike any other to the triumph of the human spirit. His simple cadences transformed the language, and his memorable characters became familiar to millions. Bunyan became a public figure, a captivating speaker, and above all, a man known for his unrelenting trust in God.

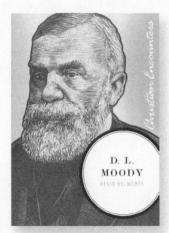

9781595550477
eBook: 9781595553782

Why America's greatest President and one of America's most celebrated spiritual giants are among the poorest of the poor is just the beginning of *D. L. Moody*, a biography with a novel-like narrative style that unveils the eternal power one life can have. Part of the Christian Encounters Series, this book reintroduces the unlikely accomplishments of a man desperate to obey God's call and shows how one committed heart can impact the kingdom of God and the spiritual heritage of a nation.

COMING IN FALL 2012

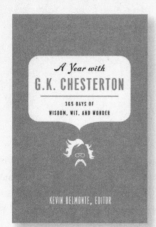

Pull a comfy chair up to a warm hearth and enjoy 365 daily offerings of wit and wisdom from G. K. Chesterton. Those who read one passage a day from the collection that follows will be glad of the chance to keep company with so thoughtful a friend as Chesterton.

ALREADY AVAILABLE WHEREVER BOOKS AND EBOOKS ARE SOLD

A powerful narrative of Chesterton's life through his literary accomplishments. Amid currents of modernity that sought to displace the Christian faith, Chesterton challenged thought leaders of his day with civility, erudition, and wit, contending that faith is the central piece of our humanity.

A comprehensive, accessible survey of Chesterton's greatest ideas and writings. With more than 850 passages showcasing his brilliance and masterful writing style, it covers topics from Academia to Painting, Politics to Architecture, Jane Austen to John Bunyan, Jesus to Fairy Tales.

THOMAS NELSON
Since 1798

thomasnelson.com